Deep Listening

Deep Listening

Uncovering the Hidden Meanings in Everyday Conversation

Robert E. Haskell

PERSEUS PUBLISHING

Cambridge, Massachusetts

Many of the designations used by manufacturers and sellers to distinguish their products are claimed as trademarks. Where those designations appear in this book and Perseus Books was aware of a trademark claim, those designations have been printed with initial capital letters.

Copyright 2001 © by Robert Haskell

A CIP record for this book is available from the library of Congress.

Printed in the United States of America.

Perseus Publishing is a member of the Perseus Books Group
Text design by Jeff Williams
Set in 11.5 Minion by Perseus Publishing Services

First printing, March 2001

Visit us on the World Wide Web at http://www.perseuspublishing.com

Perseus Books are available at special discounts for bulk purchases in the U.S. by corporations, institutions, and other organizations. For more information, please contact the Special Markets Department at HarperCollins Publishers, 10 East 53rd Street, New York, NY 10022, or call 1-212-207-7528.

Something is happening here/
But you don't know what it is/
Do you, Mister Jones?

—BOB DYLAN
Ballad of a Thin Man[1]

This book is of an entirely popular character; it merely aims by the accumulation of examples at paving the way for the necessary assumption of unconscious yet operative mental processes, and it avoids all theoretical considerations on the nature of this unconscious.

—SIGMUND FREUD
The Psychopathology of Everyday Life[2]

Contents

Preface   ix
Acknowledgments   xi

Introduction   xiii

One   Listening to the Grateful Dead, Live in Concert:
      Introduction to Deep Listening   1

Two   Slips of the Tongue or "Slips" of the Mind:
      Come Now, Mr. President   25

Three God Talk: Learning the Deep-Listening Templates   47

Four Deep Listening About Relationships: What Friends,
      Coworkers, and Employers Won't Tell You   71

Five Discovering Deep Listening:
      What Freud Didn't Know, but Almost Did   91

Six   In Defense of Whores and O. J. Simpson:
      Precautions, Ethical and Legal   111

Seven Figures of Speech in Conversation: Numbers in the Mind   125

Eight Sex and Gender: Women Under the Influence   139

Nine A Niggardly Issue? Race Matters in Black and White   157

Ten   Deep Action: Crossing the Rubicon?   181

      Notes   203
      Index   217

Preface

This book is the result of years of work that I have published in scientific journals. The time has come, however, to make my findings available to a wider audience.

Certain books and people can be important ingredients in developing one's personal and professional interests. I owe a debt to an old high school friend, Dave Dyer, who perhaps unknowingly started me on my quest to understand the unconscious mind. Dave and I worked after school on the local newspaper in Bath, Maine, the town where we grew up. During our job of counting papers, cleaning up printers' ink, and sweeping the floor, I would wax philosophical about "meaning" and the mind. One day he gave me a book on hypnosis, which in those days was quite esoteric. It was the first book that I read cover to cover. More importantly, it started me on my more tutored investigation into the meaning of "meaning."

In my quest I came across a book in the town library by an author I had only vaguely heard of at that point: Sigmund Freud. The book was his magnum opus, *The Interpretation of Dreams*, which, of course, is about meaning. But contrary to popular belief, his book is not just about the meaning of dreams; it's about how language "means" and how the mind works. Disregarding his psychoanalytic orientation, the book significantly influenced me.

Then, there's my closest friend of more than twenty years, Dr. Aaron Gresson, who shared with me his writings, brilliant insights, and ever-so-keen perceptions of what people in our common social interactions and conversations "really" mean. His supportive but critical views on my method presented in this book have also given me much to think about over the years, especially around my interpretation of unconscious racial and ethnic references in conversations. Maybe this book will do for someone what Dave Dyer, Sigmund Freud, and Aaron did for me.

Acknowledgments

I would like to acknowledge the many people who have influenced this book in some way. First, I must express my deepest appreciation to my longtime friend and colleague, Dr. Aaron Gresson, with whom, at the inception of the material in this book, I spent many hours in discussion. Though he was a most valuable critic, he was always supportive.

I need also to thank the many people who contributed examples. These include my former colleague John Heapes as well as Sarah Look, Claudette Haskell, and my daughter, Melyssa. I would also like to thank Diane Labbe for her help and Virginia Look for her invaluable "schoolmarmish" eye in proofreading the draft of this book.

Finally, I want to thank my many former students and other people who were not aware that they were providing me with examples of deep talk.

Introduction

This book and my previous book, *Between the Lines: Unconscious Meaning in Everyday Life*,[1] present a novel view of how, out of hidden and unconscious feelings, our mind creates hidden meaning in everyday conversations, what I call deep listening to deep talk. Deep listening is also a practical and concrete method for recognizing unconscious meaning that can initially be learned in less time than it takes to read this book.

For example, what if after a party or a business meeting a friend or boss starts telling a story about hyperactive children, a topic that just seems to come out of nowhere, having no apparent connection to the previous topics in the conversation? What might this story mean? I mean unconsciously? And how would you recognize and know if it had some deeper meaning? We would all like a way to figure out what people may really be saying and thinking in times like these. This book can help you do that. An added "plus" is that along the way its many examples are fascinating as well.

Now, what if we knew that the people at the party or meeting that I just mentioned had been constantly flitting about or jumping from one conversational topic to another, unable (or unwilling) to focus on anything? Would knowing this help you to decode the meaning of a conversation or a story about hyperactive children? It should. The story about hyperactive children is likely an unconscious comment on what the person thought about the party or meeting: that it was like being with a bunch of hyperactive children.

This book will take you on a fascinating and pioneering trip through the mind and the ways we creatively use everyday language in conversation to express our hidden thoughts and feelings. It's a web of meaning created by a myriad of pun-like sounds, double entendres, other every-day metaphorical uses of language, and Freudian-like slips of the tongue. The trip, however, will make Freudian slips of the tongue look like child's play.

In a very real sense, science is about decoding nature. The example par excellence is the decoding of DNA. Understanding everyday language, too, is in fact about decoding. One magazine editor called my previous book, *Between the Lines*, a "Chat Decoder."[2] So is this book. As I describe in Chapter 5, my experience in decoding "enemy" messages in U.S. Army intelligence also likely prepared me for "decoding" unconscious meanings.

What makes deep listening possible, of course, is deep talk about unconscious meaning. Deep talk and deep listening are flip sides of the same coin. This book will provide you with the language, concepts, and other simple tools that will allow you to hear things you never heard before. And what you hear will likely astonish you. Believe me. Since my discovery of deep talk, over twenty years ago now, the results of deep listening to deep talk still intrigue and fascinate me.

The implications of my findings for understanding how language and the mind work are themselves mind-boggling—and I am not exaggerating. The story of the origins of these findings is one of the more fascinating stories in the history of psychology (see Chapter 5). Although some of the deep-talk conversations in this book are inherently humorous, others I have purposely tried to style in a lighthearted manner. But don't be fooled by these entertaining motifs, for you will be witnessing some of the most profound operations of the human mind yet recognized.

In addition, the trip will also be a vaguely familiar one, especially since you already have experience with puns and slips of the tongue. Deep listening is the recognizing of puns and slips of the tongue writ large, so to speak. It's recognizing not just the double meaning of a single word or phrase, it's recognizing whole sentences and stories that have parallel meanings. The trip will also be somewhat familiar because we all have engaged—albeit unconsciously—in deep listening to such deep talk.

What you will be doing as you read this book is making what you already unconsciously know available to your conscious mind. In this regard, the ancient Greek philosopher, Plato, said that we don't learn anything new; we simply remember or recognize what we already know on some deep level.[3] Thus, because this book is about human feelings, and about how we use the words and sounds of everyday language when we talk, it will not be so much about learning something new and strange (though it's that, too) as about coming to a startling recognition.

At this point, let me note what deep listening and deep talk are not. There are circumstances where people are intentionally indirect and consciously using metaphorical-like language or innuendo. Let me be clear: this is *not* what I'm talking about here. Nor am I talking about what has come to be called "coded speech"—as in the phrase "you know how *they* are," where everyone knows who "they" are and what's "really" being said about "them." No, I'm not just talking about people being consciously indirect, or using euphemisms. I'm talking about hidden meaning that speakers aren't even aware of. I'm talking *deep meaning* here. I'm talking very deep encryption.

The study of everyday conversation is profoundly important. If nothing else is certain about most of us, one fact seems very clear: we talk a lot. But are we aware of the full meaning behind our talk? The research from various fields suggests that we are not. We take so much for granted in our daily lives, it's *as if* we are only half conscious of a great deal of the hidden meaning in our conversations; it's *as if* we're talking in our sleep. It's perhaps disheartening, but apparently true, that much of the time we don't know what we or other people are *really* talking about.

As we engage in our daily activities, most of us take part in social conversations of one kind or another, with family, friends, and colleagues at work. We are unaware of much of the hidden meaning in those conversations. At this point, let me say that everyday conversation and other verbal narratives may seem like a rather banal basis on which to make claims about the deep structure of our mind. They're not. While talking is, of course, human's stock and trade, the significance of spoken language isn't adequately understood.

It's during coffee breaks and after meetings are over, when "free-flowing" conversation is the rule, that many topics are thrown out for possible discussion. Some of these topics catch our interest, and we may stick with them for a time—while some don't. Why? Most researchers attribute this sort of "random talk" to a milling-around process intended to simply help members get acquainted. But is such topic-hopping, in fact, random? The short answer is no, it isn't. The longer answer is what this book is all about.

If we listen with a trained ear to the particular words, phrases, and tone of voice people use, we can deeply listen to the hidden feelings and thoughts that people are concealing—often even from themselves. Deep listening applies not only to adult conversation but to children's as well. This book, then, is about training the ear to hear hidden and unconscious meanings in both individual and social conversations. This is what I call deep listening.

On some level—every day, in some way—we all try to understand *how* language *means* and how the mind works. We must, because social living requires it; it's as basic as that. Survival and success in our life's goals depend on it. In philosophy the long-standing study of trying to assess the feelings and concerns of our fellow humans is called the Problem of Other Minds.

I began recognizing unconscious meaning in conversation in my small-group dynamics laboratory and have found some fascinating—indeed, often bizarre—findings. Over the past twenty-five years, in my research using T-groups (*T* stands for training), I have found that a great deal of language and conversation thought to be only literal by both a speaker and a listener is actually a kind of "metaphorical" unconscious communication that the speaker is not aware of. I found, for example, that often the ostensible literal topic of identical *twins* was a kind of metaphorical way of referring to *two* people in the conversation. But, admittedly, not always. As even Freud is reputed to have said, "Sometimes a cigar is just a cigar" (that is, not a phallic symbol).

Hidden meanings are not just found in laboratory research; they are also found in everyday conversations. Generally speaking, it's during times of informal chatter that unconscious meanings are most clearly visible. During highly structured conversations like business meetings, unconscious material may be difficult to recognize, but just prior to such meetings, during the first few minutes of ritual chitchat and small talk, or after the meeting there is often a wealth of unconscious meaning being communicated.

What I call deep listening and deep talk have not been systematically observed or psychologically explained before. Certainly there are books that purport to explain how to interpret unconscious meaning, but the method typically advanced is so general as to be almost useless, or it's a variant on a fuzzy Freudian kind of interpretation and we almost have to be trained psychoanalysts to understand and to uncover the hidden meaning. Even then, the interpretation is more fantasy than reality-based. This isn't just another of those books. This book is based on a very concrete and natural language method for recognizing and analyzing unconscious meanings in everyday conversations. And no, Freud didn't explain all this unconscious talk—but he almost did, and indeed should have (see Chapter 5).

Somewhat more technically, I have come to call these examples of unconscious language *subliteral conversations*. For short, I refer to them as *deep talk* and the uncovering of these deep meanings as *deep listening*. The term *subliteral* simply indicates word meanings that are unconsciously attached to the conscious, accepted, or standard literal meaning of words.

We overlook a great deal of what's happening in our everyday life. When we look out at our lawn, for example, we see a relatively homogeneous patch of green. But a biologist with his or her specialized knowledge looking at the same lawn will see a lot more than a patch of green lawn. The same is true for the psychologist or linguist looking at everyday conversations—and of course for ourselves as well.

Despite the fact that much of our life is spent talking to each other, surprisingly little is known about the complexity of meaning in our talk. Most people are usually just too busy talking to recognize what is unconsciously being said, and scientists are too busy focusing on grammar, semantics, rhetoric, and other more formal aspects of language. The full meaning of our words goes unheard.

In the group therapy and the small-group research literature, however, occasional and brief instances of deep talk or what I have come to call subliteral conversations have been sporadically noted and generally referred to as symbolic or metaphorical communication. Indeed, there is no shortage of books and articles on hidden meanings. But without a systematic method, such symbolic analyses become simply intuitive interpretation, and "metaphorical" utterances become mere coincidence, or random puns. Indeed, when I first began publishing my findings in peer-reviewed scientific journals, editors almost immediately dismissed them as—at best—Freudian, as coincidence, and—at worse—as "schizophrenic," as "wild puns," as " sheer fantasy," or as simply "ridiculous." You will understand why editors responded this way before you reach the end of Chapter 1.

Since those early times, I have developed an extensive systemic method divided into fifteen major categories with over sixty separate cognitive and linguistic operations for analyzing and—more importantly—for validating unconscious or subliteral conversation in everyday life. See the Appendix in my previous book *Between the Lines: Unconscious Meaning in Everyday Conversation*.[4]

This methodology provides the simple rules for parsing or breaking down the components of the stories and the language used to tell them. It also provides the rules for analyzing the parsed components and for establishing the validity of the analysis. I can't present this detailed methodology here. But in order to demonstrate that deep listening is not what early journal editors thought it to be, and to help you to understand the illustrations, from time to time I will be describing parts of my method.

There is always the danger of imputing unconscious meaning where it doesn't exist. Although this is true of analyzing the meaning of all communication, it's especially true for hidden meanings. Admittedly, many of the illustrations presented in this book strain—almost to the breaking point—the bounds of what we think is reasonable and what we think is cognitively possible.

I developed my methodology to guard against reading too much into the meaning of a piece of talk. Skeptics and critics of subliteral talk have to earn their naysaying by countering this methodology. It's not acceptable simply to say that it's all just a wild bunch of coincidences. I might note in this regard that the methods and procedures I have developed provide many more rules for analyzing subliteral meaning than we—linguists notwithstanding—consciously have for analyzing the literal and conscious meaning of everyday language.

The Usefulness of This Book

And so, it's apt to ask, of what use is understanding unconscious meanings in talk, and who is it useful for? First, let me say that it's useful for just about anyone, as there are many situations in everyday social life and at work where information about what people may be "really" thinking or feeling is difficult or impossible, but yet important to know. Deep listening can yield valuable and interesting information. The many illustrations throughout this book reveal the multifaceted nature of human relationships—indeed, of human nature itself.

The examples and illustrations I have gathered through the years not only provide confirmation of what we often suspect is going on beneath the polite surface of social conversations, but also frequently reveal new and poignant insights into age-old and near-eternal human concerns. These concerns include issues revolving around gender, sexuality, sexual preference, race and ethnicity, age, authority, leadership, religion, communication, and the individual versus the group or society. The examples thus reveal a lot to us about human relationships in all their complexity, stereotypes, and prejudices (see especially Chapter 9).

At work, fear of the boss or certain coworkers or the reward system may lead to people's withholding their true feelings about one another. Deep listening can be useful for those who manage, lead, or take part in the increasing number of small groups or teams used in the business world.

Second, my subliteral method can be used to train mental health therapists and counselors engaged in individual cognitive-behavioral, psychodynamic, or group therapy. The importance of the metaphors that clients use in psychotherapy has been recognized for some time.[5]

Deep listening can provide therapists with additional valuable metaphor-like information about patients' unconscious attitudes, the feelings and thoughts that patients may not want to reveal or of which they are not even aware.

Third, a great number of social and psychological support groups have sprung up, ranging from Alcoholics Anonymous to single-parent groups to simply people who want to talk about life and hear others do the same. Most of these groups have conversations about problems and issues that their members have. These groups are made to order for applying deep listening. Whether as a counselor or as a member, deep listening to these groups can reveal a wealth of useful information not revealed consciously. In short, this book can be useful for anyone who is interested in how the mind works.

Fourth, recognizing hidden meaning in everyday language can be fun, like recognizing slips of the tongue; indeed, it can be made into a most intriguing daily pastime for yourself and friends. The everyday social world can become your private laboratory. This can be very useful. While everyday examples are fine for learning to recognize possible deep-talk meaning, they don't provide all that's necessary for establishing its validity. Fair warning: Some of what you will hear may be things that "even your best friends won't tell you." Indeed, some may be things you don't want to hear.

I would like to make it clear that I don't use the terms *valid* or *true* to describe many of the strange mental operations that I've found and present in this book. Nor do I make such absolute-truth claims regarding the conceptual underpinnings that theoretically explain my findings. Even though I've developed an extensive method to validate subliteral conversations, scientifically speaking it's too early to make any absolute claims. But this is not to say that the analysis of subliteral conversation is just a hypothesis. Given my methodology, the history of similar findings, and the fact that many of the findings are compatible with other cognitive research and theory, the methodology constitutes something more than an hypothesis, but something less than accepted fact. And there is nothing wrong with this. Indeed, this puts my deep listening in fairly good company both in psychology and in other scientific areas of knowledge. Accordingly, research will undoubtedly continue to modify my findings.

The Format of the Book

Throughout this book, I'll be showing by examples from everyday life and from my small-group laboratory how to engage in deep listening. Many of these examples of unconscious meanings have been verified with my methodology. Others are from everyday situations where it was not possible to completely verify them, but sufficient contextual information was available to establish at least a high probability of their being valid. In addition, their analyses were in keeping with the ones that I have verified with my methodology. Still others with less exact verification can at least serve as instructive hypothetical but probable examples of what they are illustrating.

I have packed this book with examples because the best way to learn to recognize and analyze deep talk is to immerse yourself in concrete examples and let your mind absorb the patterns underlying them. Providing the complete word-for-word original data from which each illustration is derived would be ideal. Unfortunately, it would be much too cumbersome and tedious to have done so.

As you read the many examples, you may find meanings that I have overlooked. I know that as I was rewriting some of these illustrations for this book I discovered meanings that I had missed when I first analyzed them. Indeed, you will begin to anticipate some of the meanings before I present my analysis of them.

The questions this book will answer include: How is deep talk possible? What are its mental mechanisms? How do feelings and emotions influence meaning? Why haven't the mechanisms of subliteral conversations been discovered before? Are there current data and theories that relate to subliteral meaning? What can the subliteral mind tell us that's new about the mind? What can slips tell us that's new about language? How is the subliteral unconscious mind different from that of Freud's and from the views of modern cognitive science? What does an unconscious mind that creates deep talk meanings look like, and what can it tell us about the nature of consciousness? Finally, what are the implications and practical applications of deep talk and deep listening?

The myriad illustrations in this book can be read according to one's interest. First, they can simply and generally be read as interesting demonstrations of subliteral meaning. Second, they can be read as revealing, in important new ways, how we creatively use language. Third, they can be read as revealing group dynamics that might otherwise go unnoticed. Fourth, the subliteral meanings can be read as revealing a great deal about the underlying dynamics of social life. Fifth—and this is their seminal importance—they can be read as revealing how the subliteral unconscious mind works.

Chapter 1, "Listening to the Grateful Dead, Live in Concert: Introduction to Deep Listening," and Chapter 2, "Slips of the Tongue or 'Slips' of the Mind: Come Now, Mr. President," use many everyday examples. These two chapters provide an introduction to deep listening, including references to the rock group the Grateful Dead and three illustrations from a CNN news program involving Wolf Blitzer and the *Burden of Proof* program with Roger Cossack that perhaps reveal their hidden personal views about President Clinton's affair with Monica Lewinski and the congressional impeachment process.

Chapter 3, "God Talk: Learning the Deep-Listening Template," notes that throughout the course of human history one universal and enduring concern is that of a God, an all-knowing authority figure. This deep-rooted God archetype is shown to be a kind of eternal or master template in conversations for expressing deep-talk concerns about authority figures.

Chapter 4, "Deep Listening About Relationships: What Friends, Coworkers, and Employers Won't Tell You," extending the idea of a God Template, illustrates people's unconscious and hidden concerns about their peers and authorities, in conversations. For example, feelings about leadership incompetence, being manipulated by leaders, fairness and equality, and being favored. Interpersonal deep-talk examples include competition, rivalry, jealously, double standards, separation and loss, being bored, and bragging. The chapter also shows how proper names are used in deep talk to reveal hidden concerns.

Chapter 5, "Discovering Deep Listening: What Freud Didn't Know, but Almost Did," will briefly recount the author's personal journey in discovering deep listening. It also counters the initial reaction of many who think "Didn't Freud say all of this?" with the answer "No, he didn't" and briefly examines what Freud really said about unconscious communication. The chapter ends by looking at the future of deep listening.

Chapter 6, "In Defense of Whores and O. J. Simpson: Precautions, Ethical and Legal," sounds an ethical note of caution in applying and revealing deep listening and examines unconscious meanings used in two court cases, one the O. J. Simpson murder trial. Two different aspects of deep listening are discussed, the first involving ethical issues of revealing hidden meanings, the second involving the validity of unconscious meanings.

Chapter 7, "Figures of Speech in Conversation: Numbers in the Mind," shows that just as words are often unconsciously selected into conversations because they express people's concerns, numbers contained in conversations similarly carry unconscious meaning, corresponding exactly to different factions or subgroups in a conversation. The chapter provides an extended methodical illustration of a set of numbers presented in a conversation, demonstrating how the unconscious mind works using numbers.

Chapter 8, "Sex and Gender: Women Under the Influence," shows that because whenever men and woman gather together sexual tensions are present, these tensions are often revealed unconsciously in the conversation. The chapter also shows how deep-talk stereotypes are also about sexual orientation.

Chapter 9, "A Niggardly Issue? Race Matters in Black and White," is concerned with deep listening about deep roots of unconscious racial prejudice. Many illustrations are used, including examples by the novelist Norman Mailer; commentator George Plimpton on the 1974 Muhammad Ali–George Foreman fight in Zaire, Africa; the use of the word "niggardly" by a white aide in the office of Mayor Anthony Williams of Washington, D.C., an African-American; and a magazine caption of two well-known black basketball players, Kareem Abdul-

Jabbar and Julius "Dr. J" Erving. The chapter concludes with an examination of when such racial "slips" constitute racism and when they do not.

Chapter 10, "Deep Action: Crossing the Rubicon?" shows that just as our unconscious mind reveals itself through our deep listening to deep talk, so too it reveals itself through our behaviors or deep actions. Freud and others have written about what are called "action slips." This chapter examines a number of examples of deep actions, including an analysis of the ransom note left at the JonBenét Ramsey murder crime scene.

Robert E. Haskell
Old Orchard Beach, Maine, January 1, 2000
rhaskeL1@maine.RR.com

Listening to the Grateful Dead, Live in Concert: Introduction to Deep Listening

Implicit learning is the default mode for the acquisition of complex information about the environment . . . [and] there are good reasons for endowing the unconscious and implicit systems with cognitive priority.

ARTHUR REBER
Implicit Learning and Tacit Knowledge[1]

During a coffee break from a meeting, people are standing around talking, and without any apparent connection to anything that's been previously said, one person just happens to mention that he had an album of the rock group the Grateful Dead, Live in Concert. What does this mean? Is it simply a trivial comment, the kind often made during informal moments just to be social? The short answer is no, and that's what this chapter is about. The longer answer is what this book is about.

If the topic of the Grateful Dead means something other than what it seems to mean, how are we to know what it really means? And if, indeed, it means something more than what it appears to mean, can understanding such a piece of apparently random conversation be useful to you, as a friend, an employee, or a member or leader of a meeting? I will explain the real or hidden meaning of the comment about the Grateful Dead in a moment, but first, let me describe the conditions under which such hidden meanings are attached to what appears to be a simple literal piece of chitchat.

Generally speaking, it's during times of informal chatter that unconscious meanings are most clearly visible; for example, when people are standing around waiting for a meeting to start, or during coffee breaks, or in the first few minutes of "warming-up time" when ritual greetings and small talk are socially required. It's under these conditions that many topics are thrown out for possible discussion with little or no apparent logical connection between them. This social process has been called phatic communion, where conversation is used to create a mood of sociability rather than to communicate anything in particular. Most social psychologists and other researchers say the purpose of this sort of random chitchat is simply to help us test the interpersonal waters with each other, get acquainted, and find our way around the social and conversational terrain. It's our verbal sonar, as it were.

Once the context of the conversation is known, we then "map" the topic or story onto the actual conversation. In graphic form, for example, suppose there is a literal story in a conversation that's about the following:

A. 4 people in a bar,
B. 2 of whom are young men and two young women, who
C. are being boisterous, and who
D. are dominating the social interaction and conversation.

The story can be hypothesized as deep talk when the elements in the story correspond to and can be mapped onto the here-and-now conversation *where there are the same four elements as the literal story:*

A. 4 group members,
B. 2 of whom are young men and two are young women, who

C. are being boisterous, and who

D. are verbally dominating the group interaction and conversation

Some of these dangling conversations catch our interest, and we may stick with them for a while—some don't. Why? If we know how to listen, we can clearly see that such phatic topic-hopping is not random and is more than simple getting-to-know-you talk. In my research over the past twenty-five years using T-groups (*T* stands for training) in controlled laboratory conditions as well as from everyday social settings, I have found that some of our everyday language and conversation thought to be only literal by both the speaker and the listener is actually a kind of "metaphorical" unconscious communication that neither the speaker nor the listener is aware of.

Listening to the Grateful Dead, Live in Concert

In order to discover the hidden meaning of the opening story about the Grateful Dead, Live in Concert, it's necessary to understand some simple principles of the natural method I have developed to deeply listen to such language. First, we need to look at the story in relation to other comments, and second, we need to understand the context of the meeting that took place prior to the talk about the Grateful Dead.

After his initial comment about the Grateful Dead, the speaker then added, "I never go to concerts anymore because there are too many young kids there." As a part of the same topic-hopping series of comments, the chitchat drifted into talk about what people do in their spare time and about whether they just do nothing or have to be always doing something. A member said, "I feel like I am *dead* when I am not doing anything." Here we have two references by two different members to the word *dead*. Now it's important to know that the meeting the members had just left didn't reflect much planning and leadership and was perceived as not accomplishing anything; it seemed to drag on and on. Sound familiar? Essentially, then, this is what the comment about the Grateful Dead unconsciously meant:

It reveals the hidden feelings that at least two members had about the meeting. They felt the meeting was very long and boring. Thus they felt that they were not only feeling emotionally *dead* but that they were *grateful* for the coffee break. Further, the "Grateful Dead, Live in Concert" comment is likely a statement that they were not only *grateful* for the coffee break but that they now felt more *alive*. They were indeed, *the grateful dead, who now felt alive.* The initial means of deeply listening to such conversations is quite simple: Map the topic of conversation onto the here-and-now conversation and situation to see if there is a match.

But there's still more meaning to be teased out of these short comments. The member's statement that "I never go to concerts anymore because there are too many young kids there" equates to his feelings that the problem in the meeting was that some members were not acting responsibly but, rather, like kids and that during the meeting some of them either weren't listening or weren't helping the meeting to be productive. The reference to *in concert* likely refers to the fact that during the break all members of the meeting were talking at once, or acting together in concert.

In short, the topic of the Grateful Dead, Live in Concert, was a kind of poetic or metaphorical expression of some members' feelings about the meeting and the way the leader let it be conducted. It seems our mind engages in a kind of double-entry bookkeeping when it comes to creating meaning. Much of our everyday conversation, then, expresses more than the standard or literal meaning attached to it. The Grateful Dead example is a rather abbreviated one, though clearly giving an initial view of how to recognize and analyze and deeply listen to deep talk. Other examples get much more complex.

At this point I should note for readers who may be Grateful Dead aficionados, or "Dead Heads," that I'm told there is no such album entitled *The Grateful Dead, Live in Concert* (at least no nonpirated album). That the speaker used this expression, however, is not just a mistake: It's a mistake with deep meaning. As I point out in Chapter 5, "mistakes" are often used so that the literal story will fit the deep meaning that the speaker wants to express. To have merely said that he listened to the

Grateful Dead would not have been sufficient to express his feeling of being "alive" and the fact that all members of the meeting were feeling this way.

Think about this Grateful Dead example for a moment more. With this example, as well as all future examples, we must ask one simple but crucial question, a question that we seldom ask about conversations. That crucial question is this: *Out of all possible words and phrasings and out of all possible topics that could be selected into a conversation, why are the particular ones selected, and why are they selected into the conversation at that particular time?* Again, cognitively and linguistically this a critical question that's virtually never asked and consequently never answered. But it must be addressed if we are to understand the psycholinguistics of deep meaning in everyday conversations.

I have found that topics, phrases, and words aren't just selected into conversations by happenstance. Our mind is more highly ordered than that. Linguists know that word choice during a conversation occurs in a two-stage process. First, because words have multiple meanings, our brain reviews (called *lexical accessing*) all possible meanings of a word that are in our mental dictionary (called a *lexicon*). Then, from the context, our brain chooses (called *lexical selection*) the assumed appropriate meaning in the context in which it is to be used.

Finally, with respect to the Grateful Dead story, you will note that the speaker didn't just select any topic. First, the story was about a group as opposed to a single artist. This was because the deep talk was about a group of people in a meeting. Second, we must ask why the speaker didn't select a different musical group. Why specifically the Grateful Dead? Why not Metallica or the Beatles? Or the female artists known as the Dixie Chicks? Neither of these groups would have allowed him to express what he wanted to express. You will note that the Grateful Dead is an all-male group, like Metallica and the Beatles. And the meeting was dominated by the male members. None of these alternative musical groups, then, would have served to express the deep-talk meaning that the speaker was feeling—that is, "dead." Clearly, beneath the flow of our literal chitchat there is an immense cognitive and linguistic machinery operating (see Figure 1.1).

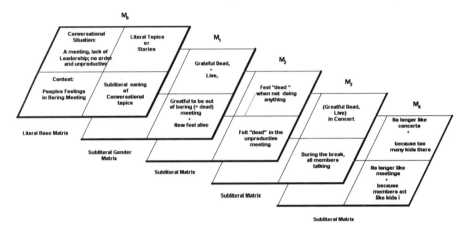

FIGURE 1.1   The Grateful Dead, Live in Concert Matrix Map

Understanding how to deeply listen to deep talk is not only simple, but more importantly, it's quite useful both in social conversations and at work. Since most people spend a great deal of time at work and therefore in group situations, let me continue using the workplace as an example. Recognizing the hidden meaning beneath office chitchat can be useful for you whether you are an employer or employee. For both those in a position of leadership or subordinates, information about what the other really thinks or is feeling about you is not ordinarily available. Survival requires that we lie a great deal.

For a boss or supervisor, knowing what subordinates think of you or how good a job you're doing is often not possible because you have evaluation power over them. You know what I am talking about here (see Chapter 4). Let's say the boss asks how you thought the meeting went. The social answer is: "You did great, boss! Good job. " The real answer may be quite the opposite. Armed with people's hidden and real feelings, a person in a position of authority can begin to look more closely at his or her leadership style and subordinates' reactions. Likewise for a subordinate, deeply listening to the deep talk of the boss can be very useful.

Hypothetically speaking, what if the boss happens to begin talking about a "Little League team that, no matter how hard the members try, they just don't have what it takes to be a winning team"? Or worse yet, what if the boss goes on to mention "one particular red-haired member of the team is a particular liability who is keeping the team from even winning one game"? Hmmm. If you have red hair, perhaps you should start looking for another job.

Deep talk, then, can be seen as a kind of coded message, and learning to deeply listen and decode it can serve as a personal surveillance system that gathers intelligence data for you. Our brain/mind seems to have evolved as a bioelectronic detection device for picking up and monitoring people's concealed feelings and concerns. Thus, it detects what's going on, in finding out what your spouse, your boss, or your friends may be really saying and feeling. Learning to decode chitchat, then, can be a valuable skill.

Another quick example from my place of work: When a person is being evaluated for work performance, it's to be expected that this person will have strong feelings and concerns. As a member of a Reappointment, Promotion, and Tenure committee, I was observing and evaluating a colleague's classroom teaching performance. I will call her Joan. Part of the topic for the day was establishing scientific validity and finding corroborating evidence. In the process, Joan stumbled a couple of times over the word *corroborating*, ending up with a pronunciation with the *cor* and the third *o* almost inaudible. It sounded like *rob-rat-ing*—which, in fact, I was doing. So Joan, revealed that she was indeed concerned with me, Rob, rating her.

Now, the importance of this particular illustration lies not in its having revealed a deep feeling or concern that wasn't already fairly obvious but, rather, in its having shown yet another mechanism of how deep talk occurs and thus how to deeply listen—or, more specifically, how to deeply listen for how proper names can be used in deep talk.

The question now is: How do you know whether what you think you heard is correct or not? This is a different and more complex problem than recognizing what seems to be deep talk. For now, suffice it to say that understanding the context surrounding the talk is very important for judging whether a piece of deep talk really means what you think it means. I will speak to this important issue of validating deep listening in more depth in the following chapters.

Even at this early point, I am sure that you now have a fairly good idea of what deep listening is all about and how useful it can be. It gets better as we go along. Deep talk can speak volumes to those ready to deeply listen.

On Speaking Volumes

While writing this book, I was talking for the first time to a book agent on the phone. I was explaining my theory of deep listening to her. After I gave her a few examples, she began commenting on the idea. Somewhat peripherally—apparently simply associating to the word *conversation*—she said, "You know what I don't like about conversations in social situations? I hate it when you go to restaurants and everybody's talking so loud." Her comment made my deep listening antennae nudge at my conscious mind. At that point, I asked myself: Was her apparent tangential comment a piece of deep talk for telling me that I was talking too loudly over the phone? I immediately answered myself: "Yes." I had been talking quite loudly. After becoming aware of this, I quickly lowered my speaking volume. Now the question is: On what basis do I think that her comment was deep talk? First, I have noticed for some time that when I am focused on explaining my deep-talk material on the phone to editors (which I had to do many times), my nervous system often shifts into high gear, with the pitch of my voice rising by an octave and my volume by a number of decibels. Second—and this is always a crucial question—why did she "just happen" to select the example of people talking too loudly? It was, after all, hardly related to my examples of hidden meaning.

Going against my experience, I decided to e-mail her, describing this episode to see if she (a) had purposefully used her example of loud talking as a kind of consciously coded speech to let me know I was talking too loudly, or (b) had at least been aware that I was talking loudly. Not surprisingly (in my experience), she denied both. She then added—with a written tone of vindication—that this was probably not a good example of deep listening because she had a slight hearing problem and always had the maximum volume of her phone turned on high, implying that she wouldn't have noticed if I had been talking loudly. While quite possible, this doesn't preclude her having failed to notice my loud volume—at least unconsciously. This is why. If she always had her phone volume on high to adequately hear normal conversation, then by definition, my voice would have been perceived as being louder than *her* "normal" hearing. The fact that she didn't consciously experience it has no bearing on her physical nervous system's registering the actual louder-than-normal volume.

In deciding to ask her for feedback, I said that I was going against my experience, because I have found that almost invariably people not only deny any awareness of their deep-talk meaning but often respond to my inquiry in an amused way and laugh it off as incredulous. Or they respond in a somewhat aggravated or defensive tone. People don't take kindly to being told that they said something that they had no awareness of saying. We know, however, that it's not only conscious impressions that can influence how someone reacts, but unconscious impressions as well. Who knows what negative impression I was creating by talking so loudly? Fortunately, I noticed it by her deep-talk response and lowered my voice. I have found that carefully listening for hidden meaning with a deep-talk ear can be very useful. This simple example speaks volumes about hidden meaning.

We can often hear deep talk in children's conversations. The unconscious mind of the child is much closer to consciousness than is the unconscious mind of an adult.[2] Thus one might expect children's unconscious *meanings* to be closer to conscious meanings than are adults. I owe this next example to my colleague, David Livingstone Smith.

In a classroom in a rough inner-city primary school in the East End of London, nine-year-old Todd was being picked up by his therapist. Even though the teacher in the class knew the therapist was coming to pick Todd up, *the teacher hesitated and was passively resisting and exerting her authority* over the therapist before allowing the child to leave the class. During this time, the other children were watching and *Todd seemed uncomfortable with his two authority figures vying.*

Upon arriving at *the therapy room, the therapist found that it abutted a noisy hallway—and during Todd's session children in the hall rattled the doorknob and banged on the door.* Not a particularly good environment for therapy. *There was certainly a sense of intrusion and a lack of privacy. In addition, the therapy room itself was a mess.* Other children had broken or stolen many of the toys, *indicating destructive intrusion of third parties into a space that's supposed to feel safe and private.*

Todd began to play with a toy castle in the therapy room, saying that he liked Robin Hood and that he never missed a film about him. He then recalled a scene from a film in which *Robin Hood and his merry men were being pursued by bad guys trying to kill them.* Robin Hood was on a horse and his merry men were on a carriage. *The bad guys made a sudden turn in the road and fell off a cliff.* Todd then started placing bad soldiers inside the castle and good soldiers outside. *The bad soldiers spoke Spanish* and the good ones spoke English. Then he made the *tower in the castle a Star Trek spaceship.* He put many soldiers inside and said that it was a safe place. He added that *bad soldiers got inside, pretending to be good,* and that it was very easy to get in. *Soldiers inside the spaceship now began to fight.* In Todd's stories, he is revealing his feelings about what transpired on his way to therapy.

First, there is *an image of a gang of bad guys pursuing some good guys, with the good guys trying to escape.* The reference to Robin Hood and his gang (= good guys) escaping the bad guys is likely deep talk about the interfering teacher (= bad guy), and about Todd and his therapist (= good guys) trying to "escape" the classroom. The stage is set here for a conflict over territory, freedom, and privacy. On a metaphoric level, the relationship between Robin Hood and his merry men and the sheriff of Nottingham is an appropriate image for the relationship between a disruptive child and the school authorities.

Robin Hood's tactic of making the bad guys fall off a cliff is likely about *eliminating interfering third parties.* (According to Smith, in children's play this elimination of third parties is typically accomplished by killing them.) That the bad soldiers took over the good soldiers' territory likely represents Todd's sense of *impingement on his private therapeutic space*, with the bad guys being the kids in the hallway banging on the door and rattling the door knob—and also being his interfering teacher.

The castle tower that became a Star Trek spaceship, the safe place where Todd put many of his toy soldiers, was then invaded by the bad soldiers, who were being dishonest and pretending to be allies. Here Todd was likely *expressing his fears about dangerous intrusions from multiple third parties* into his private therapeutic space (the teacher, the children in the hallway, and his therapist). He was feeling alone. In this scenario there is also some representation of Todd's conflicted feelings about the inappropriate therapist.

The image of dishonesty, whereby the bad soldiers con the good soldiers by pretending to be good, is likely a reference to the inadequate therapist. After all, *the therapist didn't provide much of a feeling of strength, safety, and protection; recall that the teacher initially exerted her authority over the therapist and that the therapist, in turn, was unable to procure an appropriate therapy room.*

In addition to this context, there is evidence that Todd was in fact engaging in deep talk and that Todd's therapist was referenced as a "bad guy" of sorts. First, it's linguistically interesting that the bad soldiers were Spanish, given that Todd's therapist was Italian and had a last name beginning with S. Second, during the same session, Todd told other stories that were thematically parallel to this story.

The Need to Know

As you can already see, there is nothing esoteric about recognizing unconscious meaning. It doesn't take a psychoanalyst to figure it out. A quick way of understanding and recognizing unconscious meanings is to think of what we commonly call slips of the tongue and double entendres where more than one level of meaning is revealed (see Chapter 2). Deep talk, like slips of the tongue and double entendres, provides a window into the deeper reaches of our mind. This kind of unconscious or encoded conversation has not been systematically observed or explained psychologically.

Most of us—indeed, all normal human beings—wonder what our friends or coworkers are thinking and feeling. By this, I mean what they are "really" thinking and feeling, not the public facade that's mostly presented in social situations.

We all have what the humanistic psychologist Abraham Maslow called a very primitive *need to know*.[3] This *need to know* has evolved over millions of years. There are only a few big questions that we humans would like to know the answer to, and one of these is, how does the human mind work? This book is an attempt to formulate an answer to at least a part of the big question of how our mind works.

We have this *need to know* because our social living, as well as our physical survival, requires it; it's as basic as that. Listening carefully beneath the words and stories of friends, family, and coworkers can reveal eternal human feelings and concerns of favoritism, rivalry, jealousy, competition, sexual feelings, gender issues, and leadership and authority concerns, as well as attitudes about racial and ethnic relationships (see Chapter 4).

Let me offer another workplace example. During a recent all-day departmental retreat that I attended, the chair (whom I will call Sam) was talking about the e-mails he had been sending to the administration about various issues. When Sam was finished, a faculty member interjected, saying that Sam's *e-mails really had quite a few typos and other spelling errors in them, and that he should be more careful because this reflected against the department.* Without so much as a flinch, Sam acknowledged this point and went on with the meeting. Since the faculty member had said this to Sam in a very nice manner, it appeared that Sam didn't mind. About five minutes later, another faculty member asked Sam if he would give a talk at a meeting off campus. Having inquired as to what kind of meeting it was, Sam added, *"Sure, as long as it is not like academic meetings where colleagues stand around and kick your ass for any mistakes you make."* Coming right on the heels of criticism about his own mistakes, Sam's language revealed, on some emotional level, that he did indeed care about being publicly criticized for the errors in his e-mails.

Once again, as in many such instances of deep talk, it may seem that the person—in this case, Sam—knew exactly what he was saying. In other words, it may appear that he was expressing himself in a kind of "coded speech," letting the faculty member know indirectly how he felt about being criticized. But it wasn't coded speech. It was deep talk. How do I know this? I know because a few days later Sam was visiting me at my home. When he brought up the incident of being criticized, I began to quiz him, taking care not to lead him on or give away what I was up to. (At this point he was only vaguely aware of my work on deep listening.) When I had finished, I specifically explained why I was so interested in what he was aware of during his remark. When I related to him my subliteral analysis of his delayed deep-talk response, he was quite surprised and swore that his remark was not intended as a "coded speech" or innuendo against the faculty member. In short, Sam wasn't aware of the unconscious meaning of what he had said.

Sam is generally pretty up-front about such matters; he wouldn't lie about his intended meaning. That he did actually care about being criticized was reflected in the very fact that he brought the topic up, saying that he thought the faculty member's remarks were inappropriate in the context of a meeting and that he should have expressed his concerns privately. Such department meetings take place thousands of times a week in the workaday world—and deep talk occurs during most of them.

Groups: Teaming with Deep Talk

As individualistic as we are, the fact is we increasingly live in a world of groups. Whenever people get together regularly for any purpose, they are forming a group; this is true whether the group is for playing cards, a support group, a committee, or for an extended business or team meeting. Indeed, working in groups or teams is becoming an increasing fact of life in business.[4] Just as deep listening is about individuals, there is also deep listening about the group or team. Just as there are lessons to be learned from listening to deep talk about individuals, so too are there lessons to be learned by deep listening to the state of the group or social situation.

You will note that I am referring to *the group* as if it were a separate entity. That's because it is. Similar to individuals, groups exhibit stages of development. Groups and teams have a life course. Along this life course are inevitable problems and issues, problems and issues that the group may either not be aware of or doesn't want to openly acknowledge. Deep listening to group or social conversations can reveal these problems and issues. This is important because the extent to which these issues and problems remain unacknowledged or unresolved is the extent to which they will limit a group's performance.

The lesson to be learned from deep listening to the deep talk about a group is that leaders and members can begin to work with these problems and issues revealed by deep talk (either directly or indirectly) to help the group and the individuals in it to function more effectively. Let's see how this works and what the implications of deep listening to groups and teams may reveal.

In the initial stages of a group, it's no mere accident that the conversation often revolves around problems of functioning in a *new job*, about *being newlyweds*, or about *periods of adjustment* or other topics having to do with beginnings and adjusting. These topics in the initial stages of a group are deep talk for expressing the here-and-now concerns of group members getting to know each other, including social intimacy, communications, and problems of maintaining a separate identity while merging into the group culture and norms. These simple conversations can tell you a great deal about the state of the group and its stage of development.

Suppose, for example, the talk is about *doing well* in a new job or marriage. This would tell you something quite different about the group than talk about *problems* in a new job or marriage, especially if the group's conscious and literal conversation seems to imply that members think the group is doing fine. The same talk confined to an individual member or two of the group would tell you yet something different. This deep talk would tell you something still different depending on what the surface meaning of the talk seems to say.

Just as with many marriages once the honeymoon is over, groups typically move into a period of conflict revolving around what the rules are going to be and around the emerging leadership structure. In most groups, these concerns are seldom discussed openly. Even when they are discussed, the deeper feelings underlying them may not be openly expressed. During this stage, deep-talk topics are frequently about competition and conflict. Movies may be selected as topics. Out of all the possible movie themes, the classic movie selected may be *Star Wars*. The word *Star* in the title may be deep talk about a member who is emerging as a the leader or dominant member of a faction in the group. Similarly, the word *Wars* clearly indicates hidden conflict and competition in the group. At other times the topics used to unconsciously express feelings may be about disaster movies in which groups of people are dependent on each other or about well-known groups that are breaking up. Obviously, deep listening can tell you a great deal about what may be emotionally going on in the group beneath its surface.

Assuming the group doesn't end or continue in the war or disaster mode, it moves into a stage in which members are ready to establish rules and group norms so that they can perform their job. Again, the surface talk about this process may be quite different from what is really happening. This process may begin with a discussion about *traffic problems* and the need for rules to regulate the *traffic flow*. This may be deep talk about the recognition of a need for rules to guide group interaction. If the group gets stuck on discussions about *traffic jams,* watch out. On the other hand, talk about how *Congress works out a compromise on a bill* may herald good news about where the group is heading.

When the group finally works through these unconscious or hidden feelings and issues, the members can begin performing their real work. This stage may be heralded by deep talk about how to *successfully grow plants*, about *building houses*, or *remodeling*, or perhaps stories about *family problems being resolved*. Listening deeply to a group, team, or social situation can be a powerful assessment tool.

I should point out that these stages are not as sequential or as mutually exclusive as they appear. It's possible for more than one stage to be operating at once, but to varying degrees and on different levels. In a group where the task is clear and the group is structured by a leader from its inception (as in business meetings), members may appear to begin performing immediately, but the hidden issues that I have described will often reduce performance. Moreover, different individual members may be experiencing the feelings and concerns of different stages. In other words, all the issues may be operating in any given stage.

Finally, it's inevitable that most groups will reach a termination point, either for a given session or because the group's function is over. Prior to the end of a group, or of a single social conversation, the endings may be heralded by deep talk discussions about *death, funerals, divorce*, or other topics that relate to either an ending or termination. I began to increasingly recognize that in committee meetings I could predict a motion to adjourn, even though there had been no time limit set and despite the fact that the climate of the meeting would not suggest that it would come to an end shortly. For example, in a committee meeting discussing curriculum innovation, the topic shifted slightly to *private schools that were closing down* because of a lack of interest by students in their curriculum.

My prediction of adjournment was in part based on the following: First, there's the fact that the literal topic was about *closing down*. Second, the topic was about *private schools* and the committee was at a private school. Third, a few minutes before this conversation a member had excused himself from the meeting. Someone's leaving a group is sometimes perceived (either consciously or unconsciously) as a cue to adjourn. I then began to notice in other everyday situations that topics having to do with termination, such as *death* or *leaving on vacation*, were brought up during group conversations just before the conversation came to an end.

Not all discussions about such topics as death or divorce or being abandoned herald the ending or termination of the group. They may mean something different. This is where careful deep listening to the context of conversations is important for understanding the meaning of deep talk. Instead, these topics may be deep talk about losing a group member (as we saw above) or about an absent member. The multiple ways that any given literal topic can mean different things in different contexts point out the importance of understanding the context of the situation and of having a controlling method for validating meanings heard by deep listening.

Born Free

At this point I feel the need to say a few words about some people's. skeptical reactions to deep listening. Having introduced you to the basic idea of deep listening by presenting multiple examples, you may be somewhat skeptical—if I dare put it so mildly. At the risk of appearing to be totally lacking in humility, let me say that you haven't begun to see the good stuff yet.

A major reason that belief in the reality of deep talk often meets with incredulousness and downright indignation is that it appears to be an affront to one's sense of autonomy and self-determination, otherwise known as free will. Let me explain what I mean.

Suppose after I tell you what a wonderful, bright, industrious, good-looking, and thoughtful person you are, I ask a small favor of you, which you kindly say you will do. Now suppose after an embarrassed pause at being so highly praised, you resume our previous conversation about your new job. In doing so, almost incidentally you say, "Oh, I forgot to tell you about my new supervisor. He is one of the most manipulating people I have ever met. And he's not even very subtle about it." For the sake of argument here, let's assume that this comment of yours is really your deep-talk reaction to my buttering you up (that is, *manipulating* you) by telling you how wonderful you are so you'll do a favor for me. In other words, the story of your supervisor is really about me.

Now suppose the next day we are having a conversation about my research into deep talk, and in explaining it I use our conversation of yesterday about the manipulating supervisor. I tell you that it was deep talk, with you telling me that I am not only manipulating, but that I am not even very subtle about it. The odds are high that you will deny this because it was not what you consciously meant. You further say (assuming your statements to be true) that you didn't even make the connection between being complimented and my asking you for a favor. From my experience, I have learned that you will become defensive, indignant, angry, incredulous, or all four.

In short, my attributing unconscious meaning doesn't fit what you experienced. It was ego-alien, as we say in the trade, alien to your sense of self and autonomy, just as we don't experience our dreams as being created by our self or our free will and thus disown responsibility for whatever images they may contain—especially a dream image where you kill your best friend. This is one aspect of the free will problem. Another one involves our belief in our mind being free.

As I indicated at the opening of this chapter, ostensibly random chitchat has been considered by most researchers as a kind of quantum-like talk that's not subject to Newtonian-like lawfulness, as is most of the universe around us. This belief in our autonomous free will especially applies to our mind and conversational self. But is this belief true, or does it belong with the flat-earth view of our planet? I suggest the latter is more likely the case, at least in relation to our conscious self.

There is no preordained reason why the human mind and our conversations should be any less structured and lawful than the rest of the natural universe. Indeed, as in physics, why should there not be cognitive "quarks," meaning "strings" and other fundamental structures of the mind from which all other higher level orders of meaning are generated? Indeed, this book is based on the Einsteinian assumption that "God does not play dice" with our mind, that our mental universe is just as ordered as our physical universe and is not the result of chance. Now, I am willing to admit that what I have just described may be a slight overstatement. But probably not by very much.

Remember, in analyzing deep talk we must ask why particular words, phrases, sentences, stories, and topics are selected for conversation. Why not others? Why are they selected at a particular time? And why is a particular wording expressed in the particular—sometimes peculiar—way it is? To answer "That's just the way we talk" is not to explain it at all. It begs the question. And worse yet, to answer "Whatever the intricacies are, they're accomplished by free will" is to put the analysis of conversation and language outside the reach of science.

Deep Listening and the Subliteral Mind

I would now like to initially introduce what I call the subliteral mind.[5] The subliteral mind creates what I also call subliteral language and meaning and what as a shorthand designation I have labeled *deep talk* to which we *deeply listen*. As I briefly noted in the introduction, the term *subliteral* indicates unconscious word meanings that are attached to the conscious, accepted, and standard meaning of words, that is, to their literal meaning. Hence *deep listening* refers to uncovering the meaning beneath the literal meaning and thus *subliteral*. For example, the literal meaning of the proper noun *Grateful Dead* of course refers to a rock group. The subliteral meaning—as we saw—involved the word *grateful* being used as an adjective modifying the noun *dead*.

I coined the term subliteral for my approach to unconscious meaning, language, and mind for two important reasons. First, the concept replaces traditional Freudian terms like *latent*, and *unconscious*, or *symbolic* meaning. It also replaces the linguistic term *metaphor* insofar as the term is used to describe symbolic or implied or figurative meaning in our language.[6] This name change isn't just a semantic game; it's an important conceptual distinction. This is why I developed the concept of a subliteral mind in order to carve out from a nearly all-meaningful popular notion of an unconscious mind a more concrete set of principles and procedures for understanding and recognizing subliteral meaning.

What I am calling the subliteral mind is not a vague black hole beneath our conscious mind, as much popular thinking about the unconscious would have it. The processes making up the subliteral unconscious are real. They are based in a complex of neurological circuits integrated in a multilevel series of networks all linked together. That much of our linguistic processes are unconscious is not new. It's universally accepted, for example, that most of our normal use of language is carried out unconsciously. As we speak, we are unaware of the hundreds of rules of grammar that we are using. In the subliteral mind, these unconscious language processes are linked to emotional and feeling states that somehow creates deep talk.

I should note, too, that the subliteral mind doesn't exist as a permanent unitary thing in our physical brain. Different circuits and networks are used at different times. In fact, the subliteral unconscious slips and slides from a deep unconscious state that is inaccessible to us to a partially conscious state. We will see throughout this book examples of being nearly conscious of subliteral meaning, as when people become immediately aware of a slip of the tongue they've just made.

What I mean by the subliteral mind sometimes being partially conscious is that some part may be completely conscious, as when people have conscious thoughts and feelings that they withhold from public view because of fear, social etiquette, or taboos. Under such conditions the other parts of the subliteral unconscious—the complex of neurological circuits and networks that create the cognitive and linguistic operations—are initiated in the same way as when feelings are completely unconscious. Some of the more classical terms for different levels of unconscious functioning, like preconscious, subconscious, or co-conscious, can be roughly equated to the various levels of subliteral unconscious functioning at different times. The subliteral mind, then, is often a mixture of conscious and unconscious processes and often switches back and fourth between these two states. (For more on this, see my book *Between the Lines*.)

At this point, it's useful to briefly describe the general social and psychological conditions that create subliteral conversations in everyday settings. Understanding these conditions provides cues to when subliteral conversations may be occurring.

Some Conditions and Principles for Deep Listening

There are eleven principles of deep listening. Understanding these principles will help you to deeply listen and to recognize when deep talk may be occurring. The social conditions to look for that surround conversations are ones that are informal and have little structure to them, having little or no imposed rules, agenda, or purpose. These conditions can often be seen at coffee breaks, at parties, or in other newly formed social get-togethers including free-flowing conversations that occur during new personal relationships. Social occasions of this kind could be characterized as "just hanging around, talking." Like most of social life, these conversations take place within implicit social taboos, rules of etiquette, and other social norms and expectations that tend to preclude the open expression of feelings and of what people may be really thinking.

I should also emphasize that the classic T-group leadership style is to be nondirective; the trainer/leader sits relatively silent most of the time. This creates conditions of anxiety, ambiguity, and uncertainty. At least in the initial stages of group development, the leader is the main concern of members (just as a relatively silent or noncommunicative boss at work is or a silent parent at home is). It is into this void that members of a T-group or a social or work conversation project their concerns and feelings. There are also rivalry issues for the attention of the trainer/leader just as there are in similar everyday situations.

Fragmented or dangling deep-talk conversations, then, occur under conditions of uncertainty and ambiguity and tend to create elevated feelings of anxiety and increased emotional arousal in most people. Together these conditions create a cognitive state in which unconscious emotional and linguistic schemas are activated that merge with and shape our otherwise conscious use of language. Somehow, it is out of this social matrix that deep talk is created. We will see this time and again throughout this book.

Principle #1: Conversational Conditions.   The optimal conditions for deep listening are low social structure, ambiguity, uncertainty, and anxiety. The more that a conversation floats freely, the more likely it is that unconscious processes are activated and deep talk is involved in the literal topics.

Principle #2: Knowledge of the Situation. The more one knows about the conversational situation, that is, about the social context, the people in the situation, the issues, conflicts, and expectations, the better one can map the knowledge onto the literal conversation.

Principle #3: Emotional Arousal. Under the previous conditions, when emotional arousal levels are elevated, they create a cognitive state in which nonconscious affective schemas are activated that merge with and shape conscious literal use of language.

Principle #4: Emotional Loading. In addition to general emotional arousal, subliteral material is optimally generated from specific, emotionally loaded issues and concerns.

Principle #5: Social Censoring. The more social taboos, rules of etiquette, and other social norms that preclude the open expression of feeling and ideas, the more likely deep talk occurs.

Principle #6: Silences. The more awkward silences and pauses in a conversation there are, the more likely deep talk occurs immediately following these awkward silences and pauses.

Principle #7: Conflict. The more conscious or unconscious conflict that exists between or among members of a conversation, the more likely deep talk will occur.

Principle #8: Associations. A topic is often subliteral if it's associated in time, that is, follows immediately after another topic (especially after a silence or pause in the conversation).

Principle #9: Topic Selection. Subliteral topics are "selected in" because they relate to participants' feelings that occur in the conversation. It's important to recognize that a large number of topics are possible in any conversation. The crucial question is, out of all the possibilities, why are particular topics selected?

Principle #10: Lexical Selection.   In addition to the selection of topics, the selection of a given word or phrase also constitutes a choice from a large number of possible equivalent lexical (our mental dictionary of words with their associated morphemes and sounds) or semantic choices.

Principle #11: Mapping.   Deep talk is present in a piece of literal conversation when it can be demonstrated that the talk has a parallel structure that can be mapped onto the conversational activity.

The everyday world is an incredible natural laboratory in which you can observe and deeply listen in to deep talk. Though there is no such thing as mind reading, deep listening is about as close as you will ever get to reading minds.

The best way to learn to recognize deep talk is to read as many examples of it as possible. In cognitive and educational psychology, we know that being exposed to many examples leads to developing what are called mental schemas. A *schema* is a pattern or a kind of template that helps us corral or impose an order on the apparent complexity around us. That's why I have packed this book with many examples of deep listening. As you read through them, you are increasingly creating mental schemas or templates that will help you deeply listen to conversations.

Of Wind Tunnels and T-Groups: How T-Groups Are Like Everyday Social Conversations

A T-group is a special kind of training (hence the *T*) group in which typically ten to fifteen participants learn about how small groups and teams work by actually functioning as a group. The classic style is for the "leader" not to lead, but to be nondirective. Since many of the illustrations I present come from my training groups, you may see them as not typical of the deep talk that occurs in everyday life. Not so. They are, in fact, exactly like those that occur in natural everyday settings. Comparing the illustrations I give from my T-group with those that I present from everyday conversations will clearly show that the personal concerns and cognitive operations are the same. The T-group situation is a microcosm or model of everyday conversational situations. It is a kind of magnified and dense version of everyday conversational interactions. Think of a T-group as the social equivalent to the scale model of an aircraft in a wind tunnel used by aeronautical engineers to simulate the effect of wind on the aircraft under everyday flying conditions. In the same way, the T-group is a scale model of social situations, with the special conditions that influence the T-group comparable to the wind in the aeronautical engineer's wind tunnel. In fact, all psychological experiments are kind of scale models of everyday life. The everyday world is itself a natural laboratory where everyone can observe—and experiment with deep listening.

Because the T-group is a dense micro-version of everyday social conversations, whether they are casual or work-related, illustrating with examples from these groups allows me to present a wider variety of deep talk than if I just used my personal everyday experience. Moreover, as you become acquainted with deep listening, you can add your own examples. My friends and colleagues have.

Let me close this chapter by saying that either the analyses of deep talk I present in this book are the consequence of my engaging in a kind of sheer paranoid schizophrenic fantasy or we now are beginning to recognize something about how the mind works that we didn't know before. Let's see more of what the mind does during conversation. It gets even deeper. Much deeper.

Slips of the Tongue or "Slips" of the Mind: Come Now, Mr. President

It would not be surprising if more were to be learned from poets about slips of the tongue than from philologists and psychiatrists.

SIGMUND FREUD
A General Introduction to Psychoanalysis[1]

Everyone is familiar with the idea of slips of the tongue, especially with the ones that seem to reveal unconscious meaning, otherwise known as Freudian slips. Indeed, in the popular mind, it's Freud who discovered such slips of the tongue. He didn't (see Chapter 5). One of Freud's classic examples involved the Austrian parliament president who opened a meeting by declaring it "closed," with Freud suggesting that the president unconsciously wished the meeting wouldn't take place. Such slips are "mistakes" from the point of view of the conscious and intended meaning. Other slips are considered just plain mistakes or errors in language, like the classic mechanical mistakes often called spoonerisms, after a British cleric and scholar, William Archibald Spooner (1844–1930). For example, a person might mean to say, "Allow me to *show* you to your *seat*," but actually say, "Allow me to *sew* you to your *sheet*," where *show* and *sew* and *sheet* and *seat* are misvocalized. Certainly, some slips are simply mistakes like this spoonerism and can be explained linguistically in terms of mechanical error, but not all slips. Spoonerisms and other kinds of verbal slips based on mechanical errors simply aren't made of the right unconscious stuff.

My phrase *slip of the mind* is a takeoff on the phrase *slip of the tongue* in the Freudian sense. Though both involve revealing unconscious meaning, they are not identical. Slips of the tongue are largely characterized by slips in meaning with single words. By contrast, slips of the mind are more extensive linguistically and may require complex phrases, entire sentences, and whole stories to express their double meaning; they are not in fact slips of any kind. They are based on parallel meanings. They are what I have come to call deep talk that reveals unconscious meaning. Like simple mechanical speech errors, even Freudian slips don't have the right stuff.

Our minds work in strange ways. The phrase *slips of the mind* first occurred to me when I was pondering puns and slips of the tongue in relation to our unconscious mind. As I was doing so, the analogous idea, *slips of the mind,* occurred to me. The question is, why did this concept occur to me at this particular time? Looking very briefly at that question will provide a glimpse into how deep talk is made.

First, I was of course quite familiar with the concept of a slip of the tongue. Second, the semantic association based on the initial similarity between the phrases slips of the *tongue* and slips of the *mind* is reasonably clear, especially since they both occur in the mind. There was a third factor that precipitated my association between the two concepts that I realized once I found out when I started thinking about it: At the time the phrase *slips of the mind* occurred to me, I was thumbing through the many yellow 2-by-3-inch pieces or *slips* of paper that I always kept with me to write down ideas and insights that often popped into my head at the oddest of times. Indeed, I was physically working with little *slips of the mind.*

Slips of the mind don't happen only in casual conversations. They occur in TV news programs, talk shows, and advertisements as well.

Slips of the Mind on CNN News

News reporters generally try to be objective, not letting their personal views influence their reports, but being human, this is difficult, if not impossible. Listening subliterally may tell us what the reporter's or host's real views are. Unlike casual conversation, news programs are often highly structured by scripted monologues that the newsperson can read from a TelePrompTer. In spite of this, deep talk still happens.

The well-known CNN news correspondent Wolf Blitzer was reviewing and reporting the latest news on President Clinton's alleged affair with a young White House intern, Monica Lewinsky, and a dress that she kept that supposedly (at the time of airing) had the president's semen stain on it.[2] After talking about Clinton's having to give a sample of his DNA to compare with the stain on her dress and about Clinton's not being truthful, and indeed his being charged with perjury, Wolf ended his report by saying that the president should just *come clean*.

Need I explain that on a literal level this idiom means to tell the truth, but in this context it can embody quite another meaning? On a conscious or literal level, Wolf's use of the phrase seemingly meant that he thought Clinton should stop lying about his affair with Monica and just tell the truth. But is this slip of the mind simply a slip? Or did it reveal Wolf's real feelings about the affair? I suggest it's the latter. I don't believe that this is a simple pun on the phrase *come clean* but, rather, a slip of the mind revealing the belief or attitude of the speaker. In any event, looking at the phrase itself, on a deep-listening level the phrase *come clean* could mean either that Wolf hoped (1) that Clinton's DNA didn't show a DNA match with the stain (in short, that he should have come *clean*, without a stain) or (2) that Clinton should not be having an oral sexual tryst in the workplace with a subordinate and staining her dress with his semen.

Since this is an everyday example, I don't have the history, the full context, or other controls that I have for deep talk that's generated in my groups. So how are we to know that Wolf's comment wasn't just a simple pun, and if it wasn't, how are we to know what Wolf's view of the Clinton affair really was? One simple slip doesn't necessarily (though it can) mean a slip of the mind just happened. Under the circumstances, we should follow Wolf's subsequent reports to accumulate an ongoing history and context of such deep-talk examples. This would provide additional information by which we could then begin to verify the analysis of Wolf's slip of the mind. As it happens, I do have another slip of the mind by Wolf on the Clinton-Lewinsky affair.[3]

Wolf was reporting that President Clinton's team of lawyers was about to launch an attack on special prosecutor Kenneth Starr's grand jury report that indicated Clinton lied about his oral-sex affair with Monica. Wolf meant to say that Clinton's team was about to engage in an *offensive* against Starr's report, but he slipped and said they were about to engage in *offenses.*

Again, is this just a slip of the tongue, or is it a deep-talk slip of the mind that reveals Wolf's true feelings and attitude about the Clinton-Lewinsky affair? Given the continuous reportage of Clinton's alleged sexual behavior in the workplace that many people found *offensive,* Wolf's slip was perhaps clear about what he was really thinking regarding Clinton's behavior: That they were not only legal *offenses* but were *offensive.* No sooner had he said this than an ever-so-slight twinge could be seen on Wolf's face. It was clear that he immediately realized what he had said—and perhaps revealed his personal view of Clinton's tryst: That Clinton shouldn't be having sex in the Oral Off . . . (oops, sorry) I mean, Oval Office.

Not infrequently such slips of the mind may appear so obvious that they seem to have been consciously created. I have found, however, that this is not the case. And unlike Wolf, often the speaker does not recognize these seemingly blatant slips. In transforming oral and visual examples of deep talk (that is, ones either personally experienced or ones from TV) into a print medium, one loses a great deal of information and cues for assessing whether the person was consciously creating the slip or pun. Slips of the mind can provide a surveillance system for gathering interpersonal intelligence and other deep-background information.

(The Clinton-Lewinsky oral-sex tryst reminds me of the 1972 Nixon scandal, when two reporters, Bob Woodward and Carl Bernstein, broke what has become known as the Watergate scandal with secret information from a deep-background source. The Clinton-Lewinsky tryst perhaps gives new meaning to Woodward and Bernstein's secret source of information, whose code name was *Deep Throat.*)

Yet another CNN slip of the mind referring to Clinton's tryst with Monica occurred while I was watching a program called *Burden of Proof.*[4] During all the talk about the possible impeachment of President Clinton for lying under oath regarding his workplace sexual relationship with Monica, Roger Cossack, one of the hosts of the program, made a slip of the mind that was expressed in a slip of the tongue, or so-called speech error. In talking about President Clinton's testifying before a grand jury, Roger meant to say that the event was *unprecedented*, but he slipped and clearly began to say un*presidente*d. Most linguists would call this a simple mistake and say that it was caused by confusing the similar sound and spelling of the two words which interfered with each other, ending in a speech error. These linguists are not correct, however.

From a deep-listening perspective, the meaning of Roger's slip in using the word *unpresidented* in this case likely refers to his unconscious (or at least concealed) attitude that Clinton should be removed from office or impeached. Why do I say this? First, while the similarity of sound is clear, this is not simply a meaningless speech error caused by the similar sound of the two words. Try this: Repeat *unprecedented* and *unpresidented* out loud. Note that the *prec* in unprecedented is pronounced like *press*, whereas the *pres* in president is pronounced like *prez*, requiring a different aspiration or kind of glottal configuration in your mouth. But this is trivial, really. Let's get to the real shape of the meaning here.

The linguistic explanation of this slip would be that it was simply caused by the two words' being confused and interfering with each other and that it indicated no hidden meaning. Both *unprecedented* and *unpresidented* begin with *unpre*, which is followed by either the consonant *s* or *c*, which can be similarly pronounced. These letters are then followed by the vowels *i* or *e*, which also can be pronounced similarly. Finally the words end identically with . . . *dented*. But the slip has meaning. An analysis of the linguistic mechanisms involved may explain the *how*, but it doesn't explain the *why* of the slip. To understand the *why* we have to understand the context of the slip. (See the "niggardly" example in Chapter 9.)

Since this program and the previous number of programs were about the possible impeachment of Clinton for perjury, we have a history and context to analyze this statement; there was a deep background for impeachment-related meanings. It seems probable, then, that Roger's use of the prefix *un* that was attached to *president* and the suffix *ed* indicating past tense was psychologically the equivalent of something coming *un*hing*ed* or *un*glu*ed* or *un*seat*ed*. Hence *un*president*ed*, that is, no longer president. Indeed, the adjective *unseated* has been used in a past context of impeachment. History books talk about the attempt to impeach President Andrew Johnson (1865–1869), the seventeenth president of the United States, as an attempt to unseat him.

As with any slip, having only this one example from Roger without access to his personal views means there is no way of assessing with any high degree of certainty the deeper motivation for his "slip." Roger's slip may reveal nothing or it may reveal that he either believed that Clinton should or would be impeached as the result of the scandal. Quite different meanings, but equally revealing information about his beliefs.

After this incident, I began carefully watching—that is, listening—more closely to Roger and his co-host, Greta van Susteren. It soon become evident to me that my analysis of Roger's deep talk on Clinton's impeachment was perhaps appropriate. I say this because when *Burden of Proof* first began reporting on the Clinton-Lewinsky affair, both co-hosts seemed to be trying to report in a neutral or objective manner. As time went on, however, it seemed to me their reporting became less objective. It became clear to me that Greta was more against impeaching Clinton, while Roger seemed to be leaning toward the anti-Clinton side. I say this, too, because I saw Greta being interviewed on *Larry King Live,* where she essentially stated her views. This kind of contextual information is important when assessing deep listening. (See Figure 2.1.)

CNN Un-Presidented Matrix Map

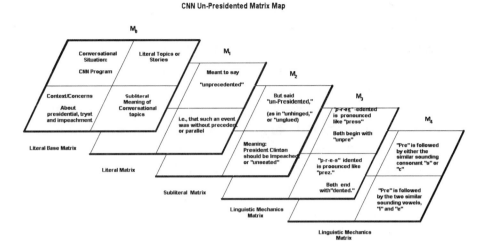

FIGURE 2.1   CNN Unpresidented Matrix Map

One more point about my analysis of Roger's slip: Analyzing slips of the mind from TV news and talk shows is a little more problematic than in natural settings. Roger's "anti-Clinton" position could have been by design on the part of the program's producers in casting Roger and Greta as taking slightly opposite positions on the issue. However, I should point out that this would not necessarily undermine my deep-listening analysis of Roger's attitude as he would have had this pro-grammed "anti-Clinton" position on his mind while apparently trying to appear at least somewhat objective. That would create the condition for his slip of the mind. As I outlined in Chapter 1, the underlying im-petus for generating deep talk is nearly the same whether attitudes or beliefs are unconscious or consciously concealed. In any event, Freud was probably right when he said that we can't keep secrets. They seep out of our every pore. Again, transforming a visual and oral event into a print form loses the tone of voice, facial expressions, and other cues by which I assessed the intent of a slip. In any event, contextual infor-mation is important to assessing the validity of the slip, and gathering more than one incident begins a pattern.

Fiddling with Words?

The following is yet another interesting illustration from the workplace, and it's somewhat more complex and problematic in terms of the complete extent of its meaning. I was having lunch with some colleagues and administrators in the campus cafeteria. Present were the male dean of the college who was a biologist, a male assistant dean, a woman associate dean, and two male faculty members. The social relationships among us had always been very collegial and informal, with all of us feeling comfortable enough with each other to joke around without having to be careful about what we said. Into this luncheon gathering entered the woman president of the university. As typically occurs when a boss joins his or her subordinates, the social climate changed.

I was engaging in social chitchat and waving my hands around as people often do when talking. It was obvious that I have a noticeable deformity in a couple of fingers on one hand. The assistant dean asked, "What's the matter with your hand?" The president noticed it, too, and immediately interjected, "Do you have arthritis or something?" I then explained that it was a relatively rare genetic condition called Dupuytren's contracture, largely affecting males with Anglo-Saxon heritage. I further explained that thousands of years ago when the Vikings swept down from the north, raping and pillaging their way through Scotland, England, and Ireland, this genetic condition was one of the historical consequences.

It was clear that this comment about raping made people feel uncomfortable. Unthinkingly, I nevertheless continued, saying jokingly that from a Darwinian perspective the raping and pillaging wasn't all bad as it helped to create diversity in a gene pool. While my statement may not have been in good taste, it was nevertheless accurate in a genetic sense. Now, at this point, the male assistant dean turned red in the face and almost had an apoplectic fit. Given the women at the table, especially the president who was strong on feminist issues, he said to me, "Jesus, Rob, you'd better be careful; you're treading on thin ground ere!" By this he meant that women might take offense at my saying that rape had a positive biological function.

An awkward pause ensued. Then, glancing at the president, I said, "It's all quite biblical, you know." Responding to being asked what I meant, I said, "You know, like the sins of the father being passed down to the sons"—literally meaning the genetic consequences of the Viking rapes being passed down to later generations, with one form of "sin" being my Dupuytren's disease. There was some nervous laughter and, again, a brief pause.

The president then posed a question seemingly unconnected to anything in the conversation. She asked if anyone knew or could recall the name of the play in which the father of a Jewish family was experiencing trouble with maintaining his Jewish traditions. The male assistant dean said it was *Fiddler on the Roof*. Shortly after this, I excused myself and left. As often happens, it didn't dawn on me until later that the entire conversation—particularly the president's question—likely carried subliteral meaning. But what meaning might it have had? Here is my take on it.

For those not familiar with the play *Fiddler on the Roof*, the basics are these: It takes place in Czarist Russia in 1905, when anti-Semitism was overtly increasing. The father is a poor milkman with five unmarried daughters to support. His eldest daughter doesn't want to consent to a traditional arranged marriage to a middle-aged butcher. After much ado, he and his wife finally consent to the daughter's wishes. The changing times are saying that children shall decide partners for themselves—a scenario that the parents see as a breakdown of traditional values. But worse, they discover not only that another daughter has married a Russian soldier of her choosing but also that he is not Jewish. This is just too much for the father to accept, so he disowns this daughter and she is henceforth shunned.

The inquiry referring to *Fiddler on the Roof*, in which tradition as well as a Jewish family's gene pool were being threatened, was likely a subliteral comment on my Viking story of rape and pillage in which tradition and gene pools were violated. Given the context in which *Fiddler* was selected into the conversation, it almost certainly did not carry positive meaning, especially given that the question was asked by the woman president—who was Jewish.

But there's more, as my colleague David Smith pointed out to me when I described to him the above initial subliteral analysis of the conversation and asked him for his thoughts on it. Unlike my own analysis, his had to do with my subliteral role in the conversation, which I had completely missed—not an uncommon occurrence with respect to subliteral conversations in general. My having added the comment about Vikings *raping and pillaging their way through Scotland, England, and Ireland* likely reflected my unconscious feelings about having the president join us. In other words, I felt that, indeed, like the Vikings, she had "invaded" our friendly "traditional purity" with each other, transforming us into a more diverse group (i.e., population). Such feelings are not atypical when a boss or authority figure joins his or her subordinates (see Chapter 3). They rang particularly true in this instance, given that the president was not widely appreciated by many faculty members.

My later biblical comment about the *sins of the fathers* was likely a reference to my feeling that I had "sinned" by mentioning rape (and its positive evolutionary function) in the presence of women. My reference to the issue being *biblical* was also possibly a reference to the president's Jewish heritage. I suspect the president's selection of the *Fiddler on the Roof* topic immediately following my comment about Vikings raping and pillaging probably has other meanings as well; but since there's not enough story detail to allow me to precisely map it onto my contribution, I have to rely on contextual information and inferences. Almost certainly the president, who is Jewish, knew the title and details of *Fiddler on the Roof* but just couldn't immediately recall it. Based on this context, I can conjecture that she felt I was somewhat like the father in *Fiddler*, who was cast as a traditionalist and even as an anti-feminist (which I am not). The theme of *Fiddler* may also have called to mind her sense of Jewishness among non-Jews (i.e., diversity).

The president's selection of the story in *Fiddler on the Roof* may have still another unconscious meaning. The verb form of the noun *fiddler*—namely, *fiddling*—carries the meaning of being "trifling" or "trivial." Was the president perhaps commenting on what she thought about my carrying on about the Vikings and their Darwinian consequences? There's yet more to this story.

Sins of the Father

I have found that when a deep-listening story is being told, it may precipitate further deep talk by the person it is being told to.

A few days after the *Fiddler* luncheon, I was having a drink with a friend of mine who was among the faculty members present at the luncheon and was telling him about my subliteral analysis of the conversation that took place that day. Holding a doctoral degree in English and literary studies, and having read my previous book, he appreciated my analysis but nevertheless seemed somewhat skeptical. After a brief discussion, there was a pause. Then without apparent connection to anything, he asked me, "Have you heard from your brothers?" I responded, "No." But as I said "No," my deep listening antennae became active. I then said to my colleague, "I think your question, however, is an excellent example of subliteral meaning." Looking somewhat puzzled, he asked, "What do you mean?"

Now, before I give you the answer to his question, I need to explain its context. He knew that about a year or so ago my daughter, Melyssa, discovered that I have two half-brothers that I never knew I had. These brothers are about eight or nine years older than me. My brothers and I had the same father. Their father and my mother had an affair and I was the product of it. Summarizing all this to him, I answered his query about whether I had heard from my brothers by saying that it was deep talk—that it was a response to my having just described to him my analysis of the *Fiddler* luncheon conversation. This is likely why his question about my half-brothers was deep talk. And this is likely what his question unconsciously meant.

First, my half-brother's father having had an illicit affair with my mother is analogous to my story about Vikings raping as they swept down from the north in the sense that the affair was contrary to traditional norms. Second, as a parallel to the Vikings' raping, my brother's father had illegitimately contributed to my mother's family gene pool, making it more diverse. Third, the illicit relationship between their father and my mother was analogous to the daughter in *Fiddler* wanting to marry outside traditional norms and, indeed, outside the gene pool (i.e., outside her father's marriage). Fourth, my birth was analogous to the Vikings passing down the genetic condition involving the fingers on my hand. Fifth, since my brothers were only "half"-brothers, they were analogous to the daughter in *Fiddler* who, after marrying outside the Jewish gene pool, would have a child who was "half-Jewish."

Finally, since I had told this friend about my biblical remark regarding the *sins of the father* having been passed down to the sons, his asking me about my brothers implied an acknowledgment of the "sin" of my father. I, of course, was the "son" to whom sin was passed down—as a result of the "sinful" affair.

Why was the president's story about *Fiddler,* and why was my friend's question about my brothers selected into the conversation? And why at that particular time? I see my friend frequently, usually over either breakfast or lunch, and perhaps only once before, soon after I'd told him about discovering I had two half-brothers, did he ask me if I heard from them.

Judging "Slips" of the Mind

In Massachusetts, a judge giving instructions to a jury about to start its deliberations verbally "slipped," saying to the jury that the defendant should be "presumed *guilty*."[7] Of course in all cases judges instruct juries to adhere to the fundamental legal principle in U.S. law that a defendant is presumed innocent until proven guilty. The judge obviously meant to say the defendant should be *presumed innocent*. The question is: Is this slip considered legally significant? In other words, is it considered to reveal the unconscious attitude of the judge about the defendant, and therefore to prejudice the case? If so, the slip would provide grounds for a legal appeal if the defendant were found guilty.

After the court clerk brought this "mistake" to the judge's attention, he quickly corrected himself by addressing the jury saying, "Ladies and gentlemen, I've picked up on a, I guess it would be called a Freudian slip." He then gave the jury the correct instructions. For some reason, the defendant's attorney didn't object to the judge's slip of the tongue. Maybe the judge thought the evidence during the trial showed that the defendant was guilty. Maybe he didn't. Maybe it was just a simple speech error. Maybe it wasn't. Only the judge really knows. But did this "slip" turn out to be legally significant. You bet.

After the jury found the defendant guilty on one of three charges, the defense attorney used the judge's slip as the basis for an appeal. He argued that it created a substantial risk of a miscarriage of justice, because it conveyed a message to the jury that the judge had concluded that his client was guilty. It's interesting to note here that Freudian slips are apparently considered real by the legal profession, at least as indicated by the *Modern Dictionary for the Legal Profession*, which defines a Freudian slip as a misstatement theorized to reveal the unconscious thought or a conflict or desire of the speaker.[8]

So, again, did the judge's misstatement harbor his hidden feelings or attitude toward the defendant's guilt? The answer depends on whom you ask. And the correct answer goes to the very core of my theory of deep talk and slips of the mind. I will hold off addressing this important point until the end of this chapter. In the meantime, the following examples (along with the previous chapter) should help you to answer the question yourself.

At this juncture, I need to emphasize two important methodological points that need to be held firmly in mind throughout the rest of this book. The first is that virtually all linguists and cognitive scientists believe that unconscious slips and puns are simply speech errors that are linguistically lawful and therefore devoid of unconscious meaning. I agree with the first part—that they are lawful—but not with the second part—that they are therefore meaningless. Some are. Some aren't. And the ones that aren't meaningless use the same mechanism as the ones that are. In short, subliteral narratives appear to use many of the mechanisms involved in speech errors and action slips, but suggest an underlying intentionality—at least in this class of subliteral "errors" and "slips."

One notable cognitive scientist who is an exception to my generalization and does believe that slips may have meaning is Bernard Baars, editor and author of *Experimental Slips and Human Error*. Baars and his colleagues have conducted some fascinating laboratory experiments on Freudian or unconsciously motivated slips. While he remains cautious, he leaves the door open on unconscious meaning. Baars says, "From some of our findings. . . . the most immediate conclusion might be that the Freudian hypothesis is just plain wrong. But that is too simple."[5] Baars leaves the door open for possible new methods that may less "blunt" (as he puts it) than current ones. I would, of course, strongly argue that my method is a new and less blunt method for investigating unconscious meaning.[6]

The second point to hold firmly in mind involves reemphasizing that the crucial methodological point and question to be asked about all deep talk examples is this: Out of all possible words and phrasings and out of all possible topics that could be selected into a conversation, why are the particular ones selected, and why are they selected into the conversation at a particular time? Cognitively and linguistically this a critical question that's virtually never asked and consequently never answered.

If, indeed, slips of the mind do reveal unconscious beliefs, attitudes, and intentions, can such slips have legal implications? For example, what if an attorney or, worse yet, a judge made a slip in court that could be detrimental to a claimant or defendant? Could such slips be used by either the prosecution or the defense? Unlikely, you say? Let see.

Deep Listening to TV Advertisements

Clearly, deep talk doesn't only occur in personal conversations. It happens on TV news programs as well. We can also observe it in TV advertisements and on talk shows.

It's no secret that unconscious meaning is often purposefully programmed into TV advertisements. It's also well-known that writers for advertising use "pop" Freudian notions about the unconscious mind and sexual symbolism to construct their ads (see Chapter 8).[9] In addition, they are well versed in how the mind associates ideas. Those who make up ads are very conscious of language and double meanings. They assume that unconscious or only semi-unconscious meanings will influence you.

One recent ad for cable TV talks about all the business advertising done on cable and ends by saying, "America is sold on cable." On one level this says, " American businesses do their selling with cable TV ads." On an another level, it says, "America is convinced about the effectiveness of cable ads"; that is, America is "sold" on it. Another ad for the brand name of vitamins called Nature Made ends verbally with a slogan that can be taken two different ways: "Nature Made me," or "nature made me." The first means the vitamins were made by Nature Made. The second one says nature made them; that is, they are natural. This double meaning couldn't have been expressed in printed form. Such ads try to influence you unconsciously.

A number of years ago I was watching what appeared to be a rather cute TV ad for dog food. But as I'll suggest, if my analysis of the unconscious meaning in the ad is correct, it ends up not being quite so cute. Many pet owners want the best for their pets. In a TV commercial about dog food, a little old lady who looked like everybody's grandmother was extolling the virtues of a particular brand of dog food that looked like hamburger. The little old white-haired grandmother says, "It's better than hamburger." At the close of the commercial she adds in a surprised tone of voice, "Better than hamburger, my word!"

Now, aside from the more obvious association of the product with an all-American grandmother figure, leading to the conclusion that not only is the dog food better than hamburger, but also thereby more patriotic, the ad is a masterpiece of construction. The literal meaning of the clause "my word" attached to the phrase "Better than hamburger" appears simply to be an exclamation, as in "My goodness, it's better than hamburger." Translated into deep talk, however, it also means: How are we to know it's better than hamburger? We know because grandmothers are true to their word. So the "my word" clause means "Take my word for it." The phrase "Better than hamburger, my word" also likely communicates to our unconscious mind the question, what's better than hamburger? Her word is. Thus, the only thing better than the hamburger is her *word*. So it must be damn good dog food.

But here is the real kicker to the whole ad: With just a little thought, the question arises: How does she know the dog food is better than hamburger?—unless, of course, she has eaten it. Now, before you say that this is ridiculous, consider the contextual fact that at the time the

ad appeared, there had been news stories about very poor elderly people eating dog and cat food to survive. Was this ad for dog food, then,
subliterally directed at the elderly? I believe it was.

Puns in the Making of Meaning

As we have seen with many of the deep-talk illustrations so far, what is
commonly called punning has been integral to meaning. In the following two examples, the use of similar sounds of words to make meaning
will be even more evident. What these two examples will also demonstrate is how we can catch ourselves in the act of deep talk.

One weekend my then-wife, Claudette, was leaving for the week to
attend law school in a neighboring state. At the time our young daughter, Melyssa, lived with me in Maine. Understandably, Melyssa was a little upset at her mother's leaving for the week, and of course it wasn't
my first preference to be left alone to parent my daughter either. As
Claudette was about to leave, I jokingly said to her, "So, you are deserting us." Almost at the very moment I uttered this comment, I knew
what I had "really" said. This comment didn't simply refer to the fact
that Claudette was leaving us alone for the week. It was a meaning-
making pun. We need to look a littler closer at the context for my comment to understand how it made meaning.

In making preparations to leave for the week, Claudette had made a
batch of chocolate chip cookies, most of which she was taking with her.
Now, chocolate chip cookies are my favorite, so I hated to see most of
them being taken away. My comment was not only deep talk about
Claudette's leaving or *deserting* us, but by taking my favorite *dessert*
with her, she was in fact also *desserting* us, that is, taking the *dessert* with
her. This is no simple pun, or a kind of verbal slight of tongue; it's a
window into the workings of the subliteral mind. What my mind did
was to make meaning out of the similarity of sounds to express an aspect of my feelings. While it's certainly true that we sometimes use the
word *deserting* to describe someone's leaving us, its use is not all that
frequent. Again, the point is, why was this word—out of many other
lexical choices—selected at this particular time?

A friend of mine, Virginia, recently visited her podiatrist to have her feet worked on. As she lay on his couch having her feet massaged, they were talking to fill an otherwise silent activity. As they did so, the podiatrist said that his clients often told him very personal things about themselves as they lay on his couch. Virginia replied that laying on a couch while having one's feet massaged was very relaxing and soothing. She said it was kind of like being in a psychologist's office having therapy, so people would naturally have a tendency to *bare their souls* to you. When she said this, she immediately became conscious of the double meaning: they bare their *souls* means they bare the *soles* of their feet to him. This may appear to be a simple pun or play on words. It isn't. Think about it for a moment.

In understanding this deep talk about souls, we must first ask (a) why the particular subject was selected into the chitchat and (b) why these particular words were combined into this particular phrase. There were many other words and phrases that could have been selected to express the meaning Virginia was expressing: that the podiatrists' patients tell him lots of personal things. For example, she could have replied to her podiatrist that his patients would *Pour their hearts out* (maybe this would have been used in a cardiologist's office). She could have replied, they would *Spill their guts out* (maybe this would have been in a gastroenterologist's office). Or she simply could have simply replied, *Yes, I guess they tell you their life stories*. But she didn't. She specifically said they *Bare their souls* to him—which they literally (soles) do.

Again, the imperative question is, why did she use the particular phrase and not any of the ones I just mentioned, or the myriad of others from our common stock of clichéd sayings? The first reason she didn't use any of the other possible phrases—and the most obvious— is that the homophones, *bear* and *bare* and *souls* and *soles* are semantically appropriate for a podiatrist. *Bear* has the meanings *to carry* and *to harbor* and *to support* weighty things like talk about souls; and of course the meanings of *bare* are *to expose* and *to become naked*. Secondly, the soles of her naked feet exposed to view are semantically equivalent to baring/bearing one's *souls,* to revealing deep personal aspects of oneself. Third, the other possible phrases that could have been

used, with the words *hearts* and *guts,* would not have been phonetically and semantically congruent with the parallel to a psychologist's
office as the word *soul* (psychology often being understood by lay people as the study of the soul). Fourth, the other phrases would not have
been as semantically congruent with the stereotypical association of
the Freudian couch with the couch she was actually lying on in the podiatrist's office.

Deep Listening to Deep Talk About Physical Events

It's not just the deep meanings in conversations that can be heard by
listening deeply. Physical events and objects surrounding a conversation are often unconsciously expressed as well. Though physically perceived, these events and objects may not be consciously noticed or
considered significant or meaningful. They are nevertheless often unconsciously processed into deep talk without speakers' being aware that
they are doing so. By listening deeply we can hear a *corpus* of these unconscious meanings.

Once more, this example I owe to my friend Virginia. She was attending visiting hours just before a funeral to view a departed brother-in-
law. As is typical, the body was laid out in the casket with the departed's
hands and arms folded or crossed. As is also typical, people attending
these solemn occasions stand around silently and quite formally. As
Virginia was standing with the others she saw the funeral director,
whom she knew but hadn't seen for some years, standing by the front
door. So she left the viewing to talk with him. Later when telling her
daughter, Sarah, about the occasion, they discussed the appropriateness
of her leaving the viewing to socialize with the funeral director. In response, Virginia replied, "*Well, it was better than just standing there all
stiff with your hands folded.*"

Literally, of course, this response meant just what it said. Socializing
with the funeral director was better than just standing around so formally. Now, if the subliteral meaning to the physical surroundings of
this occasion isn't already clear, it's this: The phrase is a reference to the
corpse itself lying there silently, stiff and with the arms folded.

With hindsight, one might think that Virginia would have realized what she had said subliterally, but like most people, she didn't. When her daughter pointed out the subliteral meaning to her, she was—again like most people—"aghast." The impact of feelings and concerns about the physical surroundings, then, are often incorporated into literal conversations. But this example doesn't end here.

Many weeks later when Virginia and I were discussing this instance of subliteral meaning, I said that when I write this funeral example up for my book, I was going to entitle it a *corpus* of meanings. She laughed and was surprised at my linguistic association of the term corpus with the funeral example. After a brief pause, she started to tell me about a writer she knew. She said that writers have strange minds, that their minds work differently from normal people. Then, almost without taking a breath, she caught the subliteral reference to me and said parenthetically, "present company excepted, of course," and continued with her story of the writer she knew. Once you start deep listening for subliteral meanings, however, you realize that in fact everyone's mind works "strangely."

Physical differences between or among people are often subliterally communicated—if only simplistically (see Chapter 9 for racial examples). A new student was inquiring about where he would find the office of a particular faculty member and how he would recognize her. As it happened, recognizing this faculty member was quite easy: Appearing to lack normal skin pigmentation, she looked albino, with very white or milky skin and hair. The person answering the student's inquiry, of course, didn't want to come right out and say that the faculty member was albino-looking, so she was described as being "very fair complected." During the course of the conversation with the student, the issue of career choices came up. Jokingly, the person said to the student, why don't you be a milkman? Obviously, milkman was not a serious recommendation. Out of all the possible career choices we have to ask why was the totally inappropriate career choice of milkman selected? From a deep-listening perspective, it's equally obvious that it was a subliteral reference to the albino-looking faculty member. Despite hindsight, it was also equally obvious that the person who offered the milkman choice was not aware of the subliteral meaning.

The following examples are from my groups, where I inform members that, mainly for educational purposes, I will be videotaping them from time to time. I also openly voice-tape each session. I also inform members that they can have full access to the tapes. I should mention that group sessions are usually conducted in a room with a one-way vision mirror. The topics that "just happen" to come up in the conversations often involve references to the *FBI* and *CIA*. In other words, despite members' being aware of the one-way vision mirror and the tape recorder, there remained unconscious concerns. The point is that even if I had not mentioned the mirror and recorder, members would have incorporated them into their conversations. As supportive evidence, in the early literature on small groups and group psychotherapy, repeated similar references to FBI and CIA have been obliquely noted and thought to be "metaphorical" expressions of patient concerns of being recorded or observed.[10]

In the initial stages of one group, the topic of conversation was *speakeasies*, illegal places to drink during the early 1900s prohibition against selling alcohol. The reference to speakeasies is again deep talk for members' concern with the tape recorder, subliterally meaning: speak easy so the tape won't record what they are saying. In yet another group, the game *charades* became a topic of discussion. You no doubt are familiar with the game, in which communicating is done in pantomime—so of course subliterally implying that the tape recorder would be rendered useless. How do I know that group members have concerns with these issues? In part, I know because on a conscious or literal level, some groups have consciously acted out these concerns by whispering and silently pointing to the tape recorder.

Here is another illustration that our unconscious often subliterally references physical things in the immediate environment into the conversation. I will start off with one of the more weird instances that I noticed. Seemingly not directly related to a discussion about raising animals, a person said, "I had a mouse that would just *peek* into the garage at the animals." You might think that this statement is a simple part of the ongoing discussion about keeping animals, and it is—but it's also more than that. Once more we must ask why this particular statement was selected into the conversation at the particular time that it was spoken. Here's the answer: During the discussion, a young woman in the group kept stretching up and down in her seat trying to see something in the direction of the door. Then the door opened just a crack and a person in the hallway who had been peering in through the small window now *peeked* into the room.

Most members were aware of what had taken place, but no one mentioned this event. It was, nevertheless, impressed upon their minds—both conscious and unconscious as the subliteral reference to the mouse that peeked into the garage demonstrates. This statement might seem like one that the person consciously contrived to kind of parody the event, but it wasn't. I checked with the person after the group session.

These illustrations not only show deep meaning but, again, also show how the mind sometimes incorporates its physical surroundings into language and social conversation. This aspect of cognition has not been recognized before. How it's possible remains to be explained.

We have seen that though both slips of the tongue and what I have been calling slips of the mind involve revealing unconscious meaning, they are not identical. Not by any means. Slips of the tongue are largely characterized by slips in meaning with single words, while slips of the mind are more extensive. Linguistically, slips of the mind often require complex phrases, entire sentences, and whole stories to express their consciously unintended meaning.

Referring to them as "slips" reveals all too clearly how they have been viewed: As anomalous curiosities, not as something more extensive with parallel meanings that reveal important linguistic and cognitive data about how the mind works. Slips of the tongue are "slips" or "mistakes" only relative to their contradicting our apparent conscious intent. Strictly speaking, they are not slips at all. They are real communications. In addition, referring to slips of the tongue as "slips" has retarded research into their real significance.

Henceforth, I will no longer use the phrases slip of the tongue or slip of the mind in referring to deep talk. So, why did I use these phrases in the first place? I used them as a bridge from something you were already familiar with to acquaint you with something new. So far most of the illustrations have been, like slips, based on relatively short examples of deep talk using play on words, short phrases, and longer topics. In the next chapter I will show how deep listening reveals more complex phrases, entire sentences, and whole stories to express extensive parallel meanings.

3

God Talk: Learning the Deep-Listening Templates

Stop here yourself for a while, that I may make known to you the word of God.

BOOK OF SAMUEL 9:27.44

Throughout the course of human history certain topics and themes have been of universal concern. These enduring themes and topics have been called archetypal. Archetypes are a kind of universal prototype or template of human experience that is somehow embedded in our mental apparatus. They are primitive modes of thought that tend to express themselves in mythological stories. Carl Jung, the one-time disciple of Freud, wrote extensively on archetypes. He believed in a special kind of unconscious mind that he called the collective unconscious. Unlike Freud's notion of an individual unconscious mind, for Jung, the collective unconscious is a depository for the experiences of the human race. Our collective unconscious may be made up of primordial archetypes.

Archetypal myths and stories seemingly reflect these ancient patterns of emotional concerns and experiences. Some of the more profound examples of these universal concerns and experiences can be found in the Christian Bible, with stories about sibling rivalry and jealousy like the one of Cain, who murdered his brother Abel out of jealousy, and the one of Jacob who cheated his brother Esau out of his birthright.

One very strong archetype is that of a God. I have come to see certain stories told in conversations as similar to myths that contain this ancient archetype of God.

In Western culture we have a set of religious beliefs derived predominately from a Judeo-Christian ethic. Many of us were brought up to believe in a God high in the heavens who is all-seeing and all-knowing. The belief in an all-knowing God or Gods, however, is more ancient that the Judeo-Christian ethic. In any event, for people raised to believe in a God who designed the universe we live in, who is able to see everything that we do, and who sits in the heavens judging us, such a God becomes by definition the ultimate authority figure, a kind of pre-technological great spy satellite in the sky.[1]

This image of God, then, becomes a very deeply rooted emotional unconscious archetype, or template, that likely forms the basis of our relationship with all authority figures. Accordingly, on an unconscious level our experience with more worldly authority figures resonates to our unconscious God template. When we are in a subordinate relationship, then we may unconsciously experience ourselves as God's children, with the authority figure as God.[2]

Think of the God template as being like the simple arithmetic formula $1 + 1 = 2$. We can plug most anything into the abstract slots of the formula and it will, of course, result in summing to 2. The basic God template looks like this:

The God Template

God	*God's Children*
Authority Figures	*Subordinates*
Parents	Children
Employers	Employees
Teachers	Students
Psychologist	Patients
Priests	Parishioners
Government Officials	Citizens
Group Leaders	Group Members

As you can see in the above figure, any authority position automatically belongs under the "God" slot and any subordinate position belongs to the "God's Children" slot. Because the T-group is a microcosm of the everyday world, I have found this God template to be quite pervasive in the stories told in conversations. Just as with the references to the FBI and CIA mentioned in Chapter 2, there is supportive evidence from the early literature in small groups and group psychotherapy, where references to God have been obliquely noted and thought to be "metaphorical" expressions of patient concerns about the therapist.[3]

Throughout this chapter, I present literal references about God that are likely subliteral references to my role as authority. Similarly, there are many references to my authority role in different contexts throughout the book. I need to point out that these references are to my role, not to me personally. Concern with an authority figure in T-groups and in social and work situations is typical.

At this point I need to reiterate the social context and concerns extant in T-group type situations. This is important information for deeply listening to the following deep talk about God. The classic T-group leadership style is to be nondirective, with the leader sitting relatively silent most of the time, strategically commenting on the group process. This is not entirely unlike many social and work situations. Such nondirective conditions often create anxiety, ambiguity, and uncertainty among participants. Consequently, in the initial stages of group development, the leader is of major concern to participants (just as a relatively silent or noncommunicative boss at work is or a silent parent at home is).

Initially not understanding a leader who seems to do nothing, members of a T-group or similar social or work situations project into this nondirective "void" their concerns and feelings: What is the leader/authority thinking? Why isn't the leader helping? Why does he or she let (as they experience it) the group flounder? Is the leader competent? There are feelings of being abandoned, and of being cheated because they are not getting what they think they should. They may feel that the course text is not helping them. In addition, there are rivalry issues for the attention of the trainer/leader, just as there are in similar everyday life situations. It's these concerns and feelings that can be mapped onto the literal conversations.

As we will see, my deep listening informed me of what some members were feeling about their group experience. On a literal level, I didn't know or at least I wasn't certain about how they were experiencing the group. Assessing individuals and group concerns and issues is often only possible by deep listening.

With each illustration in this chapter, I have included a chart that summarizes the literal topics and their deep talk meaning. You may want to look the charts over before reading the illustrations to give you an advance picture of the discussion's organization and meaning. However, if you want to remain intrigued and surprised along the way, then I recommend that you don't go to these summarizing charts until you have finished the stories.

The Mysterious Mind of God

Because the Judeo-Christian God is an all-knowing one, people often wonder what God is thinking about them. So too do people wonder what a person in a position of authority is thinking about them. The following example comes from a group discussion that was nearing its end. A number of members who had been absent in previous sessions were absent from this session as well. In response to these absences the group briefly discussed the topics of divorce, aging, and death, which are subliteral references to the absences being unconsciously experienced as separations and death. This discussion of death was followed by a more extended discussion about the pros and cons of religion. These general concerns about authority and the specific concern about the absent members are the predicating conditions that create the following deep talk.

Some members of the group felt that church was terrible because *Ministers and priests don't answer questions in church, like they should*. It was also mentioned by a few members that their *Philosophy instructor didn't really like to have questions asked in his class*. Others felt that *You just have to 'believe' what priests say, for mortals cannot understand the workings and complications of the world.* And, *At any rate, when you're young, you couldn't understand religion, anyway.* Another remarked that he could *Not believe in God when He let little children die.* In response, it was then said *Men can't understand what God is doing and thinking.* Some maintained that *Religion was too commercial,* and that *Billy Graham types make money by helping others but withhold their wealth.* Finally the topic of religion petered out, and the topic switched to divorce again.

To understand this discussion, we need to know something more about its context. The group had split into two factions: those who wanted the group to be more highly structured and who wanted me to provide structure, and those who were more independent and who wanted the group to naturally evolve (this is a standard split in many group-meeting situations). The former made frequent eye contact with me and directly attempted to elicit answers to their questions from me, but they were largely unsuccessful. From time to time, they would find ways to hurl little innuendoes at me about my not helping them. Mapping this piece of literal conversation onto the actual group situation subliterally reveals the God template at work.

Their discussing the topic of God was deep talk about my role, the authority, with the *Church* equivalent to *the classroom.* References to priests and ministers were also about me, the authority. That ministers and priests *Don't answer questions in church like they should* is deep talk about my being nondirective and not answering their questions. Similarly, the topic about *A philosophy instructor who didn't really like to have questions asked in his class* is deep talk about my not answering questions in the sessions. Having this topic mentioned twice is further support of its subliteral meaning. Both topics subliterally show that some members didn't accept the T-group philosophy of instruction: On an unconscious level, it *felt* as if *I didn't like questions asked in class.*

The statement *You just have to 'believe' what priests say for mortals cannot understand the workings and complications of the world* subliterally indicated that some members, while not completely understanding my philosophy of education and the group process, felt that it had to be taken on faith, that my nondirective stance had a valid purpose behind it. Thus, subliterally, to them my mind was mysterious—as is the mind of God.

The statement about *being too young to understand religion* is deep talk about them not having my years of experience that enabled me to understand the group dynamics. Like the previous statement, it also reflects some members accepted on faith that I know what I am doing and were not demoralized about the process. Others, however, were not of the same opinion about their experience. The remark of the member who said he could *Not believe in God when He let little children die* reflects a different opinion.

This is deep talk about some members' perception that they were not learning anything from me and my nondirective style—*that I was just letting them die.* But, again, other members were willing to stand on faith, as indicated by the statement that *Men can't understand what God is doing.* Like mortals (meaning novices) who can't understand God's purposes, so they too can't understand the purpose that a nondirective leader has in mind. This feeling was expressed as deep talk about God having abandoned them.

The total disbeliever who maintained that *religion was too commercial* and that *Billy Graham–type ministers make money by helping others but withhold their wealth* is making deep talk about *tuition paying my salary* and the perception that I was not giving anything in return. In short, my nondirective style was equivalent to withholding information from them.

The following is one way of verifying that all this deep listening is deep talk about a special kind of topic. Special topics are typically cues that there is a link between the here-and-now literal conversation and its subliteral meaning. Instead of defining what I mean, let me show you this special kind of topic. Remember the topic about a *Philosophy instructor who didn't really like to have questions asked in his class* that I suggested was deep talk about my not answering questions in the group sessions? This is one of those special topics. It's special because it is about an *instructor* and a *classroom* situation just like the actual T-group class with an instructor. Unlike the many other topics, this literal topic belongs to the same class or category as the actual here-and-now situation. That is, the group members' concerns as reflected in the literal topic about an *instructor* and a *classroom* belongs to the same situations as their concerns about the here-and-now *instructor and classroom*. It's thus a more direct linkage or parallel to the here-and-now group situation than the other topics about God or policemen or parents. I call this kind of topic a transitional topic.

Below is a summary chart of the literal topics of this entire illustration (on the left) and their deep talk equivalents (on the right).

The Mysterious Mind of God Session Template

Literal Topics		Subliteral Meaning
God/Priests/Ministers	=	Trainer as the authority figure
Children	=	Group members
Church	=	The classroom.
Priests/ministers not answering questions in church	=	Trainer not answering their questions in group sessions.
Philosophy instructor who didn't like questions in his class	=	Trainer not answering questions in the questions sessions.
Just have to "believe" priest on faith	=	Just have to "believe" trainer on faith
Can't understand what God is doing	=	Can't understand trainer's purpose
Mortals cannot understand the complicated world	=	Those new to T-group world don't understand them
Too young to understand religion	=	Not having trainer's years of experience
Not believe in a God who lets little children die	=	Not believe in a trainer who lets them "die" or flounder
Billy Graham	=	Trainer
Ministers making money	=	Trainer paid by their tuition money
Ministers who withhold wealth	=	Trainer withholding his their knowledge

If you were a supervisor or executive in the workplace, a teacher, or a parent, this would be invaluable information for you.

The Written Word of God

Let's look at another example. This group had been discussing the increased level of conflict that occurred during the previous session. When unproductiveness or conflict reaches a certain level, I typically intervene. It is this intervention that precipitated this illustration. I asked the group (1) if they had read Albert Ellis's book, *A Guide to Rational Living*, that I had assigned. I (2) suggested that Ellis had some important things to say and that reading the book would help them as a group. I then explained (3) that conflict in a group was not undesirable but was, in fact, necessary for growth, and that the problem was the management, not the elimination, of conflict. There was a very brief discussion, then silence.

Following this silence, a number of topics were introduced but didn't catch on (Again, an important point is to explain why certain topics are selected for extended discussion with others falling by the wayside). Then a member brought up the topic of religion, which the group began to discuss at some length. It was immediately clear that there were members who were religious and members who were not. The disbelievers said that *God never helped anyone* and that *the Bible is only the work of man and not to be taken as the last word*. Then someone said that *You don't have to go to church to be religious* and that *These great cathedrals that look like* [. . . name of a college . . .] *are just to brainwash you*. It was further asserted that *When you missed church, you were made to feel guilty*. Finally, it was said that *Many Christians were hypocrites, who coveted their neighbors' wives and husbands*.

Once more, we can see the God template at work: As you likely suspect by now, from a deep-listening perspective, the conversation about *God* is about *me as the authority figure* in the group. This was indicated by the statement that *God never helped anyone*, which, as in the group illustration above, is a reference to their perception of *my not helping them learn*. That *the Bible was only the work of man and not to be taken as the last word* is deep talk about their negative attitude toward *Albert Ellis's book* that I had mentioned; subliterally Ellis's book is *the Bible*. This literal reference about the Bible is also a negative reference to the other course readings that I assigned, including their textbook, which I had written.

The statement that *You don't have to go to church to be religious* is likely a deep-talk reference to the widespread belief that a person does-n't have to go to college to learn. We all know the stereotypes about col-lege courses: Ivory Tower academics versus knowledge about the "real world." The statement that *These great cathedrals that look like . . .* [name of a college] . . . *are just to brainwash you* is deep talk about *col-leges* being places of brainwashing. The statement *When you missed church, you were made to feel guilty* is subliterally about a remark I had made in the previous session about *absenteeism* in the group, indicat-ing that my remark made them feel *guilty*.

The comment that *Many Christians are hypocrites, who covet their neighbor's wives and husbands* is deep talk about a member who earlier in the session had told of *going with a married man* and who had also expressed that *she was religious* but did not go to church. It's also a ref-erence to the various sexual tensions present in the group.

Once again, this is valuable information for a leader or trainer to know. These concerns and attitudes were not evident by observing and listening to the surface level of the group interaction and conver-sation. In terms of the goals of a T-group, this "negative" talk is not in fact negative at all; it reflects a growing independence from the au-thority figure as well as an increasing group cohesiveness or feeling of groupness. If this were talk by members of a staff or business meet-ing, however, these words would very likely be spelling *d-i-s-a-s-t-e-r*. Here is a summarizing chart of literal topics and their deep-talk equivalents.

The Written Word of God Session Template

Literal Topics		Subliteral Meaning
God	=	Trainer as the authority figure
God never helped anyone	=	Trainer not helping them.

Bible	=	Course texts
The Bible is only the work of man and not to be taken as the last word	=	The Trainer/Ellis's books; are not the only truth
Church	=	Classroom/College
You don't have to go to church to be religious	=	College isn't the only place to learn things
These great cathedrals that look like . . .	=	Places of Higher Learning
[name of the college] . . . just brainwash you	=	Colleges brainwash people
When you missed church, you were made to feel guilty	=	Trainer's remark on absenteeism made them feel guilty.
Many Christians are hypocrites, who covet their neighbors' husbands and wives	=	A member who told of going with a married man, and a reference to sexual tensions in the group.

Some groups who unconsciously express their God templates generate even more complex emotional deep-talk reactions to the authority/leadership and nondirective situation. But before I continue with another example, let me explain an additional meaning of what I call God talk.

From the very earliest days of our childhood, an eternal concern we all have is separation and loss, whether the loss is separation from significant others like parents and siblings or just from familiar friends and surroundings. This concern plays out on many levels in many different situations. In fact life can be seen as a series of separations and losses beginning with the loss of our childhood, then separation from parents, and later perhaps divorce, loss of a job, betrayal by a friend, loss of our youth, and ending with the loss of our very life.

Often, people wonder why a personal loss is happening to them. We like to have reasons for what happens to us; otherwise, our lives seem meaningless and random. The theme of separation and loss runs through most human relationships. It belongs to a God template, too, in both senses of the term. This universal theme marks God talk, too. Thus God talk has three meanings: one that's literally about "God," one that refers to the universal aspect of a concern, and one that refers to subliteral aspects of language and conversation.

Lost Child of the Tribe

One of my group sessions began with a (1) member who had been absent a number of times (2) announcing that she was going to drop out of the group. She had threatened this in an earlier session, but the group had persuaded her not to do so. After announcing this again (3) she left, and the members said their good-byes to her; (4) at that point I didn't say anything. There was a long silence. A male member then said (5) that the group seems to have stabilized to 10 members. Silence, again.

A young woman broke the silence by telling us about an interview on the morning TV program, the *Today* show, where 3 guests gave their opinions on *whether or not legal records should be made available to those who were adopted as children*. She told us of *a young woman who gave up her child for adoption 10 years earlier* but *now wanted to know about the child* because it was still a part of her emotional life. She said another *person on the show had been adopted and had been looking for his parents for 30 years*. A third panelist maintained that *once given up for adoption, that should be the end of the matter; there should be no more communication between the biological parent and the adopted child*.

The male in the group then told us of children who had *been abused and then placed with foster parents*, but not given up forever. The idea was to eventually return the child to his natural parents. Long silence. The male broke the group silence by relating religion to the previous topic. He said that he *wondered about a God who lets terrible things happen, like child abuse*. On the other hand, he said, *maybe God is 'nondirecting,'* adding that maybe *He created mankind and let it 'naturally evolve.'* At this point, I interjected, saying that I agreed, explaining that *we are a microcosm of the larger world.* I again, interjected with *You know, just like in here!* The group saw the implication of my statement: To the group, I was God. The group reacted emotionally to this implication as if it were blasphemous, with the young man—half under his breath, saying, *Hmmm, God, just like an instructor,* to which he quickly added *Only on a much, much, much, much smaller scale.* Silence befell the group.

In this brief set of exchanges, a number of unconscious feelings are expressed as deep talk. The first is the group's concern about *separation and loss.* They were more concerned about losing a member than their surface reaction would indicate. They didn't overtly react or discuss the member who withdrew from the group, and on the surface, it didn't appear that they were overly concerned at all. But we can see their deep concern in the topic of *parents giving up their children for adoption.* That is, the group had lost a "child," so to speak, as indeed I had too, since I was perceived as the *parental figure* in the group. Groups often feel guilty when a member drops out. But often they secretly or unconsciously blame the leader, thinking that she or he could have avoided it. This blame was subliterally referenced by some members who *wondered about a God who lets terrible things happen like child abuse,* that is, why I let the member drop out.

Other members, however, saw the loss as not necessarily due to *a mean God* but rather in terms of their *not being able to understand God's reasons for letting the loss occur.* In other words, maybe I had my reasons that they didn't know about for letting her withdraw. That I equaled God is indicated by the particular characterization of God's motives as seen in the statements that *maybe God is 'nondirecting,'* and maybe *He created mankind and let it 'naturally evolve.'* These are strange characterizations of God. Certainly unusual.

The question is, why the use of this group language to apply to God? The answer is that these references to being *nondirective* and *naturally evolving* are from the language of their textbook and my initial lecture describing the group experience. It's certainly strange to use the term *nondirective* to describe God. Subliterally, then, the use of these particular words functions to link the literal topic of God to the here-and-now group. In this latter case the speaker was momentarily aware of the words' subliteral meaning. He was using them as conscious metaphors to extend the implication that I was equivalent to God in the group. Often, however, such linguistic linkages are totally unconscious.

A further linguistic link is the use of the pronoun *it* in referring to letting mankind naturally evolve. In terms of linguistic norms, it isn't grammatically typical to refer to *mankind* as an *it*. However, referring to a *group* as an *it* is linguistically normative. In referring to mankind, he should have left the *it* out of the sentence, by saying He let mankind *evolve*. Thus the *it* is a subliteral link to the here-and-now feelings in the group.

That the group was not entirely conscious of its equation of me to God is indicated by the response to my intervention *You mean just like in here!* as blasphemous. Yet another linkage to the here-and-now situation is that the topic came from the *Today* show, which is deep talk for *the show today* in the here-and-now group. Still another linkage that supports the topic's subliterally referring to the group is the fact that it's not by randomness or coincidence that there are *3 people* on the *Today* show, as there were *3 very dominant members* in the group. In like manner, it's no accident that the woman on the show gave up her child *10 years ago*, the exact number of the remaining membership of the group. Recall that right after the young woman left the group, the young man then noted that *the group seems to have stabilized to 10 members*.

Like most subliteral conversations, this conversation, too, reveals some of the differences between how members were viewing the group. The topic of losing children to adoption reflects a member's negative reaction to losing a group member. On the other hand, the young man who introduced the topic of a mean God causing it all at least has some doubts as to his being able to understand God's (that is, my) motivation. This is supported by the fact that in the here-and-now group the young man had been understanding the group process better than most of the other members, so on some level, he understood that the member's leaving wasn't my "fault." Here is the summarizing figure of the deep meaning of this conversation:

Lost Child of the Tribe Session Template

Literal Topics		Subliteral Meaning
The *Today* show	=	The show today in the group
Three people on the *Today* show	=	three dominant group members
Ten years ago, gave up her child	=	ten remaining group members
Adoption	=	Member who withdrew
Parent	=	Trainer
Children	=	Group members
Parents giving up their children for adoption	=	Trainer "gave up" a member
God	=	Trainer
Wonder about a God who lets terrible things happen, like child abuse.	=	Wonder why trainer let the loss of a member happen
Not being able to understand God's reasons for letting the loss occur.	=	Not able to understand trainer's reasons for letting the loss occur
Maybe God is "nondirecting"	=	Reference to trainer's nondirective style
Maybe He created mankind let it "naturally evolve"	=	Trainer who created the group and his philosophy of letting it naturally evolve

Let's now look at a final and somewhat more complex, but fascinating, piece of God talk.

Many Are Called but Few Are Chosen

In the history of humankind, one of the most enduring concerns is that someone else will get more than you will. Again this eternal template is illustrated in the Christian Bible numerous times, beginning with the stories of Cain and Abel and of Jacob and his brother. This illustration will show in detail how such concerns are expressed as deep talk. First some context.

In the previous eighteen sessions of this group, I had limited my interventions to brief clarifying remarks. As always in my groups, I focus on the group level of behavior, very rarely upon an individual. Nor do I take sides or comment on the content of discussions. In the previous session, however, I had (1) spent a great deal of time pointing out the implication of how people perceive each other. I did this by focusing on a young man whom I will call John. (Because of the length of this illustration, I'll give the more active members names.) John had been quite strongly criticized in past sessions by most members of the group. I had (2) also openly loaned him a tape recording of a group session, and (3) at one point in the session I had loaned him my pen. I should note, too, that (4) there was a colleague whom I was training in this group. These four events are the main ones responsible for creating the following deep-talk conversation.

After a few preliminary questions to me regarding a required term paper, the group began discussing whether or not they had been too hard on John during the last session. At this point *John entered the room and sat in the vacant seat on my left.* A couple of members asked him if they had *Come down on him too hard?* He replied, *No, I really enjoyed it.* John then returned the audio tape recording of the last session to me, saying that he had not finished listening to it, so I told him he could keep the tape until next session. John then asked if he could borrow my pen, and I said *sure.*

John had been outspoken in past sessions about his religious convictions. In response to further questioning by the group on his religious views, he said, *If I seem that way, it's because I have God and I go by it. You really roasted me last time. I know I can't expect all of you to act like me just because I am that way.* Another male member, Peter, said, *You really had to stand against the onslaught . . . of the devil.* Much anxious laughter ensued.

John then said, *You've all seen that TV program where people are roasted and called names. That's how you all got to me Thursday.* Then another member said, *It's hot in here*, to which a member responded, *Last week when this was mentioned, I said we were going through The Change* [metaphorically referring to a group menopause]. Much laughter and a brief silence.

Then someone questioned whether the group was adhering to the here-and-now rule [This is a rule that says all discussions must be about something within the group, not about outside topics]. A member responded, saying, *I think it's a here-and-now situation . . . you know, how we each project to others . . . am I being received the way I hear things?* At this point I intervened, suggesting that groups frequently *use an individual as a symbol of, or a scapegoat* for widespread concerns within the group as a whole, concerns the group doesn't want to deal with. Whenever a group spends session after session concentrating on a particular individual as we have, it's often an indication of *scapegoating*. There then followed a lengthy and anxious silence. When the discussion resumed, no mention was made of my comments.

Resuming the discussion, an older member who also had made no secret as to his religious convictions said to John, *I've been seeking clarification of your Christian views.* John interjected, saying, *I know for a fact that I am the only one in here that's apostolic* [Note: As I understand it, deriving from Catholicism, apostolic generally means being a symbolic spiritual descendent of the twelve Apostles by *successive ordinations* and baptisms]; *that I'm the only one who has been baptized in Jesus's name. I am quite sure.* Some members then immediately objected. But he went on to say, *You have been baptized Father, Son, and Holy Ghost, or sprinkled, but not in Jesus's name.*

At this point, a heated discussion ensued, in which John said, *I was baptized underwater in Jesus's name.* He went on to say that regular baptism was not the same; that *Just because you were baptized Father, Son and Holy Ghost . . . those are just titles. When Jesus arose from the dead, he told his disciples that all power is in the name of the Father, comma, the Son, comma, and the Holy Ghost. He didn't say 'in the 'names with an 's' on it, he said* name *(singular).* Another member replied that John was hung up on words. I once more inquired if the conversation had any here-and-now significance. I was ignored.

John then reiterated, *I know that I'm the only one in here that has been baptized in Jesus's name. Just because I am different.* At this point, a member interjected with, *If others had been baptized the same as you, you're saying they would have known it?* John replied, *Right.* Another member then asked, *If we were all baptized underwater, then would we all be the same?* He responded that *If you got the Holy Ghost, we would all be alike.* It was objected that *First you say in Jesus's name, now it's the Holy Ghost. Which is it?* John replied that *Those two scriptures went together. If you would all go to the Bible, then we would all have the same goals.*

In a delayed response to my question about the here-and-now relevance of the topic, Peter, who had previously supported John, said, *There is the same process happening in here: Jesus was scrutinized, stoned, and called crazy. It's a parallel.* There were some joking references to John as being like Jesus Christ. He denied it, of course, as did the other members—and, I might add, quite vociferously. Then a member said that perhaps John was *Jesus's son.* A member then said, *What's this got to do with the here-and-now?* to which another responded to John, *It's the way you are coming off to the group, putting yourself above us.* Someone then asked, *Because I haven't gone through the same process that you have gone through, can I be accepted in this class?* John responded, *On that train of thought, dealing with this class, yes.* The member who was asking if he could be accepted, continued, *Whatever goal we as a group have, as a class, can you accept us?*

Then, referring to me, a supportive member said, *He is our leader,* to which two other members immediately responded, *He's not my leader. He has taught me nothing in here.* Peter then interjected, *You'll change your mind when you hit the gates.* Silence ensued. I then asked, *What side of Jesus did Judas sit on at the Last Supper?* There was much laugher and puzzlement about the meaning of my comment. Then John, who was sitting next to me, *put his arm around and on the back of my chair.* There were looks of surprise at this gesture of familiarity. Silence. Addressing my question, a couple of members said they thought *Judas sat on the left of Jesus,* at least according to artist's conceptions. John added, *He sat close to Jesus because Jesus said whosoever shall sup with me on bread—and he put something in Jesus's cup—shall have everlasting life. And then Jesus told him [Judas] to go and do what he had to do—and to do it quickly.*

The discussion then revolved around whether the biblical quote about where Judas sat was correct or not. Silence. A member then directed the group into how they perceived each other. John got up and *quickly* left the group, leaving his coat and books behind. A few minutes later, he rushed back into the room out of breath and announced that he had looked up the quote and that he was right about what side of Jesus Judas sat on. The group continued, giving their perceptions of each other until the end of the session.

Now, what does all this God talk mean? I mean, *subliterally*. First, it's important to note a little more about the social contexts of human behavior. Whenever a person is perceived as having been singled out by someone in a position of authority, it's often unconsciously felt—both by the person being singled out and by the other people involved. The person being singled out is seen as special (as if the person had been specially "anointed"). Now let's begin to decode this piece of God talk in more detail [Note: Along the way, see if you can predict how many members are in this session].

John's remark, *I know for a fact that I am the only one in here that is apostolic, that I'm the only one who has been baptized in Jesus's name. I am quite sure*, subliterally means that he is the special one in the group. And he is correct. What his remark is essentially all about is (1) my singling him out by calling attention to him, (2) his being used as a scapegoat, (3) my having loaned him an audio tape of a session, and (4) my having loaned him my pen by personally handing it to him. Indeed, he was "anointed." You will note that he repeatedly emphasizes that he knows he is the special one by his saying that he *knows for a fact* that he is the only one *in here* that is apostolic, and that he is quite *sure*. The question arises, on a literal level how could he be so sure? After all, he doesn't really know the life history of all members. Yet, he repeats that he is certain. He can be so sure precisely because he is not really talking about what he knows of the members' lives outside the group, but what he has actually observed *in here*, in the group. How else could he be so adamantly certain? Thus, the prepositional phrase *in here* literally cues and is a link to the fact that deep talk is afoot.

Moreover, after already saying I *know for a fact*, why did he use the word *sure?* Why not simply say "I am quite *certain*," or "There is no doubt about it," or "It's incontestable," or any other equivalent phrasings and words? The answer is that his use of the word *sure* is yet another clue and linkage to the deep-talk nature of this conversation. Recall that when he asked if he could use my pen, I responded by saying *sure*.

John's asserting that *You have been baptized Father, Son, and Holy Ghost or sprinkled, but not in Jesus's name* subliterally means that the other group members have only been the recipients of general remarks by me (equaling Father), the co-trainer (Son) and by the group-as-a-whole (Holy Ghost), but not in a direct and personalized way by me (that is, in Jesus's name), and thus his subliteral apostolic status is derived directly from me. He had been directly and "*successively*" ordained by me.

His remark that *I was baptized underwater* means that by being focused on, he was submerged in the group process compared to the rest of the members, indeed, as no one else had been. His comment that *Just because you are baptized Father, Son, and Holy Ghost . . . these are just titles* again probably means that each member has only been the recipient of general remarks by me, the co-trainer, and the group as a whole. His comment about *When Jesus arose from the dead* is deep talk about my finally becoming active (or alive) in the group. Continuing this comment, he said that *Jesus told his disciples* (the group) that *All power is in the name of the Father, comma, the Son, comma, and the Holy Ghost. He didn't say in the 'names' with an 's' on it, he said name* [meaning singular].

That Jesus did not say in the *names of, with an 's'* (denoting a plural noun) is deep talk for all power in the group, all action being derived from me (that is, father or Jesus), not from the co-trainer (the son) or the group (Holy Ghost). The rest of the group is baptized in Jesus's name (note that *name* is singular). That this likely equals myself is indicated by the fact that my name, Haskell, does not end with an *s*. However, the co-trainer's name, Heapes, does. Further, his statement, *If you had the holy ghost, we would all be alike,* is a deep-talk reference to the fact that if I had focused on them in the same way they would all be equal.

Moreover while the Holy Ghost (which also equals the perceived messages from me) did not tell John how he should behave, it was *perceived* that he should behave in a certain manner. In response to the charge by another member that, *First you say Jesus, now it's the Holy Ghost, which is it?* John responded, *Those two scriptures went together.* This is a reference to me and my word and/or my textbook. This is indicated by the remark, *If you would all go to the Bible, then we would all have the same goals,* that is, if the group would *all go by my textbook,* then the group would all work smoothly.

The term *goal,* too, is a rather strange term to use in relation to the Bible and the discussion about religion. It's a term, however, that was repeatedly used in the textbook material. The term *goal* is thus a linkage of the subliteral topic to the here-and-now discussion. The comment of two scriptures may also be a reference to the colleague whom I was training and myself.

In my question about *What side of Jesus did Judas sit on at the Last Supper?* I was indirectly referring to John, who was sitting on my left. He was felt to be Judas because he was "betraying" his peers by always mentioning the course material, which made the others look bad. I was trying to indirectly cue them into the deep-talk nature of their conversations. John's reaching over and placing his arm around and on the back of my chair was either a conscious or semiconscious action and likely a semiconscious recognition of his understanding the deep talk.

A member's comment that he thought *Judas sat on the left of Jesus* was perhaps an unconscious recognition of John's symbolically being Judas. John's response that *He sat close to Jesus because Jesus said whosoever shall sup with me on bread—and he put something in Jesus's cup—shall have everlasting life* is likely, again, deep talk for my "sharing" the audio tape and my pen with him. And of course, he was sitting next to me. This analysis is indicated by the fact that shortly after concluding his statement that *Jesus told him [Judas] to go and do what he had to do and to do it quickly,* John got up and without saying a word—and like Judas—he *quickly* left the group. Here we have an illustration of deep or subliteral action (see Chapter 2.)

The inquiry about whether the rest of the members could be accepted in the class even though they had not gone through the process that he had gone through, John's response, *On that train of thought dealing with the class, yes,* means: from the point of view of it being a class (that is, in my thoughts) they could be accepted, but they are still not equal since they have not been favored in the way he was perceived to be by me. The remark by another member that *He's not my leader. He has taught me nothing in here* means that since he believed *that I have taught the group nothing, that he would not be my disciple.* Finally, John's comment that *You'll change your mind when you hit the gate* is deep talk for *they will change their minds when grades are due,* the time of judgment in the course.

Finally, need I note at this point that the group was composed of twelve members—my "disciples"?

Many Are Called But Few Are Chosen Session Template

Literal Topics		*Subiteral Meaning*
I know for a fact that I am the only one in here that is apostolic; that I'm the only one who has been baptized in Jesus's name. I am quite sure.	=	The only member that has been singled out by the trainer as special
You have been baptized Father, Son, and Holy Ghost or sprinkled, but not in Jesus's name	=	Other members have only been the recipients of general attention by trainer
The Father	=	The trainer
The Son	=	Co-trainer
Holy Ghost	=	Attention by the group

In Jesus's name	=	Trainer's name
Baptized underwater	=	Submerged in the group process
When Jesus arose from the dead	=	Trainer finally being active
When Jesus told his disciples	=	Trainer told the group
Jesus said all power is in the name of the Father, comma, the Son, comma, and the Holy Ghost. He didn't say in the 'names' with an 's' on it, he said name	=	All power derives from the trainer whose name does not end with an "s" as does the co-trainer's name.
If you had the Holy Ghost, we would all be alike	=	If they had been focused on individually, they would then be alike
Those two scriptures went together	=	My verbal and written words
If you would all go to the Bible, then would all have same goals	=	If all would read the textbook then would have same goals
Judas	=	Is the scapegoated member
The twelve disciples	=	12 group members
He sat close to Jesus because Jesus said whosoever shall sup with me on bread —and he put something in Jesus' cup . . .	=	Member sitting on trainer's left shared the trainer's audiotape and pen.
Shall have everlasting life	=	Shall be favored by a higher course evaluation
Jesus told him [Judas] to go and do what he had to do and to do it quickly	=	Scapegoated member got up quickly left the group
You'll change your mind when you hit the [pearly] gate,	=	They will wish they changed their view at the end of the course when grading time has come

We can see that talking about God is a prevalent substitute for deep talk for feelings and concerns about authority figures. We also saw that what I have termed God talk refers not just to talk about God but to deep "meaning" templates or "forms" in the mind. But more than this, from the illustrations in this chapter, we can see that deep talk is not just a "slip" of the mind but involves parallel universes of meaning, where multiple and intricate meanings from the deep layers of our mind are consistently tracked and mapped onto literal topics and stories.

There are, of course, other templates with their many apparently different contents or stories. For example, there are *privacy* templates, where stories about newspaper reporters, novelists, or the governmental Freedom of Information Act may all be the *same* deep talk about a single privacy concern in the here-and-now conversation. There are *rivalry* templates, as we saw in the opening of this chapter, where the archetypal stories of Cain and Abel and between Jacob and his brother are the content. There are as many templates as there are human feelings, concerns, and issues.

Deep Listening About Relationships: What Friends, Coworkers, and Employers Won't Tell You

I have been at great pains to argue that one of the most ubiquitous and powerful discourse forms in human communication is narrative. *Narrative structure is even inherent in . . . social interaction before it achieves linguistic expression.*

JEROME BRUNER
Acts of Meaning[1]

As we have seen, people's real feelings are typically not available to us. They often hold back from making their real feelings known. Often people's hidden feelings aren't even available to themselves. Without deep listening to these hidden feelings, you are at a distinct disadvantage. Your being successful as either an employer or employee may depend on this kind of deep information.

In this chapter I will extend the idea of eternal templates that humans have acquired throughout the ages to relationships with friends, coworkers, employers, and other authority figures. It is these templates of human existence that provide the emotional universal source for the enduring Greek tragedies, for the works of Shakespeare, and for other great and enduring literature around the world. It's from this common emotional experience of the conflicts and troubles in the everyday life of the human relationships that the great works of literature speak to us.

Alongside these grand templates, there are less existentially profound ones, some of which are quite mundane, even petty. Given these nearly universal concerns, it's not surprising that many of them are expressed and can be observed in everyday conversations—both literally and subliterally. In the course of daily human interactions, some of the concerns that people have are legitimate, but some seem just plain irrational. Throughout the years I have found these concerns are subliterally represented by a number of surprisingly consistent stories.

These themes include competition, rivalry, jealously, double standards, separation and loss, and others that are more positive—the positive ones, however, don't seem to be as abundant as the negative ones. Many of these interpersonal themes revolve around gender and racial or ethnic concerns (see Chapters 8 and 9). Whether rational or irrational, these themes are based on people's perceptions or feelings of what they think and feel is happening.

Of course we can't talk about authority figures without talking at the same time about those who they exert authority over: subordinates. Accordingly, I have found equally surprisingly consistent stories by subordinates about feeling like children, students, mental patients, and criminals. The themes or plots of these stories often revolve around feelings of being abused by authorities, around issues of fairness and double standards, and especially around feelings about whether the leader is competent. Thus everyone in a leadership position, whether as a parent, a boss, or teacher, needs to deeply listen about what subordinates are feeling. Though the illustrations to follow occurred in my groups and social life, watch for their sequels coming all too soon to a workplace or family near you.

Whether leader or authority figures are represented in narratives as benevolent or malevolent is determined by how members perceive they are being treated by a leader or an authority figure. This concern with leaders and authorities runs deep. Most of us learned early in life to be careful what we revealed to our parents, to withhold certain of our feelings for fear of reprisal. And many of us have wondered—at least at times—if these all-powerful figures were competent. We certainly hoped they were—and are.

At varying times in our lives we are all in positions of leadership and authority, whether as an older sibling, the captain of a team, a supervisor in the workplace, or simply as one who has higher social status than one's friends. In speaking of leadership and authority, then, "they" are us. Wouldn't you like to know that "they" are thinking about us? By deep listening to deep talk, you can.

Communicating with each other is a difficult and complicated process. Think about it for a moment. Each of us is confined to our own minds. We have no way to see into another person's mind or to feel their feelings. We are as the German philosopher and mathematician, Gottfried Leibnitz (1646–1716), said, individual Monads, completely sealed-off units, floating around the universe with no way of seeing into other people's worlds. We often don't know, for example, when someone we are talking to is bored or is competing with us, or a host of other interpersonal things. We don't know because all too often the other people may not have conscious access to what they are feeling, or because they simply won't tell us. Either way, deep listening for subliteral meaning can help us to find out what's going on in another person's universe. Such talk occurs with intimates as well as relative strangers. If we listen carefully to their talk, the finer nuances of their feelings may become clear.

What's Going On Here, Anyway?

As we carry on our conversations, not only our conscious but our unconscious mind is always vigilant for any sign of perceived insult, of being boring, of bragging, of injustice, or of any behaviors or attitudes that are outside the norms of our expectations or what we think is acceptable behavior. Our unconscious picks up on these social violations that our conscious mind doesn't pick up on.

Recall from Chapter 2 the many little 2-by-3-inch yellow slips of paper that I always used to keep with me to write down ideas and insights that I might think of at any time. While still in the early stages of developing the idea of deep talk, I was taking graduate seminars as a part of my doctoral studies. In these seminars, I frequently had these little yellow slips of paper spread out in front of me. I was constantly shuffling through them and springing forward to write something down before I forgot the idea. From time to time, I was aware of the other graduate students and the professors looking at me rather strangely.

In one of these seminars, seemingly out of nowhere and apparently unconnected to his lecture, a professor began to talk about a crazy colleague he once knew. It seemed that whenever anyone went to the colleague's office his desk was strewn with *pieces of paper* that *he would write on*—even while people were talking to him! The implication was that this was not a very polite thing to do.

It doesn't take a psychoanalyst to figure out that the professor's story was a reference to *my writing on little slips* of paper *while he was lecturing*. Although it may seem that the professor's remark may have been a conscious kind of indirect hint to me, from the context of the situation, it didn't seem to be. From a literal perspective, this was a classroom where students are supposed to take notes, so it wouldn't make sense for him to be consciously giving me a hint that I was being impolite. Being just a lowly student, I wasn't going to ask him about the meaning of his comment. Besides, he would have thought I was a paranoid. In any event, he would have likely denied that he was doing so.

This example clearly points out that in many of these subliteral illustrations, it may seem that the person must know what he or she is really saying, that statements like "I don't want to bore you" reflect one of those occasions when the speakers are conscious of what they are saying. As this analysis shows, however, in many situations speakers are not aware of what may appear to be an indirect but conscious hint.

While in a restaurant one day, my daughter, Melyssa, who was then around five years old, asked her mother and me the eternal question about how babies were born. She had always been very curious about things. Well, her mother and I explained pregnancy as best we could to a five-year-old. When we seemed to have reached an appropriate end to our explanation, there was a slight pause and my wife and I began talking about the events of the day. Then Melyssa tugged on my sleeve, turned herself toward me and asked, *What do you think of my shirt, Dad?* An innocent enough question. Or was it? On her T-shirt was a decal—at stomach level—of a banana that was depicted as a little child. In deep-listening terms, I would say that Melyssa's question was certainly *pregnant* with meaning.

Now was she conscious of her action of showing me this decal? With young children it's hard to tell. Sometimes this dichotomy between conscious and unconscious doesn't seem to apply to children. It's often a mixture. Let me describe another piece of deep talk by Melyssa. It occurred one Halloween evening. I was playfully squeezing, hugging, and kissing her. While I was doing this, she was trying to open her Halloween bag of goodies that she had collected from the neighborhood. As she opened the bag, she spied something within, and exclaimed, *Oh, it's one of those doodaddy things* [meaning a gadget or trinket that doesn't really have a precise name]. What might this apparently literal statement mean subliterally? I maintain that it was a reference to me playfully squeezing, hugging, and kissing her. Unconsciously, she was acknowledging that I was engaging in *those things that Daddy's do*, or doodaddy things. I suspect this deep talk didn't have the degree of consciousness about it that the previous example may have.

In any event, this kind of deep listening often reveals hidden meaning about what people are thinking about you and the conversation they are having with you. One evening my then-wife and I were taking an evening walk. Because I tend to be a hyper person with my brain going faster than my mouth can, I was rambling on half incoherently and stumbling over my words, mispronouncing them and repeating syllables. I had no sooner finished one of these broken sentences as we were passing a yard with one of those fences that have vertical spokes or slats, when she said—out of a myriad of things she could have said— *There's a fence with a broken spoke.* Now she wasn't just literally mentioning that she noticed that one of the fence slats was broken. She was, in fact, unconsciously commenting on the fact that I had *spoke*(en) in a broken manner. Hence, the particular phrase, *broken spoke*. Here we see the word *spoke* being used literally as a noun, referring to a connecting piece of wood in a fence, and unconsciously as a verb referring to my speaking.

When meeting someone for the first time, we often take notice of how they look and take particular note of any distinguishing characteristics. Sometimes we express our reactions to these characteristics subliterally. I was watching a TV talk show some years ago that was hosted by Merv Griffin.[2] He was introducing the actress Virginia Graham, who was a rather plump and large-framed woman. He began by describing her long career and distinguished list of credits in show business, as he often did when welcoming people. At the end of this list of credits, he added, *She's a real heavyweight*, literally meaning that she was one of the great figures in show business. He no more than had spoken the words *She's a real heavyweight* when he realized the implications of what he had subliterally said and showed his embarrassment. He had let his recognition of her weight "slip" out. This example of deep talk from the media may appear to have been consciously scripted. I have found, however, that this is frequently not the case. Again, the transformation of the visual and oral cues of deep talk into a print medium loses a great deal of information and cues for assessing whether the person was consciously creating the "slip" or pun.

Are You Boring People?

Most of us occasionally wonder whether we are boring the person we are talking with. But, of course, even your spouse or best friend will seldom tell you the awful truth. When we ask them, their answer will likely be "Oh, not at all." We have all told these little social lies from time to time. So how are you to know if you are boring someone? The answer is, by deep listening to their deep talk.

One evening, my then-wife and I and our friend and colleague were having an evening of what I, at least, thought was engrossing conversation, as we often did. The previous day, I had bought a new stereo system with two very nice stereo speakers. Now, my colleague is a very knowledgeable and extremely verbal and articulate fellow. On this occasion, we had been talking for quite some time, and he was carrying on at great length about some subject. My wife and I found it difficult to get a word into the conversation. During my colleague's monologue, she was casually looking around the room, obviously bored. At this point—and totally unrelated to what our friend was talking about—she interrupted his monologue and asked, *Where's the other speaker?*

Literally, the question *Where's the other speaker* referred to the new stereo speaker. As always, we must ask ourselves why this particular subject was interjected into the conversation at this particular time? The answer is clear: Subliterally, this question clearly meant, why is he doing all the talking? Why isn't someone else talking, too? In short, *where is the other speaker in this conversation?*

Being Perceived as a Braggart

One of the most egregious social faux pas, and one which is recognized in most cultures around the world, is to be perceived as bragging about yourself. People usually pick up immediately on such ego trips. The problem is we don't have control over how others perceive whether we may actually be bragging or not. Here's a case in point.

While sitting on my porch one day sorting through my note cards, a former student who happened to be driving by stopped to chat with me. I am not an especially talented conversationalist when it comes to superficial conversation, so he did most of the talking. He talked in a free-associating or near stream-of-consciousness manner, as much of this meaningless kind of chitchat tends to be. In between breaths, he paused for a moment, looked at all my note cards and asked what I was doing—*Was I writing a book, or something?* With a matter-of-fact tone, I quite tersely replied, *Yes, I am working on a number of things, a book, a professional article, and a talk for a conference.* He said, *Oh.* Pausing for a moment, he slipped back into his stream-of-consciousness talk. He began by telling a story about *A man he knew who was always bragging about the things he was doing.* Subliterally, he obviously perceived me as bragging. Taken somewhat aback at this, I thought to myself, "Oh, is that what you think I was doing—bragging? I thought you were the one who asked me what I was doing." So much for being able to control what others perceive.

Maybe this one will have a familiar sound, too. A few years ago my wife and I bought a small run-down summer cottage in Maine where I grew up and knew quite a few people. For the first couple of summers we were busy trying to make the cottage livable. I had to completely gut the place and put it back together. Consequently, we had no time to socialize. When the cottage was finally decent enough for company, we invited some old friends for an evening of conversation. Having not seen our guests for some years, the conversation was rapid-fire chitchat with free-floating associations to various topics. The initial small talk finally got around to discussing our cottage, so my wife and I proceeded to give our guests the "grand tour."

In the stream of conversation, one guest started telling us about a party she had attended a few weeks before. It seemed that, like us, the people having the party had just finished redecorating their home. Sandwiched in between talking about the party, and other fleeting topics, my guest said that *They only had the party to show off their redecorating work.* Unconsciously—and, again, I believe this comment wasn't a conscious snide remark—the speaker's feelings about our motivation for inviting them were clear. *We only had the party to show off our redecorating work.* As for our real motivation, of course we wanted to "show our cottage off," but human motivation is typically much more complex than this. We wanted to see our old friends, too. So much for bragging about our cottage. The human species is a strange lot.

Of Professors and Madmen

I mentioned in Chapter 2 that we can often catch ourselves engaging in deep talk. Here is another example that I caught myself doing. First to the context and then to the subliteral punch line. Many years ago I taught at a community college. We who have taught at two-year colleges at some point in our career thought of ourselves as "second-class" academics, seeing faculty who taught at four-year institutions as the real "professors." Over the years since I graduated to being a university professor, I have maintained a relationship by an occasional phone call, and more recently by e-mail, with a colleague at the two-year college where I taught. I will call him Jack. Jack was a physically imposing man who had an intellect to match. He read vociferously and was always intensely ranting and raving about something, often about some theoretical, intellectual, or social issue.

Jack would have been a brilliant scholar had he been on a university faculty. His teaching at a community college was like using a Maserati to go only to the corner store. For one reason or another, he never made this transition, however, and felt trapped. He was clearly eccentric, too. I empathized with his situation, and over the years feared that he might someday go crazy. In response to an e-mail discussion, I would occasionally send him the title of a book (as he would me). Hardly ever did I send him a book title just out of the blue. The books were usually related to our e-mail correspondence. Recently I had just finished reading an absolutely fascinating book. I went to my computer and sent Jack the title of the book *The Professor and the Madman.* This is a story about a major contributor to the making of the *Oxford English Dictionary* who did so from a mental hospital, unbeknownst to the editors. Was my unconscious mind showing an aspect of what I thought about Jack, that he was "metaphorically" speaking like a *madman?* Perhaps. Being at a four-year university, I of course am the *professor* in the title (I think).

Compliments and Remarks of Appreciation

At this point, you may have observed that almost all of the illustrations of deep listening have been about either neutral expressions of how we use language or of negative feelings or attitudes. You might be wondering if deep talk is ever about more positive and pleasant feelings and attitudes. My reply is, yes, there are positive ones, but they are quite rare—or so it seems. Why subliteral compliments seem quite rare is probably due to the fact that most people don't withhold pleasant feelings, since there are virtually no social sanctions for expressing positive feelings like there are for expressing negative ones. More importantly, unlike positive feelings, negative ones tend to be much more strongly felt. Consequently, these withheld feelings cry to be released. Nevertheless, we may also withhold compliments, either because we might feel embarrassed, because our pride may be hurt if we expressed them, or because we don't want to be seen as ingratiating. To compliment your boss might be perceived by your coworkers as brown-nosing. In addition, since most people, including myself, are more vigilant for negative feelings, perhaps I just haven't noticed deep talk about positive expressions as much as I have negative ones.

One of the first expressions of positive deep talk that I noticed occurred while I was a doctoral candidate. I was sitting in my dissertation committee chairman's office discussing an issue regarding my dissertation, when a well-known professor of small-group communications research appeared in the open doorway. He saw that there was a discussion in progress, and there was a brief awkward silence, as typically happens in such situations. My chairman beckoned to the professor, saying "Come on in, we're just sitting here talking." The professor briefly glanced at me, and there ensued another, but shorter, awkward silence as I merely looked at him and then turned away.

The professor fidgeted uncomfortably for a moment, not knowing exactly what to say. He then said, to my chairman, *Oh, did I tell you we have one of the very bright graduate students of*—I'll call him Dr. Jones (a well-known scholar)—*joining our department? She left him, told him just where he could go, too. No one has ever done that. You really have to respect her for not bowing down to him.* The professor's eyes then ever so fleetingly glanced over at me again, as sometimes occurs in those little micro moments of eye contact. After more chitchat with my chairman, the professor left.

Now, what did this conversation really mean? I mean subliterally? Was it simply a literal piece of information that the professor of small-group communications came to tell my chairman, or was it merely a piece of small talk generated by an obviously uncomfortable social situation? Or was it a piece of deep talk? If it's deep talk, how is one to assess this verbal exchange? (See Figure 4.1.)

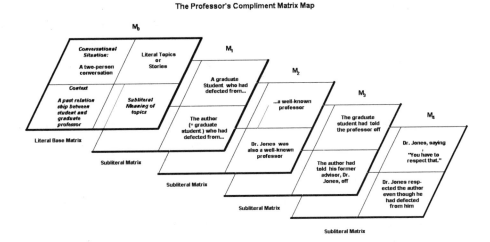

FIGURE 4.1　The Professor's Compliment Matrix Map

Since words only *mean* in a context, to understand the full meaning you need to be aware of the context that this piece of talk belonged to. It has a history outside of the social micro moment that it occurred in.

The professor who walked into the office had been my graduate adviser for a brief period of time, until I refused to be his disciple. I had told him that our relationship was not going to work out. Even at that time, I was working on my theory of deep talk and wasn't about to be sidetracked into someone else's research agenda. Like the professor in the story he told, he, too, was well-known and respected in his field and wasn't accustomed to having graduate students refuse to work with him. Indeed, most graduate students considered it an honor to be selected to work with him.

With the telling of his story about the very bright graduate student who left Dr. Jones, telling him just where he could go, and noting that no one had ever done that before, that the graduate student had to be respected for not bowing down to him, my former graduate adviser was subliterally acknowledging to me that although I had defected from him over to my chairman, he nevertheless respected me for my independence. Again, I have no doubt that he was not aware of what he had subliterally said. Pride would have prevented him for doing so. In any event, thanks, Doc.

Here's another example of hidden thoughts of appreciation. One of my groups was discussing their frustration with what they perceived as a lack of progress in becoming a cohesive group. A member suggested that *We need to read more of the text material.* As typically occurs with a suggestion to read my textbook for the course, there followed a silence. I then intervened, saying that groups often didn't read and apply the material in the text because of a norm against not *Showing each other up,* that groups had what is called a rate-busting norm. I explained that the term rate-busting is from industry, where a worker may outperform his or her coworkers, making them look bad. The coworkers then may bring sanctions to bear on the rate-buster. Silence.

They ignored what I said because to have discussed it would have created conflict amongst them. So, they just continued with chitchat. Then a member suggested that the group examine how they had been communicating with each other, but this, too, soon ended in silence. At this point, an older woman in the group said, *Why can't people be nice to one another? Why can't we say nice things to people when they do something good?* A heavy silence ensued. What did her statement mean subliterally?

In previous sessions, the older woman had complained of the lack of rules in the group and in particular of my failure to contribute to the sessions. While she complained that she was unable to understand the dynamics without help, she was always polite and courteous in doing so and was not as counter-dependent as the younger members. The previous session I had drawn a diagram on the blackboard explaining the major dynamics of groups. I had done this quietly, during a period of much small talk. Without saying anything, I returned to my seat.

As is typical in a stage where the group is beginning to develop independence from me, the group totally ignored my diagram. Only a couple of members took brief notes on what I had put on the board, and only the older woman took extensive notes. Even into the next session no one mentioned my active contribution. The older woman's inquiry, *Why can't people be nice to one another? Why can't we say nice things to people when they do something good?* was her way of subliterally thanking me for my help in explaining some of the dynamics that were occurring in the group.

As I sometimes do when I suspect that the deep talk may be coded speech that the person is aware of, I later asked the woman if she could explain why her comment came at this particular point in the discussion, since it seemed to have no connection with the previous comments. She replied she didn't know why she said it at that point. I then asked her how she felt when I had put the diagram on the board. She replied, *Grateful.* I also asked her how she felt when I had commented on the group dynamics earlier this session. She replied, *I was relieved.* I then asked if she saw any connection between her remark and my instructional contributions prior to her remark. Even with this hint, she shook her head, *No.* When I shared my complete interpretation with her, her eyes opened wide, and she gasped *Oh, my God! That's right.* So much for being the conscious masters of our intent and the captains of our language.

What's Hidden in a Name?

I opened Chapter 1 with the example of the name of the famous rock group the Grateful Dead used as deep talk for feeling bored or *dead* in a meeting and feeling *grateful* for being out of the meeting and on coffee break. This was an example of how people use names as deep talk for expressing how they feel. In being vigilant and deeply listening, then, you should always be on the lookout for names used in conversations: names of musical groups, names of famous people, titles of movies, product brands, or names of people whom the members of a conversation may personally know.

Sometimes names combine pun-like sound relations and the embedding of a name within another name. For example, one afternoon, I was at a friend's house for an in-ground barbecue. When the time came to begin to put the food in the pit my friend had dug, someone noticed that the pit was far too small for all the food that needed to be cooked. Many of the people who were gathered around agreed. Others just laughed. Then someone said that digging such a small pit was *fool-hardy*, literally meaning that it was *foolish* to have dug such a small in-ground barbecue pit. The deep-listening point here is that my friend's last name was *Hardy*. In other words, what a *fool Hardy* was. While this example is not an earth-shaking one, it show the mind's cognitive machinery at work.

An example of using similar-sounding names to subliterally express a thought or feeling about a person occurred in one of my groups that was concerned about a particular male member's experimenting on them by trying out different leadership and communication *techniques*. He was very good at adopting the different techniques mentioned in my reading material for establishing good relationships and feelings among members. Because he was just learning these techniques, at times his style seemed a bit *artificial.* Following a slight pause in the conversation, another member began talking about movies.

In particular, the member talked about the movie director Stanley *Kubrick*, who is well-known for his movie *Dr. Strangelove*, among others. Now, there are two very interesting aspects to the selecting the name Stanley *Kubrick* out of all the possible famous directors' names that could have been selected into the discussion. The first is that Kubrick was well-known at the time for the *special effects* in his movies. The second and most interesting is that the last name of the member the group was having concerns about was *Kulick*. Thus, what the group was subliterally commenting on was the *special effects–like* quality of interpersonal techniques the member was applying. Perhaps the member who selected Stanley Kubrick's name to subliterally comment on Kulick's use of techniques to try to create warm feelings in the group felt that his engaging in these *special effects* for forming personal relationships in the group was a *strange* kind of *love*.

This example was identified by a colleague whom I was training to conduct groups and for deep listening. The particular day that this example occurred, I was absent from the group. The group was composed of a mixture of hippie types, middle-class students, and two state troopers who made their identities known immediately. Members of the group were just getting to know each other and were expressing their frustration, anger, and confusion with the apparent lack of purpose and with what they perceived as a lack of leadership. During this session, a number of topics were thrown in for possible discussion but only the topic of drugs was selected for more extensive discussion. In talking about drugs, most of the hippie-type members said drugs should be legalized. The group also talked about how *The quality of service was down* in society at large and how big pharmaceutical companies like *Upjohn ripped people off.*

On one level the statement that the *quality of service was down* suggests that they thought that with my absence, leaving only the junior trainer in the group, who like myself was nondirective, the *quality of service was down in the group* even more than usual, and thus they were being *ripped off.* That is, my colleague was ripping off students just as they perceived the drug company Upjohn was ripping off customers. More particularly, it's significant that the drug company *Upjohn* was selected out of all the well-known pharmaceutical companies that could have been used. As always we must ask why a particular topic, word, phrase, sentence, story, or name is used in a particular context at a particular time. Here's the answer: It's no coincidence that the first name of my colleague, the junior trainer, was *John.* Since group members didn't feel comfortable directly asking John for help, subliterally *Upjohn* meant: *Get up, John,* and start leading us.[3]

Brand name products are also used as deep talk to express concerns. One group "just happened" to talk about an old brand of cough drops called *Smith Brother's.* Why was this peculiar name brand selected for discussion? If you haven't already begun to suspect the answer, it's this: There were *two trainers* in this group; hence *the two brothers.* But there's more. If you were familiar with the picture of the two Smith brothers on the package, you would know which brother subliterally represented which trainer. As a trademark at the time, the picture of the Smith brothers was of two bearded men, one with a black beard and one with a reddish beard. Accordingly, it's no accident that my co-trainer at that time had a black beard—and I had a *reddish beard.* No accident, indeed.

Just as to the experienced physicist certain telltale marks observed in a gas-filled bubble chamber mean the presence of a particular subatomic particle, so too someone who is experienced with my deep-listening method will be able to recognize that certain kinds of telltale marks during conversations mean the presence of unconscious or hidden thoughts and feelings.

Feelings About Leaders Being Incompetent

From very early childhood we all have a need to feel secure. We draw much of our trust in leaders from our parents and other relationships with authorities, but as I discussed in the chapter on God talk, as children we often don't understand why our God or our parents do what they do. There is often a suspicion that God and parents, and their incarnations, "leaders" or "bosses," may not know what they are doing, that they may be incompetent. Certainly those who have come from seriously dysfunctional homes where parents didn't or couldn't carry out their leadership role appropriately may be sensitized to see incompetence in authority figures. In any event, it's only a short step from not understanding the actions (or non-actions) of a leader to suspecting incompetence.

Let me begin this section with a hypothetical illustration that's based on one that I described in the chapter on God talk (see p. 54). Suppose you have been assigned to conduct a week-long training session or seminar for which *you designed and wrote the instructional materials* you were using, say, a manual for socializing employees into the corporate rules, policies of sexual harassment, and other standards like accepted modes of dress. Suppose, too, that you had taken an education course about collaborative learning, a method of learning in small groups. As a result, *you decided to conduct this training session or seminar by having members work in small groups to learn the material by self-discovery instead of lecturing to them.* Moreover, your *training session was held at an upscale old cathedral-like inn.* Suppose further that *toward the middle of the session some members began to arrive late and return late from the coffee breaks and you had to address this issue.* In addition, *suppose that you had a secret but mutual attraction to one of the members of the training session.* Now in the middle of the training session *you asked people if the sessions were going well and if they were learning something important from them.* Given that you are either their supervisor or have at least been given the mantle of authority, *most people aren't going to tell you their negative feelings.* (Even with the formal evaluations at the end of such programs, called "smile sheets," people will often still not express their true feelings—assuming they are aware of them.)

Now, suppose that during an extended coffee break towards the end of the training program, you overhear members talking about (a) *A God who never helped anyone,* (b) *That the Bible was only the work of man and not to be taken as the last word,* (c) *That you don't have to go to church to be religious,* (d) *That these great cathedrals of learning are just to brainwash you,* (e) *That when you missed church, you were made to feel guilty,* and (f) *That many Christians were hypocrites, who coveted their neighbors' wives and husbands.* Comparing these topics that were selected to talk about during the break with the training context that I described, need I say more about what the members may really be feeling? And would your understanding such deep listening be useful? You bet.

Now let me offer a real story and see how you can apply it by seeing it as a kind of analogy or parable to either a situation that you have experienced or one that you might hypothetically experience in the future. One variant on the general template about leader incompetence is the following. A widespread perception in our society (not entirely without merit, but not entirely correct either) is about college professors, that *Our research and books are really not practical* and that we *create theories in isolation from the "real world"* that don't apply to everyday life. Hence the well-known phrase, Ivory Tower, to refer to the academic environment.

During this group session, there was a discussion of marriage and the problems of two people forming a relationship. Then a discussion ensued about sibling rivalry and the problems of developing an identity in large families. One member said he *knew about identity problems* as he was a *twin.* He proceeded to say that *Psychologists don't know anything about twins. All the books I've read don't agree with my own experience.* He further suggested that *Psychologists write books that don't work. That makes me wonder,* he said, *Just how valid Dr. Spock's book really is*

[This is a literal reference to Dr. Benjamin Spock's famous baby book on child rearing]. The literal topics of problems in marriage, forming relationships, developing one's own identity in large families, and sibling rivalry were clearly deep talk for relationships, identity, and rivalry issues in the here-and-now group.

The ensuing topic was clearly about what was unconsciously perceived as my incompetence as a leader. The talk about *Psychologists don't know anything,* of course, is deep talk about *my not knowing what's happening in the group.* In saying *All the books I've read don't agree with my own experience,* the member is saying that *the books for the course describing T-groups don't agree with his experience in the group.* His remark *That makes me wonder just how valid Dr. Spock's book really is* a specific deep-talk reference to *my textbook that I wrote for the course is not valid.* Tying this discussion all together beginning with the discussion about relationships, identity, and sibling rivalry is the selection of the specific book on *child rearing.* Underlying this is the *Parent Template* which *equates to me as parent* and to *the group who are feeling like children.*

One final general deep-listening example shows how people unconsciously comment on their relationship to you. What might it mean that a group starts talking about *state employment being a rip-off to taxpayers?* Is this literal talk that means simply what it says? Or might it be saying something important to you? It's a little unfair to ask you what this piece of conversation means without giving you the context it occurred in. Does it help to know that it was in fact brought up in a group discussion just after *I returned from two unannounced absences* from the group sessions? It should. This topic thus likely reflects the members' resentment at *my being absent from the meetings and thus the feeling they were not getting what they paid for*—just as some taxpayers often feel ripped-off regarding their stereotype of government workers not having to work very hard and receiving benefits that many workers in the business world don't get.

Apply this example to yourself, if you heard this kind of topic being discussed after you returned to work from being absent for sometime. What do you do with this unconscious message? The answer might be to do exactly what you would do if you heard people literally remarking that they resented your being absent from work: You address the issue. Only in this case you don't address it directly, because they didn't address it directly. What you do is casually make known why you were absent. Their unconscious will get the message.

Remember, whenever there are themes about children, it may be a sign that the group is feeling that they have either been abandoned by the leader (who emotionally equates to a parent) or that the leader as parent is not doing his or her job and is thus experienced as incompetent, and that they feel they are being treated as children.

Discovering Deep Listening: What Freud Didn't Know, but Almost Did

*When you discover something like that, it's like discovering
a tooth with a missing filling. You can never leave it alone.*

ROBERT PIRSIG
Zen and the Art of Motorcycle Maintenance[1]

As a young man, I began writing poetry and fancied myself a budding creative writer. The metaphorical language in my poems and the way the words were juxtaposed fascinated me and opened up my mind. Understandably enough, I became somewhat obsessed with metaphor and analogy. In both my undergraduate senior thesis and in my master's thesis I researched metaphorical and analogical thinking, which were then largely considered literary devices.[2]

Even a brief glance at the history of science demonstrates the extensive use of reasoning by analogy. One such well-known analogy in science is the early formulation by the English physicist Ernest Rutherford (1871–1937) comparing the structure of the atom to the solar system, with the nucleus of the atom being like the Sun and the electrons revolving around it like the planets. In science we call this type of thinking *model building*.[3] Much later, cognitive researchers began to understand the importance of metaphorical and analogical reasoning. Cognitive science, however, still tends to be preoccupied with simple and surface aspects of analogies in science and with analogical reasoning, continuing with endless analyses, for example, of Rutherford's early analogy.[4] Almost since humans started to think systematically, philosophers like Socrates, Plato, and Aristotle have extolled the importance of similarity relations in thinking.[5]

I consider the cognitive mechanisms underlying deep listening to be the fundamental process giving rise to what we normally call metaphorical and analogical reasoning and of what we call transfer of learning.[6] A subliteral narrative can be seen as a kind of analogy in which the literal narrative is an analogy to, or *is like*, what is actually occurring in a conversation. Thus my early interest in analogical and metaphorical reasoning provided the beginnings of what I had been discovering.[7] Perhaps I was hardwired for understanding "metaphorical" meaning. I have come to believe that through evolution, our brain has become hardwired for creating invariances of meanings.

In Quest of the Mind's Kula Ring

It should be clear by now that we are often not fully aware of what we and others are doing and saying and that, therefore, much of our social life is conducted unconsciously; we often take part in social meanings that we have no idea we are contributing to. I realized this social fact when as a college sophomore I enrolled in an anthropology course. The instructor lectured to us about Darwin's discovery of human evolution and natural selection and about Louis and Mary Leakey's famous discoveries in Olduvai Gorge of human-like fossils millions of years old.

More than this he told us about the great anthropologist Bronislaw Malinowski (1884–1942). Malinowski conducted research in the Trobriand Islands, a group of small islands in the South Pacific. It was there that he discovered what he came to call a *Kula Ring*. This was an activity that each Trobriander engaged in once a year. The Kula Ring involved the ritual trading of armbands and necklaces made from sea shells. Each Trobriander always traded with a particular relative. What

Malinowski discovered was that the necklaces were always traded in a clockwise direction around the islands, and the armbands invariably traveled in the reverse direction around the islands.

Now, the kicker here is that no Trobriander knew that necklaces always traveled in a clockwise direction and armbands invariably in the reverse direction. How and why this Kula Ring came to be apparently remains a mystery. I was spellbound. The story led me to wonder if we, too, had more going on in our everyday social life than we are aware of. Just as each Trobriander unconsciously took part in a social activity, so, too, I later wondered, do we take part in unconscious meanings in which we create a kind of conversational *Kula Ring?*

The scientific process is often not the systematic and rational process that most textbooks make it out to be. What standard textbook views actually describe is what is called "normal science."[8] Normal science is what happens after an initial discovery has been made: I didn't discover deep listening by methodically forming hypotheses and then testing them as science textbooks describe "real" scientists doing. Noticing these themes grew out of my interests in cognitive psychology (the study of how the mind works), metaphorical and analogical reasoning (which even back then I saw as windows into the workings of the mind), and the conduct of T-groups. Of course in conducting T-groups I was always asking the question: What's going on here? In attempting to answer this question, I began to see that some topics in the group conversations seemed to be a kind of "metaphorical code" that could be deciphered.

A Long Day's Journey into Night: Of Secret Codes and Deep Listening

About 1972, I began to notice certain very general "analogical" or "metaphorical" themes, as I first called them, being used in group conversations.[9] As I have previously described, topics about *God* or *policeman* were frequently selected into discussions when the group seemed to be concerned about my *authority role* as trainer. It soon became clear to me that these "metaphors" were unconscious communications about feelings and concerns. Group members were not conscious of the real reason they had selected these topics. In fact when I explained this to group members and asked them, they usually laughed and attributed it to coincidence. But I thought this fascinating stuff was more than coincidence. Much more. The question was, however, whether these "metaphorical" meanings were real or whether I was reading too much into them.

In addition to my early interest in metaphors and analogies, my quest for deciphering hidden meaning was perhaps also influenced by my experience in the U.S. Army. In the days when young men were involuntarily drafted into the Army, shortly after high school I volunteered so I might have more of a choice in the job I would be assigned. After testing me for my aptitudes and abilities, the Army thought I had aptitudes in electronics and in cryptography. The latter involves decoding secret messages. I chose cryptography, of course. I chose cryptography not because I thought it had anything to do with analogical reasoning—at that point, I knew nothing of analogical reasoning—but simply because it sounded exciting. So I was assigned to an Army intelligence unit and was trained in breaking secret codes at the then newly created super-secret National Security Agency (NSA). Now most decoding is done by high-speed computers.

Just as in understanding the meaning of words, in codebreaking not only do you have to understand a kind of grammar and logic, but also the context of the messages. For example, knowing the history and whereabouts of the unit the coded messages came from helped in decoding them. It was also important to recognize the style of the person sending the code; each had a kind of "fingerprint" that was identifiable. It was hard, tedious work. There is little doubt that my Army training in deciphering codes was a factor in imprinting me to deciphering subliteral language. Deep talk, after all, can be seen as a kind of encoded secret message. So, from an early interest in poetry, I went to codebreaking. As it turned out, I was a better codebreaker than poet.

The propensity of humans to at least *consciously* encode secret messages goes back to almost the beginnings of written history.[10] As early as the Bronze Age (3500 B.C.), people in the Near East were being trained in the art of deciphering coded texts. One of the earliest and simplest forms of encoding is called an acrostic. Using acrostics, a hidden message can be deciphered by selecting the first letter of each line or verse in a text. An example of an acrostic was found in a clay tablet from the Iraq of the mid-second millennium B.C. The text on the tablet is a religious poem of twenty-seven verses, but was written to be read by someone who knew the "key" as an acrostic, with the initial syllables of each verse combining to reveal a separate or hidden message. But what I was observing was not a conscious process.

When I had group conversations transcribed into printed protocols, it became increasingly clear that somehow the intricate workings and structure of language was the key to deciphering this mind code. So I began to analyze these transcripts for linguistic and cognitive operations that would help me to decode, test, and validate my hypotheses about the meaning of these "metaphorical" topics.

As I did this, I began to notice some very strange but—and this is important—*consistent* cognitive and linguistic operations. For example, I noticed that subliteral topics were introduced *only* by members who had an emotional involvement in the concern of what the topic was about. For example, group members who were not concerned about *my taking notes* did not generate negative literal topics about *journalists*. Such topics were generated only by those who I knew had a concern with my taking notes about them. This important finding led me to still other consistent and systematic discoveries.

Another strange operation I found was that the characters in literal stories matched the status of here-and-now members in a conversation and that this could be consistently tracked by spatial or prepositional markers. For example, characters in the literal stories who were described as being either *up, down, left,* or *right* would match the status of group members in the conversations who the topic was subliterally about. That is, a character X in a literal story who was consistently described as being "down in back of" or "on the left" would—and this is important—consistently correspond to the status of a particular here-and-now group member, just as a character Y who was consistently described as being "up front" or "on the right" would correspond to the status of another here-and-now group member. The significance of this kind of spatial tracking is that being "up" and "right" consistently related to high-status members and being "down" and "left" to low-status members.[11]

I found, too, that the gender of a character in the literal story matched the gender of their subliteral counterpart in the here-and-now conversation. These findings were rather bizarre, to say the least. So bizarre that I compulsively checked and rechecked my findings and then checked them again. There's more: I found that names used in literal conversations were often like puns. For example, the proper name *Harry* would unconsciously be used as an adjective, *hairy,* that would, phonetically, describe a person with a *beard.*[12] What is more, I found that the initials of the first and last names in literal narratives would match a person's initials in the here-and-now conversation. For example, in a narrative about Walt Disney the name may be a subliteral reference to a person in a discussion whose initials were W. D. I also discovered that names in narratives may be unconsciously "misremembered" or that unconscious "mistakes" would be made so that the literal narrative would match the situation being subliterally referenced. For example, if the name of a well-known journalist wouldn't fit the subliteral meaning being communicated, then the journalist's name would be unconsciously altered to make the name fit the subliteral intent. Believe it or not.

The situation became even more disturbing to me when I discovered that numbers used in conversations were frequently used "metaphorically" or subliterally. For example, if 4 members in a conversation were dominant, the number 4 would repeatedly occur in the discussions (see Chapter 9). In other words, these numbers corresponded to a subgroup in the here-and-now conversation that was composed of the exact number of people as in the literal narrative. What is more, the story that these numbers were used in didn't simply refer to 4 members. Each person in the literal story of 4 people matched the gender composition of the actual 4 members of here-and-now conversation. In other words, if the social conversation was made up of 3 females and 1 male, the literal story would be about 3 females and 1 male—again, consistently.[13] It got even more bizarre.

I also discovered that complex numbers matched the here-and-now situation. A literal number, say *10,000,* may be selected into a narrative of a group composed of *ten* members. Subliterally, the *10,*(000) represented the *10* members in the social conversation and the three zeros in (10,)*000* represented a subgroup of *3.* As a first check on this finding, I discovered that the numbers in subsequent literal stories would change to match the absent member or members for that day.

I further discovered that within a narrative, all the different stories were variations on the here-and-now situation. It is important to note that these findings were found to be consistent not only within a conversation but across many different conversations composed of different members and situations. I discovered many other cognitive "encoding" operations. All of these consistent and systematic findings I developed into a methodology (see my *Between the Lines*).

As I began discovering these strange cognitive operations for decoding subliteral meaning, I began to feel the way I imagined the French Egyptologist, Jean Francois Champollion (1790–1832), must have felt as he began to decipher the famous Rosetta Stone, or Michael George Ventris (1922–1956), the English linguist, when in 1952, he deciphered Linear B, a syllabic Mycenaean script generally thought to be from the fourteenth to the twelfth century B.C. The rules of Linear B are so complex that a word spelled in Linear B may be interpreted and spelled out in a large number of different ways within the Western European alphabet. The Rosetta Stone, found in 1799 by Napoleon's soldiers near the city of Rosetta in Egypt, is a basalt slab that was inscribed with Greek characters, hieroglyphs, and other strange characters. It provided Champollion and other scholars with the key for translating Egyptian hieroglyphics. Having spent years studying the hieroglyphics inscribed on the stone tablet, Champollion discovered that the inscriptions were made up of both sound-signs (phonograms) and sense-signs (ideograms). He proved that hieroglyphs have not only symbolic meaning, but that they are also alphabetic for a spoken language. The language in literal narratives had been awaiting their subliteral decoding, like the Rosetta Stone and Linear B.

More than this, however, I found myself suspecting my observations—and my sanity. So were other people whom I knew. After all, I was observing that group members were talking to each other and to me in unconscious code, as it were. Whoa! This is the stuff that paranoid schizophrenia is made of. Many paranoid schizophrenics have what is called delusions of reference, in which they think people on TV are really talking about them, or, when they overhear a conversation, they think it's about them. As for seeing numbers in the talk as having hidden meaning, well, this is the stuff of occult numerology, isn't it?

Even with my consistent and systematic method of validation, however, I knew too much about the history and philosophy of science and epistemology (the study of how we know what we think we know) to feel secure. Was it possible that I had simply constructed an elaborate—but consistent—system, but one that was not valid? I painfully recalled the Ptolemaic theory of the solar system from the history of astronomy. In the second century A.D., the Greek astronomer, Claudius Ptolemy, constructed a planetary system that had the Earth at the center of our solar system, not the Sun. With its elaborate system of imaginary and ad hoc orbital epicycles, it consistently predicted very well the movement of the planets and their respective positions at any given time. We now know, however, that the Ptolemaic system was a *reliable* system but not a *valid* one.

Had I constructed a similar psychological system? I wondered if I had merely created a kind of methodological alchemy, a pseudoscience that only gave the appearance of changing literal meaning into subliteral ones, like the medieval alchemist who sought to turn base metals into gold or silver with mysterious methods.

When I confided my observations to my colleagues, some thought I was going off the deep end, so to speak. Mostly, though, they just laughed at such bizarre, but worse, "unscientific" interpretations, calling them simply wild coincidence. As my sophistication for analyzing this deep listening developed, the subliteral meaning of these conversations became even more intricate, and as they became more intricate, even I sometimes found it difficult to believe what I was finding. I was aware, of course, that psychotherapists had noticed brief instances of "metaphors" in therapy that they considered to have a kind of parallel meaning to the therapeutic situation, but nothing to compare to what I was—or thought I was—discovering.[14] Like the Kula Ring, the structure of the literal talk in a conversation is often ordered by an underlying set of individual mental activities that the participants in the conversation are not aware of.

I had to know if what I was perceiving was real. I became obsessed with a way to verify deep listening. Otherwise there was no way to contain speculative "interpretations," and my colleagues could continue—at best—to laugh. More importantly, unless I found a way to prove that what I was observing was real, I certainly would never be able to convince journal editors to publish such bizarre material.

What I needed was a systematic methodology. But there wasn't one. I began with the scientific assumption that the brain/mind is structured in an orderly fashion and that there would be a natural system underlying what I was finding. So I started a search for an orderly set of cognitive and linguistic operations that would serve as a systematic method for the analysis and validation of what I thought I was observing. The question was, where would I look?

Familiar Footprints in the Sand

I began to search the literature for unconscious meaning. I discovered that the literature on small-group dynamics, group psychotherapy, and other areas of research and practice had been spotted with brief snippets of what I was calling subliteral meaning. Some of this literature noticed, for example, that talk about well-known leaders in history like Charles de Gaulle of France was a symbolic reference to the leader in the group. Most developed was the work of Robert Bales, a social psychologist at Harvard University who was well-known for his research in small-group processes. He had labeled such symbolic talk "fantasy themes."[15] Other researchers working with him had noticed and written about such phenomena in small-group discussions.[16] Continuing my search of the literature, I discovered that very rudimentary subliteral phenomena had been laying around other fields including group psy-chotherapy,[17] psychohistory,[18] and communications[19] as unexplained curiosities. With the exception of a chapter by Bales on fantasy themes, however, there was no method for analyzing or validating examples of subliteral communication like those I was finding. Nor was there a recognition of the intricate extent or the cognitive importance of such "symbolic" communications; neither was the phenomena understood nor explained, except in general Freudian terms. Around 1979, research on unconscious communication ceased—or so I thought. It didn't, as we will see in a moment.

Knowing that others had noted similar unconscious findings—as rudimentary as they were—I finally realized I was no longer alone, just as when Robinson Crusoe, the main character in Daniel Defoe's fa-mous novel about a shipwrecked sailor on an apparently deserted is-land finally discovered footprints other than his own. If I were suffering delusions, then I at least had decent company, at least for my observa-tion of general "metaphorical" meaning—and there was some comfort in this.

Needless to say, for years I experienced great difficulty with profes-sional journals accepting my research, with reviewers calling my find-ings "schizophrenic," "paranoid," "ridiculous," and in their more kinder, gentler moments, "wild puns" or "simply coincidence." I anxiously re-called the Viennese physician Ignaz Semmelweis (1818–1865), who in the 1840s tried to convince his colleagues that they should wash their hands after doing autopsies before working with patients so they wouldn't spread infections, infections that at the time killed large num-bers of patients. Despite Semmelweis's repeated success in reducing the mortality rate by washing his hands, his colleagues laughed at him and patients spit on him. Rejected, Semmelweis became mentally deranged and died a lonely death in a mental hospital. (So, far, I am still running free.)

I learned years later from a colleague that the mental condition of one of Freud's closest disciples was considered highly suspect after he wrote a paper on what he thought was unconscious communications from patients. His claims were dismissed as his exhibiting "ideas of persecution" similar to a paranoid's perception of a television program sending him encoded messages.[20]

What Freud Didn't Know, but Almost Did— and Should Have—About Deep Listening

Almost invariably, people's reaction to deep listening is to say, but "Didn't Freud say all of this?" My answer is an emphatic "No, he didn't, but he almost did—and should have." Since Freud is probably one of the most recognized names in the entire Western world, the reason people keep insisting on calling anything pertaining to unconscious meaning "Freudian" is perfectly understandable, but it's thoroughly incorrect.

A misunderstood and overgeneralized Freud has completely permeated and become so serpentinely insinuated into popular consciousness that it often seems impossible to disentangle him from anything psychological, let alone from things unconscious. Indeed, mass media psychology has made Freud into a veritable caricature of himself. Nevertheless, I would be amiss if I didn't do at least a little genuflecting, because his work was an early influence on me.

When I first read Freud, I was not overly impressed with psychoanalytic theory in general. What did intensely impress me was his book, *The Interpretation of Dreams.*[21] What fascinated me about this book was not his dream interpretation, but rather the way Freud described how the mind worked during dreaming. Freud himself considered *The Interpretation of Dreams* his master work. Indeed, it is one of the Great Books of Western civilization. I later came to realize that *The Interpretation of Dreams* was a precursor to modern cognitive psychology, as were two other books of his: *The Psychopathology of Everyday Life*[22] and *Jokes and Their Relation to the Unconscious.*[23] These are quite different from the rest of his work. I consider them to be his cognitive trilogy.

Modern psychological notions of the unconscious mind, however, aren't derived from Freudian theory any more than modern mathematics may be considered derived from Pythagoras, the ancient Greek who is widely considered the first mathematician. Contrary to popular thinking, Freud didn't discover the unconscious;[24] neither did he discover slips of the tongue. And Freud never said he did. It often happens in popular culture that certain words and ideas are almost exclusively associated with certain authors. Those more versed than I am in literature have recognized for some time that, along with others, Shakespeare described "Freudian slips" long before Freud. Indeed, being an avid reader, Freud was very familiar with the Bard's work, and often quoted him.

Freud was influenced, too, by the ancient dream books of different cultures, which emphasized puns and play of words. He was aware that ancient "Oriental" books on dream interpretation based a great number of their interpretations on the tracing of similarities of sound, physical resemblances, and double meanings between words. He was also aware that extraordinary importance was placed on punning in the ancient civilizations of the East (just as with the sophists of ancient Greece).

Freud noted that Western books on dream interpretation, which were largely translations of those ancient Asian dream books, omitted the similarities of sound and physical resemblance between words. According to Freud's research, puns and turns of speech also occur frequently in old Norse sagas and scarcely a dream, he said, is to be found in which puns do not play a large role.[25]

It's a widespread myth that so-called new ideas or discoveries somehow are—to paraphrase Shakespeare—not born of others. Freud was a scholar who read widely and was quite aware of the many ideas about unconscious functioning that were discussed and written about during the time he began to formulate his own ideas. Like any scholar or scientist, he built on the work of others, sometimes carefully documenting his sources—sometimes not. As Henri Ellenberger noted, there are many similarities between Freud's ideas and others. For example, Freud was well versed in philosophy, including the work of the German philosopher Arthur Schopenhauer (1788–1860), to which there are many similarities. Ellenberger quoted the German Nobel laureate Thomas Mann, who had read Schopenhauer and upon reading Freud said he "was filled with a sense of recognition and familiarity." He felt that Freud's description of the id and the ego were "to a hair" Schopen-hauer's description of the will and the intellect, which Freud had trans-lated into psychology.[26] It seems that Freud borrowed liberally from the works of others, many of whom Freud specifically mentioned. But this isn't anything unusual in science.

Ideas about an unconscious mind, puns, and the unintended mean-ing of words and phrases were hanging around long before Freud picked up the pieces. I note all of this to simply show that Freud didn't come up with his ideas in a vacuum—and indeed, didn't invent most of them. It was Freud's genius, however, to organize, to systematize, and to theoretically conceptualize into a single package the existing ideas on an unconscious mind, slips of the-tongue, double meanings, and sounds of words.

Edward Caropreso and Stephen White have studied gifted children and they conclude that what characterizes giftedness is what they call an ability at "selective combination," of "combining apparently isolated pieces of information into a unified whole" that others have not seen and putting "the pieces together in a useful, relevant way."[27] As the ideas about the unconscious mind have gone beyond Freud, so have ideas about evolution gone beyond Darwin. But when discussing these newer ideas about evolution, few would ask: "Didn't Darwin say all this?" Interesting, isn't it?

Nevertheless, to most people, Freud *is* psychology, with everything else a mere footnote. He isn't. Contrary to widespread perception, Freud doesn't loom very large at all within the field of psychology. It's not only the general public that misconstrues Freud. Many of my oth-erwise-learned colleagues in cognitive psychology are held captive by Freud's ghost. Many don't want to be seen associating themselves in any way with Freudian ideas. This is understandable, because most of his ideas and his method of analysis remain largely intuitive and wildly speculative.

As I was writing this book, I received a rejection of a manuscript I submitted to a well-known psychology journal. I had written a piece on modern cognitive research, unconscious processing, and my sub-literal findings. In that article, I commented on the work of a particular researcher, noting that he was a little more liberal in his view about unconscious meanings than most of his colleagues. As it turned out, this researcher was one of the reviewers the journal editor selected to critique my article. In his signed review—which is most unusual—he was emphatic in saying, "The fact that I adopt a wider range of unconscious processes . . . doesn't mean that I am a *closet Freudian.*" *Closet Freudian?* Where did this reaction come from? When I read this comment, I was quite taken aback because in describing his work in my paper, I was extremely careful in my wording not to imply in any way that his work was related to Freudian ideas. What more can I say about the impact of Freud's ghost, and the need to exorcize it.

Why Freud Didn't Know What He Was Doing

In another context, the rogue French psychoanalyst Jacques Lacan said that Freud never knew what he was doing.[28] Despite the fact that Freud didn't know exactly what he was doing when he discovered unconscious cognitive-like operations, there is little doubt as to his insights. When we read his cognitive trilogy today, with its many illustrations of puns, double entendres, and the mind's use of numbers in dreams, jokes, and everyday slips of the tongue (Freud called them parapraxes), it's easy to understand why his followers and the average therapist today might think that Freud's notion of the unconscious mind was that it's "smart" and therefore could communicate just like our conscious mind. It isn't. The subliteral unconscious however is smart. Very smart.

Despite his recognition that parapraxes reveal unconscious meaning, Freud failed to see their true cognitive significance, seeing them as anomalous and not as reflecting the normal cognitive and linguistic operations of the mind. For example, when Freud occasionally found dreams that seemed to exhibit intellectual activity, he had to gerrymander these dreams, considering them special dreams created in conjunction with the *preconscious mind* that could engage in quasi-rational thought processes. Similarly, when he occasionally found dreams that used numbers, reversals, play on words, and so forth, he had to deny that they exhibited conscious-like thought and calculations.

In any event, considering the historical times in which Freud was working, for a man who didn't know what he was (cognitively) doing, he did pretty damn well. In fact, my colleague David Livingstone Smith found in his historical review of psychoanalysis that on a couple of occasions Freud did come close to discovering unconscious communications from his patients. His observations on the possibility, however, weren't known outside a small cadre of disciples.[29] Let's now see the various reasons why Freud didn't discover deep listening.

First, Freud didn't develop his observations because initially his theory couldn't—or Freud wouldn't—formally accommodate his observations of his actual data to his psychoanalytic theory of the unconscious. So he missed the bus. As Smith emphatically points out, "That psychoanalysts do not entertain a theory of unconscious perception is not a mere oversight on their part. It is deeply rooted in the philosophy of mind to which Freud subscribed."[30] What this means is that Freud believed—and this is crucial—that *all information found in the unconscious mind must have first passed through the conscious mind* (a very modern notion, by the way). This in itself precludes a smart unconscious that thinks and reasons like our conscious mind does. Smith also points out that Freud's theory was often inconsistent.

Second, to save his early theory of an irrational unconscious, Freud was determined to demonstrate that whatever cognitive-like mechanisms he found in dreams, jokes, and parapraxes were completely different from those found in waking conscious cognition. Maintaining this distinction between unconscious thoughts and waking conscious ones was crucial in Freud's mind. For example, Freud didn't believe that the numbers he found in dreams, and as they are sometimes found in slips of the tongue, functioned arithmetically as they do in our conscious state; he believed that numbers were simply used as symbols like any other set of symbols. The linguistic and cognitive implications of parapraxes must have bothered him, because later he emphasized his theory of the preconscious mind standing between the rational conscious and the irrational unconscious. Freud tells us that this new preconscious mind has many of the characteristics of the conscious mind.[31] With this blurring of the boundaries between the unconscious, preconscious, and conscious minds comes a great deal of interaction among them.

The importance of this blurring and interaction is that Freud now had all the ingredients he needed to systematically and theoretically recognize unconscious communication from his patients, but his therapeutic and theoretical blind spots still prevented him from doing so. (See the quotation by Freud in the front matter of this book.) In outline, this is how it could have worked.

First, Freud could have used his classic notion of an irrational unconscious for providing the emotional and motivational base in generating subliteral meaning. Second, his later notion of a "preconscious" could be seen as the storehouse for rational but denied thoughts or feelings about past and current situations; this storehouse would then be the source for subliteral meaning. Third, along with the irrational unconscious, the unconscious aspects of the ego involving logic, reason, language and perception, and secondary revision could be used as a storehouse for denied thoughts and feelings. And fourth, certain unconscious and preconscious aspects of the superego could also be seen as providing a storehouse of denied thoughts or feelings about past and current situations that could then be expressed subliterally.

Somehow out of all of this, language would be influenced by the shaping of specific words, phrases, and sentence usage as well as topic selections that linguistically express unconscious meanings by using puns, numbers, and other linguistic and cognitive-like mechanisms already found and explained in Freud's trilogy. Though Freud recognized slips of the tongue and other parapraxes, to him it was not possible that there could exist entire stories with parallel unconscious meanings (except possibly in a very fuzzy sense of interpreting dreams).

In my view, what also prevented Freud from fully knowing what he was seeing in terms of cognitive-like operations was that he was primarily concerned with inventing a therapy to cure patients of their problems as well as developing a theory of human behavior. His purpose, then, was not primarily to study the cognitive process per se.

Rather, his goal was therapeutic. The cliché, "It's difficult to serve two masters," is not a cliché for no reason.

As David Smith observes, Freud's seminal work on dreams was roughly simultaneous with and clearly related to his work on a class of cognitive-like operations that he called *fehlleistungen,* meaning "failed accomplishments."[32] This class of cognitive-like operations has been translated into English vernacular to mean Freudian slips, as found throughout what I call his cognitive trilogy. It's indeed an irony that the meaning of failed accomplishments applies to Freud's failure to formally discover unconscious communication as well as his failure to recognize the cognitive importance of the operations found in his trilogy. And so I return to the question I opened this chapter with: Didn't Freud say all this stuff about unconscious meaning. And once again, the answer is: No, he didn't, but he almost did. "Almost," however, doesn't count. Go ask Alfred Russell Wallace.

Freud's Platypus

At this point, it should be clear that while there are certainly many superficial similarities between deep-listening phenomena and Freudian symbolism, they are quite different. The similarity of subliteral meanings and cognition to Freud's findings is that they are made from similar cognitive stuff.

We have to be cautious when reasoning on the basis of similarities, however. As evolutionary biologists are aware, similarities between two animals may be based on a common origin, or they may not. This is a frequent mistake in reasoning; hence the widespread misconception of evolutionary theory that we descended from monkeys. Moreover, the almost identical similarity of eyes among widely different animals, such as the octopus and humans, doesn't mean they evolved from some common prototype. We know that the eye evolved independently in many different places and many times over the millennia.

While much of what's Freudian may reflect unconscious symbolism, not all that's unconscious or symbolic is necessarily Freudian. Again, one must be careful of similarities: If it waddles kind of like a Viennese duck, quacks kind of like a Viennese duck, and looks something like a Viennese duck—it doesn't mean it's a Viennese duck: It may be an Australian platypus.

Now, it's easy to say that if Freud had lived longer, he would have discovered and developed subliteral language and cognition. Maybe he would have. But, with one exception, none of his descendants did—at least systematically—though they, too, like Freud, had all data they needed to do so.

The Future of Deep Listening

The future of deep listening has barely begun. In order to fully understand its future we must briefly return to the recent past. In the early 1970s, however, one of Freud's intellectual descendants did discover what I refer to as subliteral communication or deep talk. As I indicated above, work on deep listening all but ceased in about 1979. Or so I thought. In 1997, I was contacted by Piers Myers, a psychotherapist in England inquiring if I was familiar with the work of the psychiatrist Robert Langs. Myers had become aware of my work on subliteral communication and said it was very similar to Langs's work. Shortly thereafter, I was also contacted by David Livingstone Smith, who had written about Langs's findings on unconscious communication.

Just about the same time I was discovering what I then called "metaphorical" themes, Robert Langs, a psychoanalytic psychiatrist, was independently discovering a similar form of unconscious communications from his patients.[33] Until very recently we were not aware of each other's work.

Langs calls unconscious communications from patients *derivatives*— because they *derive* from the unconscious. He claims that what I call subliteral communications can be used therapeutically. Consequently, Langs pioneered a new school of psychotherapy, called communicative psychotherapy, based on unconscious communications.

I had been aware of an increasing literature on patients' use of "metaphors" in psychotherapy and their possible therapeutic use, but since I am not a psychotherapist, I hadn't given much thought to subliteral narratives having potential therapeutic applications in Langs's sense. If Langs is correct, this adds another whole dimension to subliteral communication and deep listening: Deep listening could be useful to mental health counselors as a method of obtaining information from clients not otherwise obtainable from them, and as a new way of doing psychotherapy.

Here is an example of a Langsian derivative: After listening to inappropriate interpretation by a female analyst, a male patient responded to it consciously by saying that it seemed to make sense. Then, after a pause, the patient switched to an apparently different subject, telling a story about his wife. He said: *My wife is a bad public speaker.*[34] According to Langs, this is an unconscious communication to the therapist telling her that the interpretation was not a good one. The therapist is unconsciously represented as the patient's wife; the subject of the story, that of being a bad public speaker, represents the therapist's bad interpretation. Langs has developed a method of verifying derivatives. Presumably, when a valid interpretation is made, a more positively toned story will be told by the patient.

When I learned about Langs's discovery of unconscious communications and its therapeutic possibilities, however, it put me in a quandary. On the one hand, it was gratifying that deep listening was being researched and applied in another potentially significant way. Langs's insight that subliteral narratives could be used therapeutically was exciting. On the other hand, Langs also referred to his new psychotherapy as communicative psychoanalysis. This was disconcerting. I was (and still am) concerned that deep listening will become associated with pop psychotherapy and Freudian psychoanalysis.[35]

I should make it clear that subliteral cognition and communication are not dependent on Freudian theory in any way; quite the contrary, it's the underlying cognitive basis on which much of psychoanalytic thinking is based.[36] You can't read Freud and fail to see his talent for metaphorical and analogical reasoning. He was a master at them.[37]

Despite a long history of various researchers and psychotherapists sporadically recognizing subliteral-like language, such examples have been extremely rudimentary, involving general thematic or metaphorical-like meaning. They still are. Further, being considered anomalous, their cognitive significance has gone unnoticed. As two great psychologists, Heinz Werner and Bernard Kaplan,[38] wrote in their classic book, *Symbol Formation*, seemingly anomalous and atypical phenomena are often theoretically very important. An example is the role of optical illusions in the field of perception, or of speech error in psycholinguistics. Research on both of these atypical phenomena have provided grounds for extending our knowledge about perception and language. The same is true for subliteral phenomena. It will enhance our understanding of language and how the mind works.

Subliteral language has been awaiting its own method and theory to explain what it is, how it works, why it occurs, and how it evolved. There remains much work to be done. The next steps involve developing a brain-based theory for how subliteral language is possible and conducting some experiments.[39] It may turn out that the discovery of deep listening is one of the more important stories in the history of cognitive science.

6

In Defense of Whores and O. J. Simpson: Precautions, Ethical and Legal

It is difficult to make the method objective, but it is not difficult to begin to understand it and apply it. As a method, it is almost dangerously sharp. It can cut deeper than any other; hence, it should be employed with care and respect.

ROBERT FREED BALES
Personality and Interpersonal Behavior[1]

As the illustrations I've presented in this book clearly demonstrate, deep listening can be interesting, and even sometimes humorous. It can also be a powerful tool for discovering very personal hidden feelings and experiences in people's lives. So potentially powerful in fact, that I feel ethically obligated to sound a note of caution at this halfway point in the book. This note of caution refers to two different but intertwined aspects of deep listening, both of which are controversial. The first involves ethical issues of revealing deep listening. The second involves assessing the meaning of unconscious meanings.

Scientists have an ethical responsibility for their work. Or at least, I and many others think we do. The question is, what are the guiding principles and boundaries of this ethical responsibility? The Manhattan Project, which developed the atomic bomb that was later dropped on Hiroshima and Nagasaki in World War II, is perhaps the modern poster child for ethics in science. Albert Einstein, the great physicist, and J. Robert Oppenheimer, the director of the project, wrote to the president expressing their ethical and moral concerns about nuclear weapons.

More recently, the continued ethical controversies about the environment, using animals for experiments, human cloning, organ transplants, and gene splicing clearly point out the ethics involved in scientific research. These concerns have even led to the creation of professional ethicist, ostensible experts who analyze and pronounce upon what is "good" and what is "bad." Technologies of all kinds, like cloning, are outstripping our accumulated legal and ethical codes of conduct. Deep listening is a kind of technology, too. What are the principles guiding revealing what you subliterally hear?

The Ethics of Revealing Deep Listening

I remember as a first-year graduate student taking a seminar on ethics in science. I recall, too, that in the graduate seminar I posed the question: What if I happened to discover a complex chemical formula for a pill that would enable anyone to read other people's minds? Think of the implications of such a discovery. The ethical question becomes: Do I publish my formula for this pill, or do I flush it down the toilet? There were many students who felt strongly that I should destroy the formula. My position was then, and is now, that the formula should not be destroyed, because, as we know from the history of science, someone else would probably discover it eventually and might keep it secret for personal or national gain. Hitler was secretly working on an atomic bomb before the United States began to develop one.

My question about a mind-reading formula in that graduate seminar has a clear ironic aspect to it, doesn't it? I now find myself not with a chemical formula for reading minds, but with a psychological method that's similar in many ways.

Creative writers have the ethical dilemma, too, of disguising the real-life situations in their works. Remember the Woody Allen movie

Deconstructing Harry, about a writer who in his novels published all the personal information that his friends had shared with him that he should have kept confidential? While it may be appropriate to climb a mountain simply because the mountain is there, unlike scientific discoveries, it's not always appropriate to reveal subliteral meaning to a person or to others simply because it was recognized. I have many subliteral stories from friends and colleagues that I didn't present in this book. I didn't present them because I couldn't sufficiently disguise them so that the person telling the narrative or the people reading it wouldn't recognize the situation or person. In Chapter 9 I withhold the name of an author who may have revealed an unconscious negative racial attitude in his writing. I felt that the validity of my deep listening didn't justify the risk of impugning him in public.

Apparently some people have ethical problems about even suggesting unconscious may be present in a conversation, especially, it seems, if it suggests racial prejudice. At least one of my (former) colleagues ethically objects. After sending him a draft copy of Chapter 9—and an e-mail query—I have not heard from him again. I understand his objections. I just disagree with them (It's unfortunate that we can't simply agree to disagree).

There are a number of reasons why we shouldn't unthinkingly reveal such information. The primary one is that it might be harmful. First, the hidden meaning found in subliteral conversation is often hidden for a reason. A person's conscious mind either didn't want you or others to know what he was thinking and feeling, or the unconscious mind didn't want his own conscious self to know. Either way these are issues of privacy. Listening subliterally, then, is like having someone tell you something in confidence. Second, revealing the results of deep listening can be embarrassing for the person. It can also be personally or socially harmful.

That it's sometimes inappropriate to reveal deep listening is further illustrated by an incident in one of my groups. A group member revealed her feelings and thoughts about a friend of hers who was dying. Since the other member didn't really know how to deal with this issue in a direct way, there were, of course, deep-talk references to the topic. I believe it would have been inappropriate for me—even in the educational setting—to have asked the group, or the member whose friend was dying, if they recognized the subliteral connections between the topic of the dying friend and discussions in the here-and-now group.

Though the member voluntarily introduced the topic of her dying friend, and though it would have provided an added example for the group members to further understand unconscious meaning in conversation and what it revealed about the dynamics of the group, I didn't consider it educationally justifiable, ethically. If, however, the group had been a counseling group dealing with issues of separation and loss, or grieving, then it would have not only been appropriate to link the subliteral meaning of the topics to the member's story of her dying friend, it could have provided a powerful therapeutic experience. But T-groups aren't therapy groups. Still, under appropriate circumstances, sharing deep-listening meanings with someone can be very beneficial. After all, aren't we all trying to know ourselves?

On Being Hermenauts of Our Inner Space

"What do you mean?"

How often has someone asked you this question, or how often have you asked this question of someone you've been talking to? It's not only deep talk that we have to "interpret," but normal everyday literal meaning as well. This is a crucial point because I often get accused of seeing meaning where it doesn't exist—and perhaps I sometimes do. But so do we all. In fact, interpreting the meaning of words and sentences is most always a problem. But typically we either don't realize it's a problem and consequently assume a meaning that wasn't, in fact, intended, or we miss the real meaning of what a person meant—or both. We often just take the meaning of what someone says for granted. This is our default mode, as it were. To understand (read: interpret) any conversation, we always do so on the basis of the context surrounding the conversation.

A word or phrase in one context or situation may mean something entirely different in a another context. For example, how often has someone said something to you like, "But that's not what you said. You said that I was being deceitful." Then you reply, "I didn't say that at all." Then the person says, "Well, maybe you didn't say exactly those words, but it was clear that's what you meant." In these common situations the person was interpreting your everyday words, and consequently your meaning. There is no significant difference in "interpreting" or deciphering deep talk. We are just not as aware of "interpreting" everyday conversation as we are interpreting deep listening.

Creative writers and comedians know how context determines how we assess conversational meaning. Consider the following situational comedy scene: A wife enters a room where she sees her husband standing very close to an attractive woman and hears her husband say to the woman, "Your breasts are wonderful." Upon closer inspection, the audience sees a platter of chicken breasts on the table beside them (much canned laughter, here).

In the beginning, we are told in Genesis, was the Word—but unfortunately, its meaning didn't come with it. Meaning-creation is born out of our interpretation of the word. Spoken words, by themselves, are simply arbitrary sequences of sounds in search of meaning. Similarly, written words are merely a sequence of arbitrary marks or scratches in search of coherence. Only through constant and consistent association and social agreement do arbitrary sounds and scratches come to have consensual meaning. Even so, the everyday agreed-upon meaning taps only a small proportion of those associations and agreements.

The socially agreed upon meaning of those sounds and scratches is not all that precise. We make our meaning. Thus, the meaning of the words that we use in conversation are in constant need of interpretation in the specific context in which they are used. Men mean one thing by certain words, and women may mean something else entirely. Similarly, people in different socioeconomic classes and ethnic groups may mean different things by the same word.

A particular professional, too, may mean specific things when using certain words compared to people who are not members of the profession. When writing a draft of my *Between the Lines* book, an editor kept e-mailing me, saying, "Rob, be less clinical." Because I didn't use examples from psychotherapy, I didn't really understand what he meant. So I removed most of the psychological jargon. He still e-mailed me back, saying, "You're still being too clinical." I was becoming very impatient. At that point, I went to the dictionary, thinking, I'll fix him, I'll send him the definition of the word "clinical." Lo and behold, one of the meanings was *being too objective and analytical.* Now I understood what he meant. When someone says "clinical" to a psychologist, it's an almost automatic association to psychotherapy issues and language.

The specific context—the unique situation—in which a given conversation occurs can tells us its meaning in a particular context. Though we are typically not aware of it, we have to interpret the simplest everyday statements. For example, the statement "I am going to get into the pool" means little by itself. It can mean (a) I am going to get into the swimming pool, (b) I am going to join the football pool, or (c) join the car pool, and so on, depending on the context in which the statement is made. When we utter such a sentence, the conditions surrounding the conversation act as a rule to inform us which meaning should be selected out of the many possible meanings. Obviously, if it's 98 degrees outside and you are sitting beside a private swimming pool, you can safely assume that the person who made the statement is not talking about a football pool.

Take the statement "Well done." What does this statement mean? Without context, it means nothing. Now, what if we know that the statement was made in the context of discussing food. It could still mean two different things. First, it could mean "well done," as in "you did a good job." Or it could mean, "I would like my food cooked nicely," or that I want my meat cooked thoroughly. We are always interpreting meaning.

Finally, though I have developed a systematic method for analyzing and validating deep listening, since it's not an exact science, the subliteral analysis of a piece of literal conversation may not be correct. This is where the ethics of revealing a piece of deep listening meets validating it.

In Defense of Whores (A Cautionary Tale)

A biologist friend and colleague of mine (whom I will call John) was talking to me on the phone. The conversation came round to a novel he was working on. I asked him what the title was and he said he didn't really have one. I replied that I almost always have the title before I begin to write. After continuing to press him, he responded, hesitating, saying somewhat whimsically that he had kind of been thinking about one: It was *In Defense of Whores*.

Now, what does this mean, subliterally? To understand the hidden meaning beneath the words of this book title, you have to understand the context of our relationship.

First, John and I joke and banter around with each other most of the time in a kind of academic equivalent to the macho verbal game called the "dozens" (a social repartee originating with young African-American males where participants see if they can out-insult each other).

Second, over the past few weeks we had been briefly discussing—in a "dozens" kind of exchange—my previous general-audience book about unconscious meaning in conversation.

Third, I had been trying to talk him into writing a popular or general-audience book on environmental issues, so that the public would understand his research-based view of the environmental problem. I had often complained to him about "pop" psychology propagated by practitioners who don't conduct or understand research. He said his field had the equivalent problem with environmental practitioners who consult with businesses.

Fourth, he had always refused to write such a book because he thought it would be "selling out" his values as a scientist. The phrase he had used in the past was that to write such a book would be *prostituting one's self.*

Fifth, during the time I had been writing my book, he had, indeed, jokingly chided me on selling out to "pop" psychology.

Sixth, when he mentioned his tentative title, it seemed like he had just made it up in a kind of stream of consciousness.

Now, given these six contextual cues, I suggest that his title *In Defense of Whores* was a subliteral reference to my writing a popular book, namely, that I am an academic "whore" who sold myself in the market place. The upside, however, of the subliteral meaning of his title was that on some level he was *defending* whores. So, in this sense, it was a kind of backhanded compliment to me (and perhaps an unconscious recognition of possible merit in writing popular books). What are friends for, if not finding redeeming value in you even though they may disagree on some level with what you are doing. (It's possible that he was consciously aware when making up the title. When I talked to him later, however, it seemed that he was not aware of the deep talk. In any event, at worst, this illustration serves as an initially instructive hypothetical example.)

It may seem that the meaning of John's deep talk was clear. But, as with many subliteral meanings, clarity is not always what it appears to be. I am not backing off the analysis of my friend's story, I am just going to clarify the *intent* of it. The subliteral meaning of a story and the *intent* underlying it are sometimes not the same. This point is crucial for fully understanding the *implications* of a subliteral piece of talk. The human mind is incredibly complex, as are human motivations. Where humans are concerned few things—if any—are as simple either as they appear to be or as we might like them to be.

When confronted with the deep talk in their conversation, most people will adamantly protest, "That's not what I meant at all; I had nothing like that in mind whatsoever." Our mind, however, is made up of multiple levels. While my colleague's conscious meaning of *In Defense of Whores* was what he literally meant, there was, of course, also the deep-talk level that he wasn't aware of.

Now, as he protested to me when I pointed out the subliteral meaning in our conversation, *How could you think I was criticizing your book, when I helped to disseminate your work to the campus community?* This he certainly did, but again, in his playfully insulting "dozens" kind of way via e-mail. In any event—and this is a most important point—though my deep-listening analysis of his deep talk was correct (I believe) in terms of the parallel between being a whore and my "selling out" by writing a popular book, the typical implication of the negative intent underlying the deep talk is probably not correct.

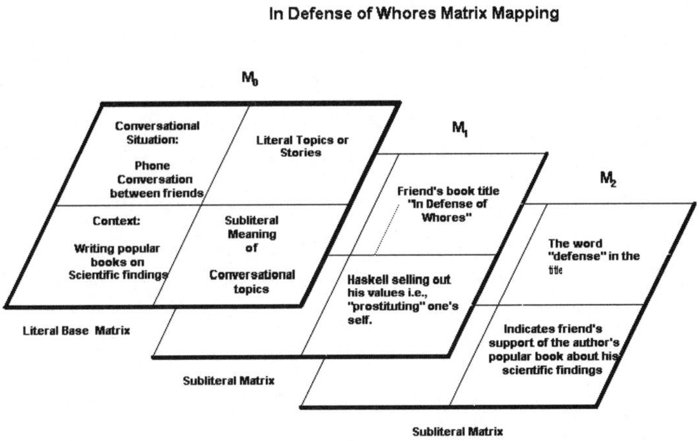

In Defense of Whores Matrix Mapping

FIGURE 6.1   In Defense of Whores Matrix Map

It's in analyzing this last aspect that we must be most cautious. The latter doesn't automatically follow logically from the former. Let me explain why my friend didn't harbor the negative intent that my deep-listening analysis appears to imply. (See Figure 6.1.)

First, John did make my book known to my colleagues on campus. This was an unusual gesture for an academic. Second, we respect each other professionally. Third, he has no need to be envious; he has published a great many well-received papers and books and was inducted into the prestigious American Association for the Advancement of Science (AAAS). And as we often joke, being a biologist, he is after all a "real" scientist as opposed to a psychologist.

Finally, and most crucially, I have often found that deep talk is often not congruent with what is known about the person speaking. So how then do we understand the apparent negative attitude implied in my friend's title *In Defense of Whores?* The answer is as follows:

We are all recipients of cultural conditioning, of social beliefs, stereotypes, attitudes, and so forth (see Chapter 9). Many of them are deeply ingrained in our unconscious by years of movie images, magazine pictures, and other people's comments (they may also be simultaneously conscious as well). I first became aware of this when listening to sublit-eral stories involving females and ethnic minorities. Some of the people creating the stories I knew were not sexist or racially prejudiced. But years of conditioning (still) about women being emotional and irra-tional and African-Americans being lazy and less intelligent provide a massive storehouse of deep unconscious and thereby involuntary *asso-ciations* that may automatically surface in deep talk. I found that often these deeply ingrained stereotypes and beliefs sometimes reflected prejudice but other times might merely reflect the recognition of dif-ference about a person or group being subliterally referenced.

The same can be said about the origin of John's deep talk. Many acad-emics have been conditioned to not respect popularizers of scientific findings. This is due to many reasons, but one is that it's believed com-plex findings have to be oversimplified to be understood by nonscien-tists. In this process, it is thought that the purity of science and truth is compromised. Another is that the media often draw sensational impli-cations from the findings that are simply incorrect. Perhaps the most perceived egregious negative belief is that receiving money corrupts the integrity of the scientist (Unfortunately, there is a sufficient kernel of truth in these beliefs to reinforce the negative attitude about populariz-ing). So, regarding John's deep talk, it was most certainly just the reflec-tion of these deeply ingrained academic stereotypes, images, and beliefs.

Now, I'm willing to admit that it's possible that on some very deep unconscious level John's comments did reflect envy and negativity (but I doubt it). As we saw in Chapter 4 on human relationships, feelings of rivalry run archetypally deep. I certainly have experienced these twinges of envy, while at the same time sincerely wishing a colleague well. We all have such multiple programs running simultaneously.

Two more points regarding the meaning of deep talk: First, these ar-chetypal twinges are thus not really significant interpersonally. Second, giving significance to these "possibilities" without clear external indica-tions to support them is sheer irresponsible speculation. If in the past John had shown jealously and rivalry with me professionally, then his title, *In Defense of Whores*, would be meaningful in terms of intent—but he hadn't. Never. Not even a tiny bit.

Certainly there is enough irresponsible speculation in our society already without contributing to it. I can't emphasize this cautionary tale enough in analyzing the meaning of deep talk. It's clear, then, that there is (a) deep listening that may look like it has subliteral meaning, but doesn't, and (b) deep listening that has subliteral meaning but that is not interpersonally significant. This is why we must be extremely careful when imputing unconscious meaning to a person.

More importantly these hasty "interpretations" can not only lead to serious personal and social consequences but legal ones in the court of public opinion.

O.J.'s California Dreaming

Perhaps only in California could the situation I am about to describe occur, especially in a court of law. I doubt if there is anyone reading this book who doesn't recall the O. J. Simpson criminal case in which he was accused of killing his former wife and her male friend. Though the case was not about subliteral meaning, it was about pop psychology, Freud, and the unconscious mind's revealing hidden meanings. During the case, you may remember that Judge Lance Ito admitted into evidence testimony presented by a former friend of O.J.'s that O.J. had confided in him about a dream he had of killing his wife. Aside from what most research-based psychologists would agree was an outrageous ruling admitting a dream as evidence, what amazed me was that apparently O.J.'s Dream Team of lawyers didn't protest too loudly (if they had, the dream would certainly not have been admitted).

According to pop psychoanalysis and psychology, the dream presumably meant that O.J. had unconsciously harbored a fantasy of killing his wife. This interpretation may seem quite reasonable to many people. After all, didn't Freud say that dreams were the result of unconscious wishes? Well, yes, he did—kind of, or sort of. Few psychoanalysts today agree with Freud's "wish" theory of dreams. In any event, in point of fact it's absurd that a dream of this nature could be entered into a legal proceeding. I say this not being a total disbeliever—like many of my experiment-based colleagues—that some dreams may have meaning, with an emphasis on *may*, and a further emphasis on *under certain conditions* and for *certain purposes*—maybe.

Interpreting the unconscious meaning of dreams, despite Freud's seminal book on the subject, is extremely problematic under the best of circumstances—whatever they might be.[2] There are over 160 different schools of thought from which the dream could be interpreted with not only different but conflicting meanings. Maybe O.J. did harbor such homicidal feelings toward his former wife; maybe he didn't, too. Even within pop psychoanalysis, one interpretation would say that the dream simply used the "metaphor" of *killing* as a symbol of O.J. wanting to *kill his feelings* about his wife or reflect a separation "wish."

The question is what would Freud really say about this dream being used in a court of law? Would he agree with the popular notions of what people think he would have said?

Freud Redeemed

To avoid never-ending dueling interpretations or quotes of what Freud might have said based on his general views of dreams and unconscious meaning, I rummaged through his works—without much hope that I would find what I was looking for—to see if I could find a dream like O.J.'s. with both killing and a legal proceeding involved. I didn't find one.

I did, however, find a dream about killing someone. And pop Freudians won't like what I found. In Chapter 1 of Freud's *The Interpretation of Dreams,* where he reviews the literature on dreams prior to 1900, he cites one scholar mentioning an emperor who put one of his subjects to death because the man had dreamed he killed the emperor. Alas, Freud didn't say whether he thought such a dream justified the emperor's killing his subject.[3] But I kept rummaging. Then, near the end of the book, Freud did comment on this dream. This is what he said: "*I think . . . that the Roman Emperor was in the wrong when he had one of his subjects executed because he had dreamt of murdering the emperor.*"[4] He thus would likely have said the same thing about O.J.'s dream being admitted into evidence. But we don't know for certain, given just the one comment by Freud.

Being somewhat compulsive, I kept rummaging around Freud's works hoping against hope to find a dream that involved killing and a legal proceeding. Though, again, I didn't find such a specific dream, on page 73 of his *A General Introduction to Psychoanalysis*, I found a slip-of-the-pen example that's appropriate since we are talking about what meaning to apply to unconscious meanings.[5] It involves a legal proceeding as well as Freud's own words about whether it should be used as legal evidence.

The case was about a physician who conducted research on highly dangerous diseases. To carry out his work he had to order cultured specimens. The physician once complained to the laboratory that made the specimens about the ineffectiveness of the cultures they sent him. In doing so he made a slip of the pen and instead of the words "In my experiments on *mice* and *guinea pigs* (i.e., *Mausen* und *Meerschweinchen*)," he wrote, "In my experiments on *people* (i.e., *Menschen*)." This slip, says Freud, attracted the attention of the doctors at the institute but they didn't draw any conclusion from it. Freud asks, "Now, what do you think?" Should his fellow colleagues have taken the slip of the pen as evidence of a criminal act and started an investigation?

As it turns out, the man had indeed been murdering people with his deadly cultured specimens. Freud then says that "such a slip of the pen would certainly rouse great suspicion in me." Shades of the O. J. case, right? Not quite. Freud then goes on to evaluate the possible meanings of this unconscious meaning. He says,

> [T]here is an important objection against regarding it as a confession. The matter is not so simple. The slip of the pen is certainly an indication but, alone, it would not have justified an enquiry. It does indeed betray that the man is occupied with the thought of infecting human beings; but it does not show with certainty whether this thought is a definite plan to do harm or a mere phantasy of no practical importance.[6]

Freud recognized only too well the central problem in assessing the meaning of unconscious communications, whether they are from dreams, slips of the tongue or slips of the pen: They shouldn't be used as legal evidence.

Freud also recognized that it's very difficult to tell whether such communications are fantasy or reality-based. If only Judge Ito had been adequately informed by research-based psychologists and not the clinical darlings the popular media are so fond of. If only Ito had not suffered from the ever-popular "Freud syndrome." And how are we to now assess the illustration in Chapter 1, where the judge made a slip of the tongue to the jury about a defendant being "presumed guilty"? I think the answer is clear.

Freud's caution and his reasoning about not jumping to conclusions with unconscious communications apply directly to validating the meaning found in deep listening.

Figures of Speech in Conversation: Numbers in the Mind

The genesis of number is hidden behind the impenetrable veil of countless prehistoric ages. Has the concept been born of experience, or has experience merely served to render explicit what was already latent in the primitive Mind?

TOBIAS DANTZIG
Number: The Language of Science[1]

I approach this chapter with great fear and trepidation because to suggest that numbers used in conversations have unconscious meaning is, at best, to be aligned with the wildest of psychoanalytic interpretations and, at worst—and more likely—with ancient and New Age numerology. Indeed, to suggest that numbers in conversations may have unconscious meaning conjures up suspicions of a kind of psychological alchemy. Given the history of psychoanalysis and of occult numerology, my fear and trepidation is perhaps understandable. Nevertheless, I have found that numbers mentioned in conversations can function as subliteral "figures" of speech.[2]

How do you explain, for example, the repeated occurrence of the number 5 in a conversation where only five people are active in the discussion? Or how do you explain the repeated occurrence of the number

14 in a seemingly casual conversation when the conversation is composed of exactly fourteen people? Further yet, how do you explain the number 14 in the literal stories changing to the number 13 after one person excuses himself to leave early? It doesn't take a mathematician to figure out that there was unconscious subtraction going on. Further, what does it mean and how do you explain the repeated occurrence of other numbers that "just happen" to come up in the course of stories or ostensibly unrelated conversations that correspond exactly to the various subgroups or factions in the conversation?

In this chapter I will show that conscious and literally intended numbers contained in stories and topics during conversations are often unconsciously selected into the conversations because they express people's concerns with the various factions or subgroups within a social conversation. Accordingly, the number 5 appeared in a conversation as a consequence of some members' concern that 5 people were dominating the conversation. Just as words and topics function as deep talk, so do numbers. And just as with using subliteral language, people are not conscious of the deep-talk meaning of the numbers that they "just happen" to use in their conversations.

In some ways, understanding the deep-talk function of numbers in conversations is more important than recognizing the subliteral meaning of words, phrases, and stories. I say this because words are notoriously vague, always leaving room for different meanings being attributed to them. Unlike words, numbers are quite precise and concrete; they have clear boundaries. Accordingly, analyzing numbers' hidden meaning is much less problematic—if, indeed, somewhat more controversial.

The importance of subliteral numbers isn't only their unconscious meaning. They have another very significant function: They provide a structure, a concrete framework for cross-checking and validating the analysis of subliteral language. Subliteral numbers function as a cognitive map, a kind of cognitive grid system for finding our way around the sea of subliteral word meanings.

Because most professionals and laymen look askance at numbers being "symbolic," it's important to present a fairly extensive and complex method for systematically analyzing and validating deep listening to numerical references in conversations. Providing a concrete framework for cross-checking and validating deep talk, this chapter will show how our minds create an incredibly systematic and coherent construction of subliteral meanings.

Before we see *how* numbers subliterally "mean," it's useful and, I think, quite interesting to look at how numbers have been thought to express symbolic meaning throughout history. My main purpose for looking at this brief history is to clearly separate my subliteral analysis of the unconscious meaning of numbers from any hint of ancient and New Age numerology or the often fast-and-loose psychoanalytic interpretation of numbers. I'm talking cognitive operations here.

A Brief Look at Numbers as Mystical and Symbolic

Neither the field of psycholinguistics nor the broader fields of the psychology of language and cognition have recognized numbers as carrying meaning outside the literal referent in the literal conversation or topic that they are a part of: *five apples* simply means five apples, no more, no less. I will categorize the scant literature on the psychological meaning of numbers into five basic areas, four of which, because of their occult and quasi-occult character, have been responsible for the scientific neglect of numbers as being valid cognitive data.

Because of the occult-like nature of past approaches to the meaning of numbers and the lack of an appropriate controlling method with which to perform a systematic analysis and validation of them, understandably no "respectable" cognitive scientist has or would consider conducting research on the unconscious meaning of numbers—until now, that is.

The first area concerned with the meaning of numbers is what I will call the *mystical* or *cosmological*. This includes the ancient belief in the mystical and secret meaning of numbers. This belief was propounded by a pre-Socratic Greek philosopher and mathematician, Pythagoras (582–507 B.C.), who applied mathematics to the study of musical harmony and geometry, both of which he thought reflected the structure of the universe (Recall the Pythagorean Theorem from grade school: The sum of the squares of the lengths of the sides of right triangles is equal to the square of the length of their hypotenuse?). He is generally considered the first mathematician. The school he founded became a secret mystical order. His followers believed in the transmigration of souls and discovered the numerical relationships between musical tones and numbers. They also believed that the essence of all things involved numbers and that all relationships, including abstract concepts like justice, could be expressed with numbers.[3]

With all due respect to Pythagoras—and to more knowledgeable historians than I—out of this early belief in the mystical quality of numbers evolved both medieval and contemporary occult groups who believe numbers to possess mystical and cosmic meanings. This is known as numerology. Numerology believes that each number has a cosmic meaning. From ancient to modern times, numbers have been assigned to each letter of the alphabet, to names, to birth dates, and so on. Even each person's "soul" is thought to have a number.

Another area of the meaning of numbers is what might be termed the *mythical,* which includes the meaning of numbers used in primitive myths and folklore, where they are believed to possess both universal and concrete significance.[4]

In addition to mystical and cosmic meaning, numbers have been thought to have psychological meaning. One area is what may be termed the *pathological,* which includes schizophrenic thought processes where numbers are often believed to possess both personal and cosmic significance.[5] Another area is a general *psychoanalytic* view of the meaning of numbers. This includes numbers as they function in dreams as well as other psychoanalytic interpretations. Historically, the idea that numbers may possess psychological meaning has largely been the purview of psychoanalytic theory. In addition to Freud, other psychoanalysts have noted instances of numbers possessing symbolic meaning.[6] By and large, their interpretations were that numbers held *universal* symbolic meaning. For example, the number 5 has been said to represent psychological integration. Examples from this approach, however, are not only few in number but are analyzed by the loosest of free associations, with rules for their combination, transformation, selection, addition, multiplication, and subtraction at the intuitive discretion of the analyst. For example, the psychoanalyst Emil Gutheil[7] says that the number 3 equates to male genitalia. Other analysts give numbers meaning based on similarity of sounds, with, for example, the number 50" equating to "filthy."

Outside of occult numerology, it was Freud in his *The Interpretation of Dreams*[8] who discovered that numbers have psychological meaning. His aim being principally therapeutic, he seems to have not been overly concerned with numbers as having real cognitive significance outside of their representing dream thoughts. Because of serious methodological shortcomings, and a small number of instances, Freud's findings are limited with regard to the method of recognizing numbers' unconscious meaning and their scope. The procedure he used for validating the unconscious meaning of numbers was a very loose method of free association. But, as we saw above, long before Freud, it was widely believed that numbers possessed religious or cosmic meaning. Freud's attempt to analyze them from a psychological perspective was seminal.

A more modern and cognitive area is what may be termed the *associative selection* area. It includes a few scientific statistical association studies.[9] No psychological meaning, however, is attributed to numbers. Finally, my findings suggest that numbers not only have unconscious meanings reflecting here-and-now concerns in social conversations but they make use of fairly sophisticated *cognitive operations*.

Numbers in Mind

Rather than present stories with multiple numbers in them from different conversations, I will instead present references to a single subliteral number from one ongoing conversation. I do this because presenting multiple examples from a single conversation allows me to show you how the numbers are integrally and structurally related to other subliteral aspects of the conversation. It also allows me to provide you with some modicum of demonstration of how my method of validation works. In addition, it allows me to show you how subliteral numbers can help to validate deep listening to what appear to be just literal words, phrases, and sentences. At times the analysis of numbers gets just a little tricky. Bear with me. It's worth it.

The following analysis of numbers is about a subgroup faction in a conversation from one of my groups. The conversation was characterized by the repeated use of the number 3 in the various topics and stories that were told in the group. There were thirteen stories, which I have grouped into four parts. Together these story variations on the number 3 reflect a primary emotional concern of the nondominant members in the discussion about the 3 dominant members, concerns which reflect peer jealousy, rivalry, and disagreement about how the group was being run. All of these stories are really one unconscious topic generated by a single emotional concern about the 3 dominant members in the group. I will refer to these three dominant members as the *triad*.

The numerical theme of 3s is just one number out of an array of numbers in the same conversation that subliterally correspond to the membership subgrouping, which included myself and the 12 members who were present during the particular session, thus totaling 13. Broken down, the membership included: 1 very active older woman and 10 young women (eighteen to twenty years of age), totaling 11 women; 5 of the young women, along with the older woman, were active, making a total of 6 active women. A total of 7 members were active, 8 counting myself. There were 2 males, counting myself. Within this group discussion, there were 3 very dominant members: a slightly older male, an older female, and myself.

The session was characterized by the general themes of bars, of drinking, and of being drunk. These themes will become important as we go along. With this said, let me now begin to parse the thirteen specific *triadic* themes.

I should note that there were other numbers that were mentioned in the session. Along with the number 3, these other numbers make up a very complex *matrix* of both semantic and numerical topics that are all integrally connected. *This matrix of connections among the numbers plays a very large role in the validation process. It constitutes a system of interrelated connections among the numbers that wouldn't exist if the numbers were simply coincidental or without subliteral meaning.* This system is the essence of my validation method.

I am primarily limiting this chapter to the number 3, however, because to include the others would be technical and tedious, though I must explain a few of the integrally related other numbers.

Parsing Deep Talk About Numbers

I labored long and hard on how to present these subliteral numbers. If I present my complete methodology, it tends to get too complex. On the other hand, if I don't present some semblance of verification, the numbers may seem not only arbitrary but just too weird for words.

Presentation of these numbers in more detail would probably tax your mind far beyond what is necessary to illustrate their subliteral meaning. I know that tracing the extensive matrix of subliteral numbers still taxes my mind, even after all these years.

Following section, divided into four parts, is an advanced summary of each of the thirteen topics involving the number 3:

I.   (1) We Narrowed Them All Down to *3 Different Options.*[10]
(2) The *3 Lucky Spots Bar.*[11]
(3) About *3 Weeks Ago.*
(4) It Started Snowing *3 Hours Before.*
(5) *The 3rd Stream* Was Playing.
(6) The Bartender Can Refuse If He's Served You, for Instance, *3 Drinks.*[12]
(7) *On the 3rd* Day They Said, "We're Just Going to Bus All of You."[13]

II.   (8) *3 of the 10 People* (Who Came into the Bar) Were Really Drunk . . . and They Wouldn't Serve Any of Them.

III. (9) *3 Seniors* Were Drunk on an Airplane During Their High School Class Trip."[14]
(10) *3 Old Greyhound Buses* That Took People from the Airport.[15]

IV .   (11) Being *Under 21 Years of Age.*
       (12) LCB Men Were Coming, Like in *2 or 3 Weeks.*
       (13) This *1 Girl Who Was with These 2 Guys.*

The general overview of these thirteen topics references the number 3 and other numbers that are integrally related to the number 3. All thirteen topics are subliteral references to three members who are dominating the conversation. (See Figure 7.1.)

It's important to know that these "numerical topics" are from a transcribed tape recording of the session that the numbers are from. This made it possible for me to systematically account for every time any number was used in the conversation and the precise context it was mentioned in. This in turn is important because it eliminates bias in selecting only certain numbers to attribute meaning to.

I should now give you advanced warning: Even the following fairly straightforward analysis of the subliteral meaning of the above numbers may prove to be somewhat of a rough trip, so hold on tight to your mental stability (you may end up thinking I've lost mine). Here goes:

Sum of the Numbers in Mind

Stories 1–7

The first seven stories are relatively simple subliteral references to the 3 dominant members. (For additional analysis you may want to go to the corresponding endnote to each topic.)

Story 8

This narrative about *3 of the 10 People (Who Came into the Bar) Were Really Drunk . . . and They Wouldn't Serve Any of Them* deserves more attention, as do the remaining stories.

The significance of these literal numbers is in showing the integral connection between the primary number 3 and another subgroup. The number 10 corresponds to the 10 young female members. Combining

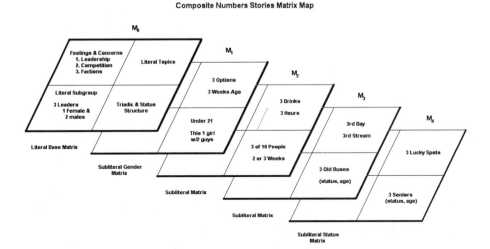

FIGURE 7.1 Composite Numbers Stories Matrix Map

the *3* plus the *10* totals to *13*. The significance of the number 13 is that it corresponds to the exact number of people in the group that day, including myself. On a literal level the number 3 is included within a total number of 10 (that is, 3 of 10 people), but in subliteral thinking the numbers are separate, thus adding to *13*.

The *literal* arithmetic structure of the number 3 being a part of the number 10 would not have fit the *subliteral* meaning, which added up to the total group membership. In other words, to have said something like *3 people came in and sat down with the other 7 people at the bar, which made a total of 10 people,* would have precluded the *subliteral* adding of 3 and 10 to total the 13 members.[16] (See Figure 7.1.)

Stories 9–10

The significance of the next group of literal stories, (9) *3 Seniors Who Were Drunk (on an Airplane During Their High School Class Trip)* and (10) *3 Old Greyhound Buses (That Took People from the Airport)*, is that in using the terms *seniors* and *old* subliterally correspond to the age differential of the triad, which was composed of myself, an older woman, and a male who was slightly older than the remaining ten female members.

Stories 11–13

These stories are considerably more complex numerically, and this complexity is methodologically telling. (11) *Being Under 21 Years of Age* is a literal story about being too young to legally drink. Like the direct references to the triad using the number 3, it also subliterally references the triad. This is indicated by taking the number *21* and separating it into two single numbers and adding them together: *2 plus 1 equals 3.* In addition the use of the word *under* in the topic of *Being Under 21*—with the *21* being the triad—refers to the fact that the group was *under* the influence of the triad. But it gets even deeper. Much deeper.

The reference to the number 21 breaks the triad down into its appropriate numerical as well as gender components, with the 2 subliterally representing the *2 males* and the 1 subliterally representing the *1 older woman*.[17] Now, you may be wondering why the 2 couldn't represent the older female and the older trainer, with the 1 representing the younger male. It's possible but not probable. First, I have found that when two members of the same gender are part of a subgroup, they are typically referenced by a single number. It would be unusual for a male and a female to be referenced by a single number in this kind of context. Second, this particular gender grouping is congruent with two other stories in this group session, stories you should consider before you brush off this gender and grouping aspect of the number 21 as being too far-fetched.

Consider story (12), *LCB Men Were Coming, Like in 2 or 3 Weeks.* Here, we once again see the triad subliterally referenced and broken down into its numerically correct subgroups, only this time the subgroup of the 2 males being subliterally mentioned without the 1 female in the *2 weeks* part of the story, and the female being subliterally included only when the entire triad is referenced by the *3 weeks* part of the story. It's also possible that the 3-letter acronym *LCB*, literally referring to the Liquor Control Board, also subliterally references the triadic structure, since Liquor Control Board represents authority. But I won't push this last point too hard even though I have other similar data indicating that acronyms can be used in such a subliteral way.

Finally, the numbers in story (13), *This 1 Girl Who Was with These 2 Guys*, like the examples above, not only add to *3* and thus subliterally reference the triad numerically, but also, as in the above story of being under 21 (i.e., 2 + 1 = 3), indicate the correct gender of the here-and-now triad—only this time explicitly by using the nouns *girls* and *guys*. The *1 girl* represents the *1 older woman*, and the *2 guys* represent the *2 males* in the triad.[18]

Again, you might be wondering why the older woman is referenced as a *girl*, especially since in stories 9 and 10 the literal references to *seniors* and *old* correctly indicated the older age of the members they subliterally refer to. To make a long story into a short one, I have found that sometimes terms are used generically. That is, terms like *girl* are used as simply a gender reference, not a reference to age, and the context of the reference will typically indicate when a term is being used generically.

It should be clear by now that while the linguistic structure of deep talk is consistent and determined by rules, the rules are often determined by the context they are used in. The important point is that the rules are applied consistently. If sometimes there seems to be inconsistencies and contradictions, it's likely because I haven't yet discovered all the rules. And if sometimes the rules seem strange, it's because nature's mind is not the same mind that logicians use. (See Figure 7.1.)

If, at this point, your mind is still working and hasn't turned into the consistency of oatmeal, there are a number of additional interesting observations to make regarding these 13 subliteral references to the triadic leadership structure of the above conversations. First, the total number of topics, 13, may represent the 13 members of people in the group that day (including myself).[19]

Second, with the exception of the first two topics, which were initiated by the male member, the remaining 11 topics equal the total number of females in the group. Methodologically, it's interesting that all 11 topics were initiated by the females. The question is whether it's just co-incidence that the total number of topics, 13, equals the 13 members in the group and that the 11 stories—all initiated by young females—equals the exact number of females in the group. Perhaps. Lacking further examples of this kind from other groups, I am willing to concede that this particular analysis may be coincidental, though given the highly structured nature of these subliteral findings, it's reasonable to hypothesize that these two findings are real.

As for all the numerical references to the number 3 being coincidental, this is another matter altogether. At this point, would you seriously contend that the 13 statements with the number 3 are not subliteral for the triadic leadership structure of the group, that they are coincidental? I think not. At least I think it wouldn't be reasonable to hold such a position.

If we look back upon the 13 stories and their relationships, it seems clear that for this series of consistent and structurally integral numbers to occur, each numerical representation and its other consistently associated aspects and corresponding meanings must somehow be *mapped, tracked, and stacked systematically throughout multiple levels of meaning and through the various story permutations, all remaining invariant with respect to the specific set characteristics (for example, age, gender) and meanings.*

In addition, there must exist a set of underlying operations that function as if there were a set of transformation rules creating this invariance of feeling and meaning. Exactly how all this is neurologically possible, I confess that I don't know (though I am working on it). The fact is, however, these cognitive operations happen.

If the other deep talk presented in previous chapters seemed strange, but you were willing to suspend your prejudices, this chapter on subliteral numbers may have put you over the edge. I don't blame you. It's deep. Very deep. Even after all these years of working with this material, I sometimes look at the complex cognitive operations that I've consistently found and say to myself, "WHAT!—G-i-v-e m-e a b-r-e-a-k!" The fact is, however, I have to believe what the evidence suggests, not only from my systematic method of verification, but from similar corroborating cognitive and linguistic operations found in dreams, primitive myth narratives, and the works of great poets.

A famous German philosopher, Martin Heidegger (1889–1976), once said that every poet poetizes out of a single poem.[20] The work of any poet, painter, sculptor, or novelist, then, can be said to spring from the depths of his Being, and an artist's complete work is a working out of, or variations on, a fundamental theme or feeling. In the same way, a conversation "poetizes" out of a single concern. (Exactly what unconscious "poem" this book originates from, I can't say.)

Sex and Gender: Women Under the Influence

If there's no meaning in it, said the King, that saves a world of trouble, you know, as we needn't try to find any.

LEWIS CARROLL
Alice in Wonderland[1]

It's certainly no secret that one of the most enduring of human concerns when men and women gather together is sexual tension. We certainly didn't need Freud to tell us that where males and females are, there shall sexual tension be. Contrary to pop psychology, at their base these concerns have less to do with things Freudian than they do with things Darwinian. As Charles Darwin clearly showed us, the role of sex is cardinal to our survival as a species. While this seems obvious enough now, I don't think we really understand the emotional depths to which these concerns are ever-present and concealed.

There are strong taboos in most social situations prohibiting the direct expression of sexual feelings. On top of these taboos, there are also intricate biological and social rules defining the "mating game." Given these primal and social forces, it should come as no surprise that unconscious feelings and attitudes about sex would be some of the stronger forces generating deep talk. Some of these sexual feelings are unconscious, some are not, some are simply hidden from social view.

Some are realistic, and some are stereotypic. Listening subliterally, we can often tune into these otherwise hidden sexual tensions, concerns, and perceptions. Just as deep listening to all stories and conversations can be useful and informative, so can deeply listening to conversations between the sexes be useful for recognizing underlying gender dynamics that might not otherwise be evident.

Women Under the Influence

One enduring concern when men and women gather is social and sexual dominance. This relative balance of power and its influence in social situations depends on a number of factors, including the kind of situation, the topic being discussed, the assigned roles, and the relative number of women and men present. Given the history of humankind, the primary, or at least the overt, concern typically revolves around male dominance of, and influence over, women.

In one of my groups, there were only two male members other than myself. One of the males had been quite verbally dominant throughout the sessions. The female majority of the group, while wholly disgruntled with me for not providing structure, was respectful (that is, retained a dependency to my role). Members of the group were dissatisfied with what they perceived as their lack of progress in becoming a cohesive group. At this point, the group went on semester break. The dissatisfaction with the group increased upon their returning from the break. As a consequence, the group was not working as a unit and couldn't seem to even return to the level of functioning that they had achieved prior to their break. They felt bad and often obliquely apologized to me.

The essential here-and-now concerns of the group were: (1) the group had "died" over the vacation, (2) an artificial attempt was being made to bring it back to life, (3) members were ambivalent about the manipulation to revive it, and (4) members continued to be concerned about dominance and control.

There was considerable talk about *It's like what we had has come apart.* They felt that *The group has died*, and expressed their feelings that *Coming back to life after vacation is difficult*, that it was *Like beginning all over again*. Then after a flurry of topics, the group settled upon discussing an old late-night movie entitled *A Woman Under the Influence*. The next topic was about the movie *Dr. Frankenstein*. What might all this literal talk mean subliterally? And how might you make use of it.

In discussing the movie *Dr. Frankenstein*, a number of specific deep-talk references were revealed about the feelings of the group members, especially the women. The basic subliteral structure was: The *monster equals the group*. The discussion about *Dr. Frankenstein also equals a reference to me*. I am, after all, a "Dr." Thus, the talk of *Bringing the monster back to life* is deep talk for *resuscitating the dead group*. That it's *A difficult task even for Dr. Frankenstein* means that *it's a difficult task even for me*.

In further talk about Dr. Frankenstein, it was also said that *Scientists must have patience*. This is a double deep-talk reference. First, I (that is, Dr. Frankenstein) must have *patience*. This is a play on words suggesting that, like any doctor, I must have *patients*. This was the first deep-talk reference to their feeling that I am *working on them*, that I am artificially trying to make the individual parts (members) into a single body (group). In other words, for Dr. Frankenstein (me) to construct the monster (the group), he must have used a lot of bodies (patients, or members).

Also, there was talk that the group, like the monster in the movie, had to be *Shocked* to bring it to life. Finally, *the dominant male member* equals *Igor*, Dr. Frankenstein's (that is, my) helper. After I had advanced the general interpretation that the group was the monster and that I was Dr. Frankenstein, a couple of members immediately, but jokingly, referred to the dominant male member as "*Igor*." This demonstrates that deep-talk meaning is often not far from consciousness.

The statement that *It's like beginning all over again* means *it's like bringing the monster in the movie back to life*. The group and the monster are also like movies; they were all *directed and constructed* and therefore *unnatural, artificial*. The themes of unnatural and artificial are a frequent perception about T-group functioning.

The deep-talk meaning of the movie *A Woman Under the Influence* equaled *the women in the group being dominated by the males*. (See Figure 8.1.) At first glance, it may appear that the two movies subliterally dealt with separate issues, with *A Woman Under the Influence* subliterally addressing gender issues, and *Dr. Frankenstein* subliterally addressing other issues about the group as a whole. But because these two movies were mentioned together, they were psychologically connected. Just as *A Woman Under the Influence* dealt with the group issue of the two males being perceived as dominating the largely female group, so too, *Dr. Frankenstein* dealt with domination and gender as well. Dr. Frankenstein (meaning me) and his assistant, Igor (meaning the other dominant male), dominated nature (the females). Both movies were thus about the domination of the females in the group.[2]

On Being Cocky

The following story is from a single-parents' group that met once a week to discuss the problems of being a single parent. The group was conducted and later analyzed by a colleague.[3] A female member of the group was the mother of a seventeen-year-old daughter who was her only child. She was a devout Roman Catholic. Her husband had died over a year ago, and during the last several years of her marriage she didn't engage in sexual intercourse with her husband; nor had she been sexually intimate since her husband's death.

Her daughter had recently started to date a boy quite steadily and seriously. Throughout the sessions, she expressed constant worry about her daughter's having intercourse with the boyfriend and about her daughter's becoming pregnant. She repeatedly said that she couldn't trust her daughter, even though she was in all other respects very trustworthy. She feared that her daughter would violate her deeply held religious values with respect to not engaging in sexual relations until after marriage.

The counselor suggested to her that *Sometimes a parent without a partner becomes jealous of a child (daughter) who she thinks is, or may be, getting what the parent isn't*. The sexual connotation of this comment became obvious and the counselor mentioned the implication. Her re-

Women Under the Influence Matrix Map

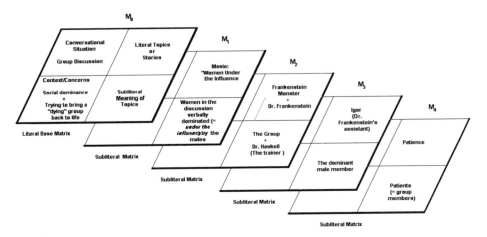

FIGURE 8.1   Women Under the Influence Matrix Map

sponse was: *I think . . . guess? . . . you're right.* She then quickly switched the topic since time was running out for the session. Just before the group got up to leave, however, she said: *You know . . . [her daughter's boyfriend's name] . . . belongs to a club called the Explorers* (suggesting that he wasn't a delinquent), but, she emphasized, *He is cocky.* The session ended. So what does all this reveal about what the woman was feeling unconsciously?

The woman had directly revealed her emotional issues around separation and loss. First the loss of her husband and now the psychological loss of her teenage daughter to a young man. She had also directly revealed her sexual frustration and tentatively admitted a jealousy: Her daughter might be enjoying what had been missing in her life, not only for the sixteen months following her husband's death, but also for the last several years of her marriage—sex.

A subliteral analysis of her last statement about her daughter's boyfriend belonging to a club called the *Explorers* and the further emphasis that *He is cocky* can be seen as deep talk supporting her tentative agreement with the counselor's interpretation that she was perhaps unconsciously feeling jealous of her daughter, who might be having a sexual relationship.

Consider this: Phonetically, the term *Explorers* can be parsed into *explore* plus *her*, and the reference to *cocky*, given the context, subliterally likely means *cock* in the vernacular, referring to a male's penis. The mother thus feared that the penis of her daughter's boyfriend would *explore her* daughter, an event which would simultaneously violate her conscious religious values while unconsciously she desired a sexual relationship herself.

If this example seem to be stretching meaning a bit too far, remember: to say that the woman was simply mentioning the word *Explorer* and just happened to select the word *cocky* doesn't explain anything. Scientifically we need an explanation for why the particular word *Explorer* was retrieved from memory and used at the particular time it was, and why the particular word *cocky* was selected for use, especially in relation to the particular context of the conversation. (Do you really believe that if the woman's daughter had been a son, with his girlfriend seemingly as assertive or self-confident as she perceived her daughter's boyfriend to be, that she would have used the word *cocky* to describe the girlfriend?)

The Eternal Seduction Triangle

One of the deepest human dramas played out on life's stage is about sexual seduction and intrigue. Since the beginning of time, sexual seduction is one of the grand eternal archetypal dramas in human *affairs* (the pun *is* intended). Seductions can be obvious, or they can be subtle; they can be conscious or unconscious; and they can be carried out verbally or just with our body language. They can also be real or simply in the mind of the beholder.

In groups of mixed-gender composition sexual seduction and rivalry dramas are not uncommon. These dramas of sexual seduction and rivalry especially seem to go with power and authority: Followers often lust after a leader, and leaders lust after their followers, as on-the-job sexual harassment complaints often clearly show.

So you think you know when you are being sexually seductive, or when someone is being seductive toward you? Think again. Seductions often happen unconsciously. Though this illustration occurred in one of my groups, watch for its re-run coming to a workplace near you.

In a previous group session I had changed my seat, explaining as I did so that a group leader should always be able to see each member clearly. At the start of the following session, an attractive young woman sat in the seat directly across from me. With a nervous laugh she said, *We can really look into each other's eyes now*. There followed a heavy silence to this comment, which carried obvious flirtatious implications.

Then, in an apparently unrelated vein, a slightly older attractive woman sitting next to the younger female said to the group, *I have a problem that I would like your opinion on*. She told of going with a married man who was *Separated from his wife*. Continuing, she said *The other night she [his wife] was peeking in through this window* at them. Since it was rather warm in the room, *I took off my blazer jacket*, placing it on the back of my chair. Almost immediately, the older woman who told of going with the married man *took off her pullover sweater, sharply exposing as she did so the outline of her prominent breasts against her tight jersey shirt*. Then, returning to the topic, a male member said that he thought she ought to talk about her problem and *Get it off her chest*.

What this conversation means is likely already obvious. Seduction is at work here. Let's look at it in a little more detail, for it will provide the "evidence" that makes my subliteral analysis credible.

Throughout the group sessions, the two women had exhibited a great deal of grooming and primping behavior (called "preening" by those who study animal behavior) by fixing their hair, smoothing out their skirts and blouses, and so forth. Such behavior in social situations is considered by many psychologists and anthropologists to be sexual in connotation—a kind of flirting invitation, as it were. Throughout the previous sessions, the younger woman had made eye contact with me more than other group members. In addition, the two dominant young men had been vying almost openly—with each other and with me—for leadership of the group (which consisted of eight young women and five young men).

The young female's statement to me that *We can really look into each other's eyes now"* was a literal or conscious link to my comment the previous session that a group leader should be able to see each member clearly. Subliterally, of course, it was either a romantic feeling or fantasy on the part of the younger female member for me, or feelings she believed that I may have had toward her. It's also a verbal expression of her previous behavior of trying to make frequent eye contact with me.

The discussion by the older woman about her *going with a married man* is deep talk about her feelings toward the younger female's previous remark to me of *Looking into each other's eyes*. Subliterally she considered *the younger female's remark as an overture to linking up with a married man* (me). It thus suggests a typical rivalry for my sexual attention (as the "powerful" leader). The act of *removing my jacket was perceived as seductively undressing*.[4] The older woman then *taking off her sweater equals an unconscious, reciprocal, seductive undressing* response in this sexual drama.

Just as in the story she related about the eternal triangle of husband/wife/lover, so too, in the group the young woman, the older woman, and I correspond to the sexual triangle in the here-and-now group conversation. In addition, the older woman's comment of *going with a married man* puts the younger woman (that is, the wife) and me (meaning the husband) on notice that she, too (the third part of the triangle), was in on the competition.

The young man's remark to the older woman to *Get it off your chest* is deep talk for him noticing her breasts when she removed her sweater. (For a similar example using a similar phrase, see the section below. Similar examples add supportive evidence that the example is not an aberration.)

The older woman's recounting an event about the wife of the man she is going with *peeking in the window* is equivalent to *her observing* the ostensible relationship between myself and the younger woman. In other words, just as the wife was peeking in at the husband and herself, she was watching the younger woman and myself. The remark about *peeking in* was stimulated by the younger woman's earlier comment to me of being able to *look into each other's eyes*. The main dynamic this deep talk reveals is the rivalry between two female members for a leader's attention.

This conversation also illustrates the shaping and selection of topics and words by the physical events that take place during a conversation (see Chapters 1 and 9). For example, the remark *Get it off your chest* was precipitated by the older woman's physically taking off her sweater and exposing the outline of her breasts on her shirt.

Finally, the particular remark by the older woman about her male friend's being *separated from his wife* was physically predicated on the young woman's *changing her seat from sitting beside me to sitting across from me,* that is, separated from me. In terms of imagery reflecting physical action, the remark by the older woman about the wife who was *peeking in through this window* was precipitated by (a) my remark the previous session about sitting so I could see all members clearly, and (b) the younger female's opening remark to me of *Looking into each other's eyes now.*

All of these correspondences are lent further validation by more specifically examining the grammatical aspects of the language used. For example, the remark about the wife who was *peeking in through this window* is significant. The use of *this* as an adjective referring to a person or thing that is present, instead of either the more appropriate indefinite article *a,* as in peeking in through *a* window, or *the* window, or *that* window, or *my* window, changes an event in the past to one that is happening now. This temporal shift psychologically links the literal topic to the here-and-now situation in the group.

TV Talk Shows and Commercials

Deeply listening to TV talk shows also can reveal deep talk. Most talk shows are, after all, relatively unscripted conversations. Some years ago on the late-night Johnny Carson show, Carson was welcoming Dolly Parton, a well-known female country western singer. As she walked toward him, it was obvious that she had extremely large breasts. Carson seriously welcomed her, saying, *Sit down and take a load off your feet.* This is a phrase that's sometimes used to mean "have a seat." But given the context, he had no more than gotten the words out of his mouth when he apparently realized what he had "really," that is, unconsciously, said: *Those huge breasts must be heavy to carry around. You had better sit down and relieve yourself of that load!* You could see his face turn red. He fumbled around trying to cover it up, but to no avail.

When he recognized what he had really said, Carson blew the scene by socially revealing to his guest his withheld perception of her physical appearance. This example illustrates what is perhaps a rather common perception males have of big-breasted women: that they need to relieve themselves of their burden. (Recall the *Get it off your chest* illustration above.) The example also clearly illustrates the process of hidden perception slipping into the conscious mind and determining the shape of the language used. While it's possible that Carson's remark was scripted (as he was known to do), it was reasonably clear from his face turning red that it wasn't scripted. It is nearly impossible to fake blushing.

Deep talk can also be seen in commercials. Indeed, it's no secret that advertisers consciously use symbolism—Freudian and otherwise—in their ads. A great deal has been written on symbolism and the use of puns in advertising. While most of the following TV commercials may seem fraught with Freudian symbolism, I will be more concerned with how those who create the ads subliterally communicate meanings to your unconscious mind. The people who design and carefully construct advertisements consciously know that meanings get wrapped around our psyches in various ways, some obvious and some not so obvious. The illustration I am about to present shows how advertising writers know exactly what they are doing with the double meanings of words.

When the Reynolds Company first introduced a new product to wrap food to keep it fresh (The product is now well known as Reynolds Wrap), it ended its ad by simply saying, *Reynolds Wrap, The Best Wrap Around.* When I heard this phrase, I initially heard what the Reynolds ad designers wanted me to hear, namely, that the Reynolds product was the best on the market. But it wasn't that simple. Not by a long shot. The ad generated at least two other levels of hidden meaning.

The first is based on sound symbolism, or a kind of pun. This meaning tells listeners that the talk they are listening to is the best. That is to say, the words they are listening to constitute the best (w)*rap* around;

the words are truthful. The connection here, of course, is to the defini-tion of the word *rap*, meaning to have a conversation.

The ad's last meaning, I believe, was intended to be a sexual associa-tion. That is, the phrase *wrap around* is semantically connected to a network of sexual associations. The non-conscious subliteral connec-tion is to sexual intercourse, as in one's arms and/or legs being wrapped around one's partner when engaged in sexual embrace: Indeed, Reynolds implied that this kind of sexual wrap-around is the *best* wrap-around (I am tempted to add my own commercial here: that deep talk, too, is the best (w)rap around).

If all this talk of subliteral sexual content to ads sounds far-fetched, the history of advertising clearly shows that since the early 1950s it has been heavily Freudian, with advertising agencies making use of their understanding of psychoanalytic symbolism. In addition, the field has made extensive use of the understanding and adaptation of association psychology, where ideas and images are connected to each other by as-sociations we have to them. Advertisers' belief is that using unconscious symbolism will function like a subliminal message or a post-hypnotic suggestion causing viewers to buy their product. We must remember that ads are constructed very carefully. Nothing—neither words nor objects in the background—is put into an ad that isn't very carefully se-lected for a reason. Every detail of an ad is consciously designed. With this said, let's now look at what I consider a more bizarre example of deep listening to sexual communication in another ad.

Yes, another good illustration of the conscious use of double mean-ings that advertising writers hope will bypass your conscious attention is an ad that ran a number of years ago. As I explain the ad, it may seem terribly obvious, but people only half-watch such things, thus often missing the subliteral meanings. I checked with a number of my friends who had seen the ad and they seemed genuinely surprised at my analy-sis, even though they had seen the ad numerous times.

The ad was for a new roll-on deodorant for women called Tickle. This ad employed almost inclusively visual images instead of lan-guage. The elongated container had a huge ball-like top. A white fe-male with an ever-so-slight French accent says, *This is like no other one; it has a bigger ball than most.* Then she touches its head with the tip of her finger very hesitantly and coyly, quickly withdrawing her finger from it as she giggles. The next scene shows another white woman slowly sliding on a turtleneck sweater. The final scene shows an African-American female in a baseball field, throwing a baseball into her baseball glove. This collage of images is no accident, of course.

The elongated container—like so many women's cosmetic containers—was an "obvious" phallic symbol with a huge ball-like head. More than this, the container was made to look like what is called a *French tickler*, a male prophylactic device, a "safe." A French tickler is so named because it has minute protrusions along its shaft to increase stimulation of a woman's genital area during intercourse.

Hence the *French accent* and the product's name *Tickle.* Saying *it has a bigger ball than most* suggests a big penis. What is more, saying that it has a *big ball* on its tip is subliterally connected with an associated meaning for sexual intercourse, as in *to ball* someone. In standard Freudian symbolism, a bald-headed male signifies sexual potency, presumably because within a kind of dream language a bald-headed male is a walking erect phallic symbol.

The *forbidden fruit* of touching the male penis is symbolized by *the woman's touching the container's head quickly and coyly, withdrawing her finger while giggling*—after *tickling it.* Still more, the male penis has been popularly symbolized as a worm. The scene with the women slowly and slinkily sliding a *turtleneck* sweater over her head is subliterally connected by association to the imagery of the *foreskin of the penis* being pulled back from its head. As a supportive linguistic association, there is even a fairly well know joke (among males, at least) about the male penis being a worm with a turtleneck sweater on.

In the final scene, the black female in the base*ball field* is throwing a *white* baseball into a *colored* glove, that is, a *vagina.* Again, *ball* is associatively connected to *bald,* and *field* is associatively connected to *feel.* In deep-talk terms, the *white baseball is the head of a white male' penis penetrating an African-American vagina*—in other words, a white male having a ball, or *balling,* a black female.

Subliterally tying the ad altogether is an associative matrix of visual-similarity-implied sounds. We have *tickle-turtle-giggle, ball-bald, field-feel*. Other more peripheral subliteral associations related to the baseball imagery are: *scoring* as in a male successfully seducing a female, or *winning* her and being *safe* at the plate as associated with the *safe* or prophylactic, which in this case is a *French tickler*. The association of *sliding into* home base, of a double header, that is, a *big-ball* game, and of repetitively throwing the base*ball* into the glove all are associated with the sexual intercourse activity of going *in and out*. Of course the implied baseball term *strikes* is associated with sex and aggression as is the ball's being *thrown* into the glove. Are we to seriously believe that all these images and associated sounds are accidents? No, they are not. Unfortunately many people still don't believe such analyses of ads.

Poetry, too, is full of such intentional and unintentional use of language. Such conscious uses of language make it clear that if we know how to use language like this on a conscious level, it shouldn't be surprising that it occurs on an unconscious level.

Playing It Straight

Just as in our perceptions of ethnic and racial relations, many still harbor stereotypes and other feelings about a person's sexual orientation. Recently, a woman I know was in a store that she frequents and was waiting to pay for her purchase. In front of her was a man wearing a T-shirt with *Secret Service* embossed on it. He was inquiring about a product. The woman knew the store clerk, who is gay. Though the clerk's demeanor was not the typical stereotype of a gay male who acts extremely effeminate, his behavior could be seen as such, and thus it wouldn't be unreasonable for someone, especially a macho male, to suspect that the clerk might be gay. The clerk had just finished a long and rather dramatic explanation of a product to some other customers. It was then the man's turn.

As the clerk was answering the man's question, the man said to the clerk, *Be straight with me, now,* by which the man literally meant, don't just give me a sales pitch to sell the product, is it really good? The woman observing all this said the clerk did a subtle but clear double take on the man, asking him to be *straight* with him. The three common meanings of the word *straight,* of course, are to be (a) socially conventional or normal, (b) to be honest, and (c) to differentiate someone who is heterosexual from someone who is homosexual. The gay clerk certainly consciously understood these meanings. The question is: Was the man's *Be straight with me* remark a subliteral statement reflecting that he unconsciously recognized—or at least that he was hiding his belief—that the clerk was gay?

Not having more information, I can't absolutely assess that the statement was in fact deep talk. However, given (a) that the instance occurred in a small, and rather provincial town, (b) in a state where there had recently been a referendum on gay rights legislation, and (c) where there had been beatings of gay men, it seems reasonable—being a member of this provincial linguistic community—to assume that the selection of the word *straight* was no accident. Judging from the clerk's double-take, it certainly didn't seem an accident to him. The clerk's unconscious tuned in on the possible subliteral meaning, which then became conscious.

Then there is the matter of the man's T-shirt embossed with the words *Secret Service.* After the man's statement, the clerk asked the man if he was in the Secret Service. The man said he wasn't. Why would the clerk ask the man if he was a Secret Service agent? Perhaps the clerk's subliteral mind's picking up on the word *straight* was in part based on the words embossed on the man's T-shirt. While in most states it's no longer illegal to engage in homosexual activity, it's still illegal in some states to engage in anal sex (called sodomy). Perhaps the clerk on some unconscious level was reacting to this illegal association with a possible officer of the law.

Finally, the noun *service* used as an adverb as in "to service" is also used by both gay and heterosexual males to refer to providing sex activity to another, as in servicing someone. In fact, in most dictionaries this is one of its meanings (but it's usually defined as having sex with a female). If the illegal aspects of my analysis of term *servicing* seems far-fetched, consider that in the area where this deep talk occurred, every so often there is a news item that the police are cracking down on an area where gay men meet to have sex, to *service* each other. (I don't recall similar news items about heterosexual gathering places, like Lovers Lanes—at least not since the *Happy Days* of the 1950s.)

Yet another example of a gay stereotype. A female in one of my groups, who was being trained to work in counseling groups at her workplace, asked me, *Were you absent last time on purpose in order to see what our response would be?* I replied, *No, I wasn't absent on purpose.* I was just about to explain that during each group I plan to be absent a couple of times during a semester, when the dominant male member of the group sarcastically interjected, saying, *Oh, come on, don't give us that.* There followed a heavy silence because typically statements that appear to challenge a leader are both consciously and unconsciously felt by other members to be "dangerous." They fear that the challenge may bring retaliation not only to the member who made the statement, but upon them as well (shades of family life and parent/child relations).

Then apparently unrelated to any previous topic, the female member began talking about the counseling group where she worked, saying she *Feels so sorry for this one member. He is a homosexual and announced it at the first meeting,* adding, *This made me wonder if he really felt comfortable with it.* She went on saying that in the counseling group there's *A male member who is always making remarks about this homosexual, but the fellow who is homosexual will not respond to them. He just sits there passively. I feel so sorry for him.* She then explained that she didn't know whether to say something to the male who was making the remarks about the homosexual or not, as she was *Just beginning to establish a good relationship with him in the group.* Silence. Some small talk ensued, and the session ended.

The context for this conversation was this: In previous sessions, the dominant male member had frequently made derogatory and chiding remarks to me to which I didn't respond. Each time this occurred, she looked aghast at me, clearly expecting me to reply to his remarks. She had also mentioned in previous sessions that she felt that she and the dominant male member in the group were just beginning to establish a comfortable relationship. The deep-talk picture should be coming into focus now.

The older woman's reference to the gay male in her counseling group is deep talk about me, as, like him, *I will not respond but just sit there passively in the face of remarks by the dominant male.* Thus, the dominant male member in her counseling group who was always making remarks about the homosexual equates to the dominant male member in the here-and-now group who makes remarks about me. Therefore, her remark of *Feeling so sorry for this member* reveals her feeling sorry for me.

Members frequently feel perplexed and sorry for the trainer in group situations where the trainer is nondirective and passive. (The British group analyst Alfred Bion once said that groups don't understand a leader who neither fights nor runs away.) That the gay male announced his role at the first meeting of her counseling group corresponds to my announcement during the first meeting that my role was not that of an active member (implying that I would be "passive").

The woman's wondering whether the gay male at work was comfortable with his role equals with her wondering whether I am comfortable with my role, that is, being addressed in such a manner by the male in the group. Her statement about not knowing whether to say something to the male in her counseling group because she is just beginning to establish a working relationship with him equals her concern about saying anything to the male in the here-and-now group because, as she said in a previous session, she is *Just beginning to establish a relationship with him.*

This episode demonstrates the dynamic of the woman's feelings toward (a) me in terms of a person and as a trainer and (b) the male member. It may also reflect some concern she has for another group member who could be construed as being gay. No one bothers him, but he did just sit there passively. Once again we can see that the particular language that is unconsciously selected linguistically signifies the topic's linkage to the here-and-now group. In the woman's statement about a male in her counseling group who is always making remarks about a gay male, instead of saying *the* homosexual, or *a* homosexual, she used the pronoun *this* in referring to the gay male. Thus, she psycholinguistically shifted the reference to subliterally reflect a here-and-now meaning. Likewise, in the statement, *But the fellow who is homosexual will not respond to them*, which literally refers to the other male's comments, the *them* subliterally, means: In my nondirective leadership style, I do not respond to members, that is, *them*.

There is yet another level of deep listening to this episode. During the group discussion, I didn't feel as if I had identified all aspects of the subliteral meaning connected to the gay male topic. I asked the woman to make an appointment to see me in my office. In response to my request that she reiterate the story she told about the gay male in her counseling group, she said that he did not return to the counseling group. She went on to say that *He's very intelligent.* As a matter of fact, she said, *He's the most intelligent person in the group so I guess he wasn't getting anything out of the group.* During the session, just prior to meeting with me in my office, the woman had expressed that she *Wasn't getting anything out of the group and that she felt like not coming to the group any more.*

It's likely that in the woman's own unconscious mind, she identified with the gay male; that is, being older than most of the members, she felt she was more *intelligent*, in the sense of having more experience, and that like him she, too, felt like not attending the group any longer. Further support that the gay male subliterally corresponded to me is the woman's comment that *He's the most intelligent person in the group so I guess he wasn't getting anything out of the group.* Contextually, groups often mention that professors are very intelligent. More specifically, groups often talk about their belief that since I have conducted these groups for years, I probably don't learn anything new and am probably bored (neither of which is correct).

The literal topic about gays, then, becomes a multi-leveled set of subliteral meanings and a window into the deep-rooted stereotypes in our culture. The stereotypes here are that gays are (a) effeminate, (b) passive, (c) emotionally female, (d) deviant, and (e) highly intelligent. Just as with racial and ethnic stereotypes, these deeply rooted emotional beliefs become generalized to other situations that are perceived to be similar.

All these subliteral topics were transformations of basic concerns about sexuality, including domination, competition, stereotypes, sexual preference, physical touching, and disrobing, with each different topic being a permutation or variation revolving around a single complex of emotional concerns. We also saw that subliteral transformations were carried out using various cognitive and linguistic operations. These included the use of movie themes reflecting here-and-now meaning, pun-like sounds, the use of words that have multiple underlying meanings, the physical events precipitating corresponding or subliteral topics and meanings, the use of plural and pronoun shifts, and oronymic use of words. *And once again,* we saw that much can be learned about particular unconscious feelings and thoughts and interpersonal relationships by deep listening.

9

A Niggardly Issue?
Race Matters in
Black and White

*Gump's first encounter is with a 'white feather' . . . his first
human encounter is with a black woman wearing 'clean
white shoes'. . . . Gump identifies himself as a descendant of
the southern Confederate founder of the KKK.*

AARON DAVID GRESSON
"Reading Forest Gump"[1]

As we come into the twenty-first century, we live in an age in which the earth has been reduced to a global and incredibly diverse multicultural village. Ostensibly it's an age of enlightenment, an age in which education has supposedly replaced superstition with facts. But in social gatherings of mixed ethnic composition, prejudicial feelings, attitudes, and concerns are ever present in most people, regardless of skin color or ethnicity.

As with our individual lives, so too our work and social lives have become increasingly made up of different groups of peoples from around the world who not only look different from each other but who have different beliefs and cultural practices. It's important to understand and recognize behaviors and attitudes toward different peoples if we are to reduce personal and global conflict in our lives.[2]

Many non-minorities think that racial prejudice has been almost eradicated since the civil right movement that began in the late 1950s. Certainly, with the exceptions of the still-active Ku Klux Klan and other white supremacist groups—and on the other side of the race issue, the Nation of Islam—it's nearly impossible to get someone to admit on a questionnaire survey that they are prejudiced against certain ethnic and other minorities. But the issue of prejudice and discrimination looms, if not larger, at least as pervasively and certainly more subtly. We have driven some of it underground, just as we have driven some sexist prejudice underground.

As the extreme and overt forms of prejudice decline, the breadth and depth of more subtle and unconscious forms of prejudice and discrimination seem to increase. Even now we tend to exaggerate and selectively experience something that we fear or dislike. A Gallup Poll[3] in 1990 showed that most white Americans believed that African-Americans made up 32 percent of the population and that Hispanics constituted 21 percent, when in reality the figures were 12 percent and 9 percent. Perceptions haven't changed. When I asked my students and friends what percentage of the U.S. population they thought were African-American, I received answers all the way from 20 percent to 50 percent. Amazing, isn't it? Perceptions of the race issue in the United States remain deeply divided.

We saw this division in perceptions of the race issue during the 1995 trial of black football star O. J. Simpson on charges of killing his white ex-wife and a white male friend of hers. The vast majority of whites felt race was not an issue in the trial process. Conversely, the vast majority of African-Americans felt that race was integrally involved.[4]

One way to uncover these more subtle and covert forms of prejudice is by listening to conversations with a subliteral ear. In this way, we can hear both current and vestigial remains of these feelings and stereotypes causing much of our racial and ethnic conflict and misunderstandings. I have been listening to such subliteral racial and ethnic stories for years.[5]

It's widely recognized that in everyday conversations certain euphemisms are consciously employed to cryptically talk about ethnic out-group people such as "you know how *they* are." Similarly, certain phrases in a conversation may consciously be used to represent *black versus white* prejudices, stereotypes, and concerns such as topics about *city versus rural* or talk of *inner city* and *welfare*. This is simply called "coded speech," by which everyone knows what's "really" being discussed. But, again, I am not talking about coded speech, I am talking deep stereotypes.

I have found in mixed racial groups of African-Americans and whites that literal topics associated with color often creep into chitchat that on the surface seems to have no bearing on race. Why would references to the color black be selected into the interracial chitchat? For example, why would talk of *chocolate ice cream*, or *black eyes*, or *electrical blackouts* be selected into a "mixed" racial conversation?[6]

And as out of date as it may sound, why would the apparently literal topics about people being *lazy* or about *eating watermelons* creep into conversations with no conscious awareness of these topics' being stereotypic racial references to minority members in the conversation? It's as if the very physical presence of an African-American acts as a stimulus that automatically evokes multiple layers of prejudices, stereotypes, and other concerns. Some of the stereotypes that the deep-talk illustrations in this chapter are based on may seem to no longer exist— to be from a time long past. Let me assure you that this is not the case.[7] Many of them are still operating on deep unconscious levels.

Before I begin to more fully illustrate deep listening to racial stereotypes, however, I need to sound a note of caution regarding interpreting conversations that seem to reflect prejudice. While prejudicial and stereotypic attitudes can be revealed subliterally, I have found that often deep-talk references to ethnic stereotypes may not necessarily mean that the person speaking is prejudiced in a negative sense. Such references may instead reflect the activation of cultural stereotypes that most of us have had ingrained in us through mass media that may be automatically evoked (see below and in Chapter 6). This caution applies not only to all subliteral references in conversations, but it especially applies to racial topics. I also need to clarify some terms before we begin.

The Meaning of the Terms Prejudice and Race

The terms *prejudice* and *race* are widely misunderstood. Most people think of prejudice as reflecting something negative. This is because the everyday usage of the term in relation to racial and ethnic issues has overridden its psychological meaning. *Prejudice* means simply a pre-judgment about something before looking at all of the relevant information. It can thus be positive, too. A related meaning is a preconceived preference, opinion, or idea. Finally—and this is the meaning generally applied—*prejudice* can mean an irrational dislike or hatred of a particular group of people on the basis of their ethnicity/race, gender, sexual orientation, or religion. I use the term *prejudice* here not as a simple prejudgment but rather in the typical sense of a negative or adverse prejudgment, one that negates or devalues an individual or group. This prejudgment is precipitated and organized by both conscious and non-conscious belief systems made up of negative stereotypes and attitudes. It's in this sense of the term *prejudice* that a person is said to be racist, sexist, and so forth.

People who subliterally generate stereotypes may not be overt racists or bigots, may not discriminate, and may in fact be involved in civil rights activities. Such subliteral references may simply denote a person's ignorance about a negative meaning or a buried culturally conditioned stereotype that was automatically evoked. We may think of this distinction as racial but not racist. I might note here that this distinction is my own. It uniquely comes out of my findings on subliteral talk and is an important distinction both in terms of prejudice and in terms of our cognitive structure. I will explain this more concretely at the end of this chapter.

The term *race* is also problematic. I use the term as it's typically understood by the majority of the population, which apparently includes many scientists. Race is considered to be a significant biological and genetic distinction defining a group of people who belong to an ideal or "pure" genetic pool. I use the term here because it's the accepted medium of semantic exchange and therefore convenient in communicating the subject of this chapter. However, I consider the concept of "race" to be a myth, as the anthropologist Ashley Montague argues in his book *Man's Most Dangerous Myth.*[8]

Deep Listening to Ethnic Prejudice

Race does matter.[9] One day my closest friend and colleague, Dr. Aaron Gresson, and I were standing outside smoking our pipes. Gresson is African-American. A white woman who was also standing there said, *I love the smell of pipe smoke; it smells so good.* She then turned and looking at Aaron and said of his tobacco, *It smells like there's vanilla in it.* Once more we must ask, why did this come into the woman's mind out of all the possible topics and other things to say? Even if the tobacco did smell like vanilla, she perceived other characteristics of the situation as well. And why didn't she simply chitchat about the weather, like most people do? The likely deep-talk meaning is that my fairly light-skinned black friend is part white, not only in his genetic heritage but in his socializing—hence the remark about *vanilla.*

Outside the sports world and Hollywood, it's still relatively unusual to see a white male and a black male chumming around together. On one level, I think the woman's first statement, *I love the smell of pipe smoke; it smells so good* provides a positive context for her racial deep talk. In addition, most whites do not have the stereotype of African-American males smoking pipes. So the statement *It smells like there's vanilla in it* also likely means that Aaron was engaging in a white man's activity. In addition, her remark may have been an oblique reference to her feeling that Aaron was an "Oreo," the phrase used to describe a black person who is culturally white, like a chocolate Oreo cookie that has vanilla (white) frosting inside. Because of the positive first statement, however, I doubt this "Oreo" meaning. Nevertheless, human motivation and perception is complex, so this statement likely reveals a number of feelings and attitudes, even conflicting ones. All in all, this deep listening about race matters was likely relatively benign in terms of prejudice.

Other similar references may not be so benign. One of the most enduring beliefs about many minority groups, especially African-

Americans, is that they are genetically different in significant ways. Thus, when a person is perceived as being of "mixed" genetic heritage, for some people this becomes important. In a group discussion where one of the members was perceived as being genetically "half black and half white," the topic turned to talk of *animal pedigrees*, with an ensuing discussion of *pure strains* versus *half breeds* of dogs. Later in the same group conversation, there was mention of the pipe tobacco called *Half and Half*. I don't belief these ostensibly literal topics are coincidental. These literal topics of *animal pedigrees, pure strains* versus *half breeds*, and of the pipe tobacco called *Half and Half* are deep-talk references to a person in a social conversation who is perceived as being of genetically mixed heritage. In other words, it's no accident that these topics were selected into the conversation.

Clearly, these subliteral topics are not on the same level of consciousness as typical talk about *city versus rural* or *inner city* and *welfare*, where everyone knows that race is "really" being discussed. The use of the quantitative metaphor "half" is used, because historically—and I think even now—prejudiced thinking by whites maintains that people who have any African-American heritage, however small, are considered black. (Actually, a light-skinned "black" person is almost never considered to be half-black. In fact, a person who is thought to have any African-American heritage at all has generally been considered only black.) The use of the metaphor "half" is a strange kind of unconscious math that rounds off any fraction into a whole number. At the very least, this deep talk about genetic matters is not benign because it shows that race matters. That such racial stereotypes are still operating today may seem hard to accept by many whites. To most older African-Americans, however, the fact that these stereotypes are still operating is no surprise.

Norman Mailer and George Plimpton
Versus George Foreman

While I was working on this chapter, I was watching a recent documentary on the 1974 Muhammad Ali-George Foreman fight in Zaire,

Africa.[10] Ali, who was much younger than Foreman, was attempting a comeback for the championship title. Ali won the match. During the documentary, George Plimpton and Norman Mailer, the U.S. novelist, were extensively interviewed, since they had both been in Zaire for the 1974 fight. In two descriptions made by Plimpton and Mailer, deep-talk racial references were evident to me.

The first—and perhaps somewhat more subliterally problematic comment—was one by Plimpton. It occurred in the course of his describing the then reigning champion George Foreman as a giant of a man whose image or persona was bigger than life, so to speak. He went on to say that when such a figure loses he seems to "shrink" to the size of a ___ (you fill in this blank and see below) ___. Now any number of words were possible to describe Foreman's shrunken persona or status. He could have selected the word *midget* or *dwarf*, or said that Foreman seemed to shrink to the size of *Tom Thumb*, or made any number of other typically associated descriptions to the word *shrunk;* or he could have simply said that when larger-than-life figures fall from their status, they seem to shrink in stature and left it at that. He didn't.

Plimpton said Foreman seemed to shrink to the size of a *pygmy*. Pygmies, of course are a group of equatorial Africans standing less than five feet tall. Why was pygmy selected to describe Foreman's *shrunken* persona instead of the many other alternatives?

First of all, being an upper socioeconomic class recipient of private prep schools, Harvard, and of Kings College at Cambridge University in England, Plimpton was certainly aware of the long history of the English in Africa. Second, the term *pygmy* is obviously more congruent with racial associations than are the other terms that I suggested above. In addition, the term *shrink* has stereotypical associations with *head-shrinking* cannibals.

When I began describing this incident, I said it was somewhat more problematic than the one I will describe in a moment. This is so for a number of reasons. The first one is (a) Foreman is of African heritage, and (b) the fight did take place in Africa. Therefore one could say the term *pygmy* was quite logical and had nothing to do with race. I don't buy this explanation—not for a moment. I don't buy it because Foreman is not an African but an American, in the same sense that Plimpton is American but of Anglo-Saxon heritage. And what if Foreman had been white? Would he have been compared to a *pygmy*? Highly unlikely. The fight was billed as a "rumble in the jungle."

Further, I don't think that my interpretation of "head-shrinking cannibals" is stretching the analysis. During the documentary a most peculiar segment involving an African witch doctor's prediction of Foreman losing kept being woven into the story. By the same token, I don't ever recall (though I am no avid follower of boxing) stories of psychic mediums being woven into documentaries on boxing matches in the United States. So is Plimpton's use of the term *pygmy* racial? Certainly, I believe it's racial. I don't believe it's racist or reflects prejudice, however, in the typically negative sense. The use of the term likely reflects (a) an automatic activation of a cultural racial stereotype, (b) though it's possible that it also reflects an actual deep-level unconscious belief in the stereotype.

From all that I have gathered about Plimpton, he doesn't appear to be racially discriminatory in his everyday behaviors. Regardless of racism and prejudice in the negative and active sense, at the very least the incident certainly shows that race matters. There are many different shades of prejudice.

The second illustration of deep listening to racial material in the documentary was evident in the commentary by Norman Mailer. After showing and describing Foreman repetitively hitting a punching bag during practice (the big "heavy bag") in the same spot with great force, Mailer said that Foreman's great punching strength left the bag with an indentation the size of ___ (you fill in blank and see below). Again, any number of words were possible to describe the size of the indentation. Since it was a sports event, he could have said that the indentation was the size of a *softball* or perhaps a *soccer ball*. But he didn't. Mailer described the indentation as *Half the size of a small watermelon*. Recall that eating watermelon is historically and classically associated with African-Americans in the United States. So, we must ask again: Of all possible objects, why was a fruit selected to compare the size of the indentation, and second, why the particular fruit watermelon? Why not a cantaloupe?

More importantly for assessing the validity of the deep-listening meaning, note that Mailer's mind had to make the watermelon stereotype fit the actual size of the indentation. The indentation was not in fact as big as a typical watermelon. Nor was it the size of a small watermelon. It was *half the size* of a *small* watermelon. It's very peculiar phrasing to say that the indentation was not only "half" the size of a watermelon, but it was "half" the size of a "small" watermelon. What's significant here is that Mailer's mind had to linguistically gerrymander the size of the watermelon to make it fit a stereotype. I suggest that this was no accident.[11] Why not have said *twice the size* of a *grapefruit*?

But is this a racist comment in the typically negative sense? Probably not. Over the years, Mailer has been known for his "liberal" and "hip" views (he even wrote a book in the late 1950s entitled *The White Negro*). As with the Plimpton incident, at the least Mailer's comment shows that, on some level, race remains a significant matter. So does deep listening to Plimpton and Mailer's interviews at least inform us about the automatic activation of cultural racial stereotypes? You bet. Are they racist? Probably not—at least in the negative sense.

A Niggardly Question?: Racial or Racist—or Not?

In January 1999, a story about a potentially explosive racial incident involving the use of the word *niggardly* in reference to a financial budget was widely reported. Ordinarily, this word might not be newsworthy, despite its seeming association to the so-called N-word, "nigger," even taking into consideration the ethnically sensitive times we live in. However the word was used by a white aide in the office of Mayor Anthony Williams of Washington, D.C., an African-American. Some blacks attending the meeting immediately walked out in protest when hearing the word *niggardly*.

The incident elicited considerable national media attention, including two pieces in the *New York Times*, one by a reporter[12] and one an opinion piece by Steven Pinker, a widely respected M.I.T. cognitive scientist *cum* linguist.[13] Most of the press, along with Pinker, did not find any racial (stereotype) or any racist (negative) intent by the white aide.

More importantly, the NAACP issued an almost instant press release agreeing that the white aide's use of the word *niggardly* had *no racial or racist meaning*. After all, the NAACP's reasoning went, the word means "miserly" and has absolutely no grammatical linkage or linguistic history that would suggest anything racial. Indeed, the word was simply coincidental. End of newsworthiness. So the African-Americans who thought the term was racial were thought to be overly paranoid, or at the very least over-sensitive, right? I don't think so. At least, not exactly so. It was a clear piece of deep talk.

From my deep-listening perspective, the significant question that was again left unasked was this: Why was the particular word *niggardly* selected into this particular context as opposed to its many other synonyms, especially given the ethnic composition of the meeting? Indeed, why was *miserly* not used, or *stingy*, or *tight*, or *tightfisted*, or *penurious*, or *penny-pinching* or *frugal*, and so on? This is the significant question that must be answered if we are to fully understand the racial implication of what happened in Mayor Williams's office.

As most linguists agree, a large part of our everyday use of language, including accessing and selecting words, is accomplished unconsciously. This is especially the case with our use of complex grammar. (Out of the many hundreds of grammatical rules that you use everyday, how many can you recite?) While sometimes linguists can demonstrate on the basis of the context surrounding a conversation and syntactic consistencies why a particular kind of word will be selected into a conversation, they can't explain why a particular word is selected. Herein lies the ghost in the disavowing of any racial intent of the white aide's use of the word *niggardly*.

There are three significant alternative interpretations of the word *niggardly* in the context in which it was used that—in the rush to disavow any racial undermeaning—were ignored. First, despite the technical meaning of the word, the white aide's use of the term could be an indication of unconscious racial prejudice just by the white aide's mind selecting a word sounding and looking similar to the word *nigger* or *niggardly*. Secondly, it could have been a "simple" automatic linguistic association expressing the *recognition of a racial difference* in the meeting, without any negative prejudicial intent. In this second case, it would certainly be "racial" but not "racist." In other words, the mind simply by association expressed a perceptual difference it perceived in its immediate environment. Third, it could have been an *automatic activation* of a cultural stereotype. Let me briefly explain how I come to these alternative explanations and their racial and social significance.

As Steven Pinker correctly noted, the similarity of sound and sight of the two words *niggardly* and *nigger* linguistically access each other via associations. The reason for this is—again as Pinker pointed out—that any word selected during a conversation occurs in a two-stage process. First, because words have multiple meanings, our brain reviews (called lexical accessing) all possible meanings of a word that we are aware of from our past experience. Then, from the context, our brain chooses (called lexical selection) out of all the possibilities the assumed appropriate meaning in the context of its use. In addition, Pinker correctly noted that the "*ar*" in the word *nigg(ar)dly* is often pronounced "*er*" as in *nigg(er)dly*. Pinker used these linguistic facts to concur that no racial meaning was present. This would seem to put this racial matter to rest. But the ghost in this linguistic theory remains.

As I have explained previously, the perceptions, feelings, and concerns that we harbor about a situation or person influence our unconscious word choice. No one will deny that the color white is perceptually quite different from black, and that many of us still harbor various concerns on various levels about these differences. What I am suggesting is that these racial differences and concerns about those present in the mayor's meeting *unconsciously determined the lexical selection* of the word *niggardly* in this mixed racial meeting. Now, it's crucial to emphasize that without knowing much more context about the aide and the history of the people involved, admittedly there is no way to know with certainty whether the use of the word was an unconscious association to race in the racist sense.

In disavowing any racial meaning to the word *niggardly*, the analyses were correct, as the technical definition of the word carries no racial meaning. The linguistic analysis based upon associations was also correct. But socioculturally, I believe, the disavowal was not correct. Like most of the above examples, the phrase likely reflected culturally primed *automatic* racial images most of us have had ingrained in our minds. Either way—racial or racist—the *niggardly* remark is likely significant in terms of cultural prejudice. It shows that such images are still ingrained in our psyches.[14] So, while the statement may not mean that the aide was individually racist (though it might; see below), like the watermelon example, it certainly reflects our cultural history of racism.[15] As for the all-too-swift and strong disavowal of the incident by most people, to paraphrase Shakespeare: Me thinketh they disavowedeth too much.

On Big Bucks and Gaming

One day in the mid-1970s my friend Aaron and I were returning from a leisurely talk on a wharf overlooking an expanse of ocean near my cottage in Maine. At that time, a black person in the area was a rare event (relatively speaking: It still is—I mean black representation is below the 1 percent level). As we passed a neighbor's cottage, a family was playing a game of lawn tennis, with the men playing against the women. As we approached, their game was nearing its conclusion. While we walked slowly past the players, they briefly and quietly responded to our friendly "hello" with stares of obvious surprise at seeing a black man.

While still trying to play tennis, the players were straining their necks to look at my black friend. Just as he and I walked past, the game ended. The male team had lost. It was clear from a flurry of brief comments that they had wagered money on the game. Then the patriarch of the family turned, looking at me and Aaron, and loudly exclaimed, *There goes that buck*, literally meaning he had lost a dollar bet on the game (or whatever the real amount was as represented by the dollar or buck). From a deep-listening perspective, however, the statement *There goes that buck* was a nonconscious expression of a racial stereotype—and in this case probably indicated prejudice.

One of the oldest racial stereotypes is that of the large black male being sexually potent and animalistic by nature. It's well-known that large male game-animals are seen by many as sexually potent and are often referred to as *bucks,* as with a male deer. Indeed, Native American males were often historically referred to as *bucks.* Similarly, it's well-known that, large black males—who were stereotyped as sexually potent— were also historically referred to as *bucks* in the same animalistic sense. Thus the literal phrase *There goes that buck* subliterally referred to my black friend as a black male buck.

Once again, out of a nearly infinite number of responses the white man may have made, we must ask why was the particular phrase *There goes that buck* selected as we were walking past him? Granted, the word "*buck*" is a common one used to refer to a dollar. Any number of topics, words, or phrases were possible to describe losing a dollar bet. The man could have said, *There goes that dollar,* or *Well, we lost that bet.* Why this specific phrasing? What's the rule that determines its lexical selection? I am suggesting the selection rule is the unusual racial context the man found himself in. In linguistic and cognitive terms some deep structure or internal racial representation or memory schema functioned as a rule for generating the specific syntax and semantics of the statement. In this case it was the image of large *buck* game animals. By the way, my friend was rather large in terms of being overweight.

Almost any dictionary will reveal the meanings of the word *buck,* in this context as referring to some animals, as a highly spirited young male, and as a disparaging term for a Native American or a black male. We even have the phrase *buck fever* that refers to the excitement at the first sight of game while hunting. After reading this example in my book *Between the Lines,* people have said to me that, while the incident is instructive in showing how language and the mind work, it refers to an old, outdated stereotype that no longer exists and therefore doesn't tell us much about the current state of racial stereotypes and prejudice. Unlikely.

Since the publication of *Between the Lines,* I have found further, more current evidence for my deep-listening analysis of the use of the word *buck* in a racial context, which show the term is still in the cultural lexicon. In a book by a well-known psychologist, the author describes the activity in the emergency room of the famous Bellevue Hospital in New York City on a "hot Saturday night, when the place is *jumping* with the *raw* problems of city living." The author goes on to describe the scene by saying that people are crowded into the hallways when "in walks yet another teenager, this one literally out of his mind from drugs." Apparently enraged and on alcohol and PCP, "the young *buck* jumps around all the medically ill like an overactive *ape*."[16]

Now! Aside from this quoted passage's demonstrating that even in the 1990s the term *buck* was still linguistically active and was used to describe young sexually macho males. By itself the passage doesn't necessarily apply to racial stereotypes. We need more information about the context of the statement to find its probable meaning. Part of the information we need is knowing that the emergency room of Bellevue Hospital is widely known for serving the surrounding population of poor African-Americans and Hispanics. Thus we have a 1990s probable example of the term *buck*'s being used to describe young black males (I am not aware of Hispanic males being specifically referred to as *bucks*). Because the psychologist connects the use of the term *buck* with *ape*, and given the generalized knowledge of a large African-American population who come to the Bellevue emergency room, I think it's reasonably clear that the association is again specific to black youth. (It's also possible that this is an outright illustration of consciously coded speech.)

In addition, I should point out that the author used the term *buck* in the singular, not the plural. This is likely an important piece of linguistic evidence. Recall that the author said, in walked "another teenager," implying there were other teenagers—likely of various ethnic backgrounds—there. Using the term *buck* in the singular is thus not a reference to young macho males in general. More likely it's a reference to a particular kind of teenager: a black male teenager. So, is this a racist statement? Without further contextual information about the author, it's not possible to say with any reasonable certainty. But I don't think it's merely another automatic activation of a culturally ingrained stereotype.

As I have been cautioning all along, what may appear to be racist may in fact not be racist at all. A so-called racial incident from the sports world that received quite a bit of press in the 1980s is an excellent example of the problem of automatically assuming a comment to be a racist slur. During a play-by-play description of Alvin Garrett, a Washington Redskins wide receiver who is black, the sportscaster Howard Cosell described his running down the field by saying, "Look at that little *monkey* run."[17]

The immediate reaction is to see this remark as a reference to the stereotype of African-American's descending from monkeys and apes. Again, in earlier decades, blacks have often and openly been likened, not only to *bucks*, but to *apes* and *monkeys*. So, was Cosell's remark indicative of a deep personal racial stereotype? Probably not. Once more, the context of such a remark must be considered. Contrary to much of the popular media, it probably wasn't racial because of Cosell's individual context of using the phrase: Cosell apparently used this phrase frequently not only to describe white players, but in his own family to describe children running. Indeed the phrase is one in our everyday vernacular that's used to describe little children who can run very fast.

Cosell's remark, however, could have been racial in the sense of being based on an automatically activated cultural stereotype of African-Americans. Even used with reference to children, *monkey* is still an association with our *primate* ancestors, isn't it? Or with blacks as being like children, as was historically implied? Finally, since Cosell didn't use the phrase all the time, the questions remains as to why he "automatically/unconsciously" selected it in certain situations.

If someone still thinks that I am reading too much into the use of the outdated term *buck*, then consider the following.

Big Bucks Basketball

This example comes from a 1992 issue of *People* magazine. There is a picture of two well-known black basketball players, Kareem Abdul-Jabbar at seven feet two and a half inches tall and Julius "Dr. J" Erving at six feet seven inches in a mutually intimidating in-your-face posture (see Figure 9.1). The article that went with the picture was about the large salaries of star basketball players (by implication black players). The bold-face caption on this picture read: "BIG BUCKS BASKET-

BALL." Yes, again, I am quite aware that the phrase "big bucks" is common vernacular for "big money." I am also aware that "Dr. J" played for the Milwaukee *Bucks*, but those facts don't change the psychological selection process I am talking about—they contribute to it.

There are still many other phrases that could have been selected for the headline. (As it happens there was another headline to this same photo. See below.) Whether the writer was aware of the racial/racist implications of this headline or not, I can't say. There are two possible takes on this example, both of which represent racial stereotypes. The first is that the headline *Big Bucks Basketball* is the deep-listening equivalent of the *There goes that buck* example, that is, it reflects an unconscious stereotype. A second possibility is that the writer knew exactly what he was doing and thought he would put one over on the reading public. Writers and artists often consciously "slip" hidden references into their work.

An even more current example using the term *buck* to refer to an African-American male occurred on the nightly news in 1999.[18] NBC's Pete Williams was reporting on the progress of locating the suspected abortion clinic bomber, thirty-one-year-old Eric Rudolf (who is still hiding out in deeply wooded mountainous terrain). Rudolf's sister-in-law, Deborah Rudolf, was being interviewed. In describing him she said he harbored racial prejudice. As evidence, she said hesitatingly—you could plainly see that she was embarrassed to be vocalizing what she was about to say—that whenever he saw an interracial couple, where the female was white, he would remark, *Look at that big black buck*. Unlike the other examples, there is no mistaking the consciously intended racial meaning in this news item, and the currency of the term *buck* in relation to African-American males.[19] But there is still more to this story of big bucks.

Net Profits: Big Bucks B-balls

The identical photo of Kareem Abdul-Jabbar and Julius "Dr. J" Erving was used in an earlier Time magazine piece, but without the "BIG BUCKS BASKETBALL" headline.[20] In this earlier version the headline

Composite "Buck" Matrix Map

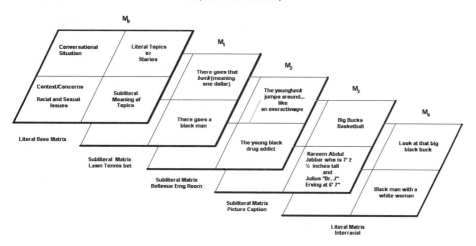

FIGURE 9.1 Composite "Buck" Matrix Map

read: "NET PROFITS." Now, the pun/double entendre on the word *net* in this headline was obviously a conscious one, referring, of course, to money and the net that surrounds the basketball hoop. The psychological processes responsible for this literal double entendre, however, are likely the same as those that created the substituted "Big Bucks Basketball" headline in the later *People* magazine article.

Given the rather obviously conscious double meaning in this headline, it's not too unreasonable to suggest that the double meaning of the "Big Bucks Basketball" headline, if not consciously constructed, then at least as a "slip," it was created by a habitual tendency to make such double meaning headlines. Having been a journalism major in college for a very brief time, I did learn that this double entendre-ing was quite prevalent in the field. Given this, it is not unreasonable to assume that there was unconscious racial meaning beneath the "Big Bucks Basketball" headline.

Now for the rest of the story, a story that you may think is just a little too bizarre. So be it:

The wording in the *Time* story of "Net Profits" is also interesting subliterally because the end of the short article refers to Abdul-Jabbar as "b-ball's" top scorer. The letter *b*, of course, stands for the word *basket*. Though this abbreviation is sometime used, I suggest that here it's the subliteral equivalent of the "Big Bucks Basketball" headline. It's likely that "b-ball's" is an association to African-American males' testicles; that is, the vernacular refers to them as *balls*—again harkening back historically to the stereotype of large black males being sexually potent.

If this reference to black testicles sounds absolutely outrageous, perhaps even irresponsibly outrageous, consider all that I have explained in this book up to this point about subliteral cognition and all that I have shown in this chapter relative to the activation of racial stereotypes. Consider, too, that behind this wording is a long racial history in the United States of black men's sexuality being of great concern to many white men; indeed when black men were lynched, their testicles were sometimes removed, even mutilated. In addition, consider more specifically the context of the article itself.

First, the article opens talking about basketball's being a fixture of every *Fractured-asphalt school yard in the country*. The phrase "fractured-asphalt school yard" is clearly a stereotypic reference to ghetto (read black) kids all playing basketball in hopes of becoming stars one day. Indeed, this phrase clearly seems to be coded speech for the issue of race. Second, as I have shown, the stereotype of African-American males and sexuality forms a backdrop for the entire short article.

Third, a further sexual association in the piece is its mention of a pay-TV benefit for the *War on AIDS*, which, fourth, specifically mentioned Magic Johnson, the black basketball player who contracted AIDS by his admitted penchant for heterosexual forays.

Fifth, it should be noted that *b-ball's* was used in specific reference to the black player, that is, in the possessive case. In short—in deep-listening terms—the ball(s) belonged to a someone. Finally, for those editors who may be reading this, the abbreviation *b-ball* was not used for the longer word *basketball* to conserve space in the column. There was considerable white space at the end of the piece.

If the deep-talk meaning behind this illustration still seems farfetched, I should note this analysis is at the very least congruent with the kind of word associations that laboratory research for over a hundred years has demonstrated.[21]

Now let me make three final subliteral references from the article that also may seem far-fetched. First, regarding the use of the phrase *b-ball's*, is it coincidence that the repetition of the letter *b* is in reference to the name Abdul-Jabbar with its repetition of the letter *b*?

Second, note that the article pointed out that Kareem (Abdul) Jabbar and Julius Erving were competing for a *Six-figure* prize? Again, given what I have illustrated so far in this book, is it coincidence, too, that each of the names K-A-R-E-E-M (ABDUL) J-A-B-B-A-R, and J-U-L-I-U-S E-R-V-I-N-G contain *six letters*, yielding a further deep-level cognitive connection to the deep talk? Perhaps. But I doubt it. What this last apparently bizarre illustration shows is the same kind of cognitive machinery that was demonstrated in the chapter on subliteral numbers.

Finally, think about this. The headline NET PROFITS, being published first, could have lead to the second BIG BUCKS headline. Magazine editors often scan other magazines. At the very least, these stories harbor subliteral racial references and reveal cultural concerns with race. At worse, they may reveal individual prejudice.[22] (See Figure 9.1.)

Automatic Activation of Stereotypes Versus Prejudicial Negative Beliefs

Throughout this chapter, I have alluded to some of this deep talk about race as not necessarily reflecting prejudice in the negative sense on the part of the speaker but instead reflecting the automatic activations of ingrained cultural stereotypes.

Before I explain further, however, let me make as absolutely clear as I possibly can what I mean when I say that some apparently racist remarks are not in fact racist. I am not trying to explain away racial prejudice or to provide racists with a rationalization for their prejudiced beliefs and attitudes that slip out in their talk. Sometimes unintended remarks do reflect unconscious racism; sometimes they don't. More often than not, however, they probably do on some level. What I am trying to accomplish here is to bring a much needed sense of proportion to the prejudice issue. This is the only way it can begin to be resolved. The lack of proportion by both African-Americans and whites surrounding this issue is partly why we have failed to resolve it.

Early on in my subliteral research, I came to see that some of what appeared to be racist comments were not racist or the consequence of prejudice as we commonly understand it. In an article I noted that, "listening to apparent casual verbal reports in a systematic and linguistically informed manner continues to reveal both personally current and psychosocially *vestigial* remains of racial conditioning."[23] The operative word in my quote is *vestigial*. In biology the term refers to a part of our body that may once have had a function but which no longer does. Our appendix is usually considered such a vestigial body part. It's imperative to understand this distinction not only for validating and analyzing subliteral conversations but more importantly for understanding the nature of prejudice.

My deep-listening approach to studying unconscious meaning and the role of language is made-to-order for use in everyday life. Even though I have developed an extensive and systematic method for analyzing and verifying my analyses of deep listening, as with any new idea, it's always a good sign if there are related and corroborating research findings—especially laboratory experiments. Findings from controlled laboratory experiments are, after all, typically seen as being "real" science. Since my early view of vestigial expressions of racial stereotypes, there have been some fascinating experiments that both explain and provide support for my analysis of unconscious racial prejudice. For those who are already convinced that unconscious prejudice exists, the experiments will still be fascinating. For those who are skeptical about our unconscious creating hidden meaning and influencing our behavior, the findings may prove helpful.

An early, but very telling, study was conducted in 1976 by Birt Duncan with University of California at Irving students.[24] He showed them a video tape of a white man and a black man having a rather low-key argument. In one version of the video the white male was seen lightly shoving the black male. In another version, the black male was seen lightly shoving the white male. In the video with the white male lightly

Composite "B-balls" and "Six Figure" Matrix Map

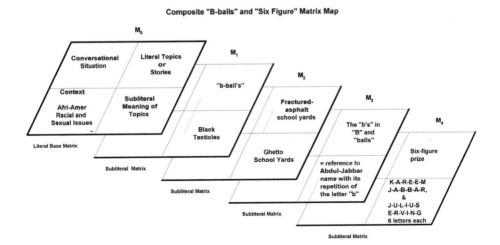

FIGURE 9.2   Composite "B-balls" and "Six Figure" Matrix Map

shoving the black male, only 13 percent rated the incident a violent act. However, in the version where the black male was seen lightly shoving the white male, 73 percent rated it a violent act. If some readers believe that this reflects outdated attitudes, consider the studies below. But first let me comment on the mental processes presumed to undergird this study.

The cognitive processes undergirding the findings of this experiment are similar to those involved in the famous Rorschach or so-called ink-blot test where people are asked what an ink-blot shape reminds them of. The processes are also similar to another famous test, the Thematic Apperception Test (T.A.T.), in which ambiguous pictures are shown to people who are then asked to imagine what is going on in the picture. The idea is that when a situation is ambiguous (that is, it can mean many different things) people "project" meaning from their own un-conscious onto the picture. In other words, a young person who has unconscious fear of authority may respond to a T.A.T. picture showing a young person standing in front of a desk with an older person sitting in a chair behind it with a story about a student's being called down to the principal's office to be reprimanded. In contrast, a young person with no such authority concerns may tell a story about a student discussing a sporting event with a coach.

The same processes apply to the above experiment involving the somewhat ambiguous video tape; unconscious prejudice is projected onto the version of the tape where the black male is seen lightly shoving the white male. Many other experiments have shown that people with unconscious stereotypes and prejudice are more likely to overtly project their prejudice when shown ambiguous pictures if they are angered, in a hurry, or otherwise feeling stressed. It seems that under those conditions we cognitively regress to our more unconscious concerns.

Now for the two other very revealing experiments showing unconscious prejudice. White volunteers who believed they were not prejudiced in any way were connected to electrodes that registered minute facial muscle activity.[25] They were then shown pictures of both whites and African-Americans and asked to imagine interacting with them and to select who they thought they might like the best. With most subjects who indicated liking the African-Americans, their facial muscles belied their beliefs—at least on some level. When the pictures of blacks were shown on the screen, these subjects' frown muscles registered more active than their muscles that were used when smiling. This was not the case when shown pictures of white people. Similar experiments have been conducted using gender and age as the focus and have shown the same results. Indeed, findings are similar for any person who is not considered a member of the subjects' in-group.

Under experimental circumstances such muscle responses are nearly impossible to consciously control. This technique of measuring muscle activity is not new. We have known for sometime, for example, that when we even just think about hammering a nail our arm and fingers produce consciously undetectable minute muscle activity as if we were already hammering the nail. It seems we unconsciously telegraph our intentions—indeed on many levels and about many things. Experiments like these demonstrate not only the existence of unconscious processes, but also that these unconscious processes can influence our overt behavior and judgment.

In another experiment with a group of volunteers, researchers flashed either words or pictures onto a screen at a rate too briefly for them to consciously "see" what appeared on the screen (This technique is called "priming." You may also note its similarity to subliminal perception). Words or pictures were flashed that represented racial minorities. With the second group, no images were flashed during the presentation. What the researchers then did was to anger the subjects. They then asked them a series of neutral questions. Subjects who were exposed to images of an African-American male were more likely to respond in a hostile manner to annoying questions than those who were also angered but who weren't primed with racial images.[26]

More recent is the work of Anthony Greenwald at the University of Washington and his colleagues. He has developed a method called the Implicit Association Test (IAT) using stereotypic ethnic names associated with either whites or blacks.[27] His meticulously designed research has found that whites unconsciously (automatically) select (prefer) white names and, indeed, associate positive attributes to white names and negative attributes to black names. Greenwald has developed a similar test using photos of whites and blacks. These experiments can be seen as supporting my deep listening about race matters.

That unconscious racial concerns are still with us, then, should be beyond reasoned dispute.[28]

10

Deep Action: Crossing the Rubicon?

Just as our unconscious mind reveals itself through deep listening, so too, it reveals itself through our behaviors or actions. Freud and others have written about what are called "action slips." Freud presented a number of such action slips in his classic and quite readable *Psychopathology of Everyday Life*. And Donald Norman, a well-known and respected figure in psychology, has also written extensively on action slips.[1] Most researchers view them just like speech errors, as simple mistakes, like your opening the refrigerator door instead of the oven. Freud, however, saw them as analogous to verbal slips of the tongue that reveal unconscious meaning. You may recall that in Chapter 6 I presented a revealing slip of the pen by a murderer that Freud reported. But this chapter is about more than action slips. It's also about outrageous analyses of unconscious meaning. In the final section of this chapter, I will present an analysis of apparent unconscious meaning revealed in a famous ransom note. I will begin with a couple of simple examples of deep action.

Slips of action can often be found in newspaper articles. While I was being interviewed for a feature newspaper story on my idea of deep listening, the reporter kept asking me if I was picking up on any "slips" of unconscious meaning he may be making in our conversation. He was very curious about this. Actually it would probably be more accurate to say he was concerned. I said, "No, I hadn't recognized any." When the story appeared, however, there was a clear action slip. A deep-talk episode that the reporter had included in his article involved the issue of gender. When the story appeared, instead of the word *gender*, the word *genetics* had been substituted, presumably by mistake. I don't believe, however, that this was a simple mechanical typo. Think about this: After the initial syllable *gen*, to type the remainder of the word *gender*, that is, *der*, requires only the left hand, whereas to type the remaining syllables of the word *genetics*, or *etics*, requires both hands to be used—and twice, not just once.

In addition, the word *genetic* was not a totally irrelevant word to substitute. After all, it's our *genetic* makeup that creates the concept of *gender* (at least as popularly understood). Moreover, what this action slip likely expressed is that whoever made the slip probably doesn't believe—as is currently widely held—that the differences between males and females are largely due to learning or socialization as indicated by the term *gender* (which technically indicates a social role), but instead believes male and female differences are natural or *genetically* caused.

It's frequently the case that handwritten words are illegible enough so that when we go to type them, their ambiguous character becomes like the well-known Rorschach or ink-blot test, with a typist projecting onto an ambiguous word his or her own unconscious meanings. This is especially true of controversial or emotionally laden material. In typing some of my old handwritten notes for a chapter I was working on, the typist misread the word *psychically and* typed *psychually*. Does this word bring anything particular to your mind? It should, especially if you speak the word instead of just looking at it.

If nothing comes to mind, let me provide some context to this example of deep action. First, it's important to note that the typist seldom made such typos, or "mistakes." As illegible as my handwriting is, she would usually figure out what I meant or leave a blank space on the page. On this occasion, however, she didn't. Second, the notes that she was typing were for a chapter on deep listening about race and prejudice. Thirdly, and more specifically, the notes were about the historical stereotypes of black males.

When I quizzed her, asking if she noticed anything particular about this combination of letters, she looked at them and with a quizzical look on her face and said, "No." She did say that while she was typing the word, at first she thought it was *physical* I asked her to look at the word again. But she still had no recognition of its subliteral meaning. However, when I asked her to pronounce the word *psychually* quickly, with a look of great surprise she said, "Oh! *s-e-x-u-a-l-l-y.*"

The word *psychually*, then, was a fusion of four unconscious thoughts. The first is about something *physical*, the second is *sexual*, which obviously goes with physical. Third, since the subject matter of my notes was deep-talk expressions of racial references about black males, the word automatically activated sexual associations in her mind. Fourth, since she was well aware of my theory of subliteral meaning, I think the typing of the syllable *psych* may have been an unconscious leakage of her deep recognition of the racial association. Otherwise, why didn't she combine what she consciously thought was the word *phy*sical with the unconscious word *sexual*, ending in the mistake *phy-ually* or *phys-ually*? Moreover, words beginning with *phy* or *phys* begin with an "f" sound which would not have provided the needed "s" sound that *psych* does. Nor would *phy* or *phys* have provided the glottal stop in the back of the throat produced by pronouncing both *psych* and *sex*(ual) which when coupled with *ually* produces the phonetic equivalent sound as *sexually*.

This subliteral action slip doesn't necessarily mean that the typist is prejudiced; more likely the slip reflected—as we saw in Chapter 9—an automatic activation of a cultural sexual stereotypes of African-American males.

Subliteral meaning, then, can be expressed not only by words but by our written words. As we have just seen, typographical errors are not necessarily mechanical "mistakes"; they can be the translation of sublit-eral meaning into "slips" of the fingers. Instead of our tongue, our fin-gers become the delivery system. In the next example, we will see a more subtle translation process into a not-so-subtle action.

Crossing the Rubicon?

Let me be up front with you on this one. The following illustration of deep action is a very speculative and imaginative one. It's right on the border between being quite possible, on the one hand, and an example of what shouldn't be done with analyses of unconscious meaning on the other. The analysis resides, however, on the acceptable side of rea-son. In any case, in principle (or in theory) the analysis is a sound one. Whether it's valid, I can't say. I can promise it will be interesting.

This example is so uniquely bizarre that I have given it its own head-ing. Reading through this book, you have seen many examples of deep listening that in their own right certainly deserve the adjectives *weird* or *strange*. But this one might appropriately be called *bizarre*. I am talking mega-bizarre, here. Despite this, it struck me as compelling. You be the judge.

The Milwaukee *Journal Sentinel* ran a story about a man accused of bludgeoning his father in the head, almost killing him.[2] It seems the man had gone without food, water, and sleep for days while he was working on a master's thesis for his job as an industrial arts teacher. Despite the grotesque and tragic nature of this story, as it was reported, there doesn't appear to be anything too extraordinary about the alleged crime, except that the man had tried to kill his father—though even this doesn't seem all that extraordinary these days.

As I continued to read the background on this news item, however, possible subliteral meaning began to nudge at me. So, I contacted the reporter and he sent me the complete police report.[3] The man was a teacher at nearby a high school and lived on Rubicon Street. His mas-ter's thesis was about technology and education, with a strong religious twist to it, involving beliefs about being able to kill people and reunite with them in an afterworld. According to the police report, the man believed that if he killed his young daughter, there would be some mother somewhere in the world who would be killing her young son and this would somehow unite cosmic opposites and be good for the world.

He apparently became so obsessed with his thesis, that his father said he had reached the point of trying to prove his beliefs, talking about killing his family to prove his theory.

While discussing this thesis with his father, the man pointed to a golf bag in the garage. When his father followed him into the garage, the teacher attacked his father. You may be thinking that the man bludgeoned his father in the head with a golf club from the golf bag. But he didn't. He used a hatchet. Is it coincidence that the man used a *hatchet*? Perhaps not. But as I continued to read the police report, I became acutely aware of the possible subliteral nature of this story: On some level, it's possible that the man's choice of a hatchet in trying to kill his father was unconsciously influenced, that his choice was made of the same stuff as the action slips described in the previous section of this chapter and of the same stuff that I have described throughout this book. But with a bizarre twist. Consider the following context surrounding the incident.

First, the name of the town where the act was committed is *Menomonie*. The name is derived from the Native American *Ojibwe* language and the town is historically steeped in this heritage. Second, the man was a teacher at the local high school, *Arrowhead*. Third, while it wasn't clear from the story whether his master's thesis and his belief that after death people could reunite with their relatives in an afterworld was specifically derived from Native American folklore or not, such belief is generally consistent with some Native American spiritual folklore. Fourth, a *hatchet*, of course, is an instrument typically associated in the United States with American *Indians*. Indeed, in many dictionaries, hatchet is linguistically associated with *Tomahawk*, a short-handled ax used by many Native American peoples. What we have here is an association matrix with Native American folklore and culture.

So, the use of a hatchet may not have been completely fortuitous. If it isn't already clear, what I think is possible is that the man's delusional mind was influenced by his environment, which was heavily about *American Indian* culture, religious beliefs and folklore, and *Ojibwe language*, with names like *Menomonie,* his own *Arrowhead High School,* and knowledge of *Tomahawks*. After all, why didn't the man use one of the golf clubs he pointed to as a weapon, instead of a hatchet?

On top of all this, the man was somewhat delirious from lack of food and sleep. In addition, given the general context, I wonder if the name of the street the man lived on also unconsciously played into his delusion about crossing over from life to death? Recall he lived on *Rubicon* Street? The term *rubicon* has come to mean crossing or exceeding a limit that when passed allows no return.[4] Again, coincidence? Perhaps. But note: This man's perceptions and associations are precisely the same kind of stuff paranoid schizophrenics often allude to in their delusions and hallucinations.

At this point, let me say that I am only too aware that my analysis of this story sounds far-fetched, if not completely ludicrous. But in conjunction with my subliteral findings, it may not be as far-fetched as it first appears. We have already seen in Chapter 1 that unconscious beliefs, physical events and conditions like tape recorders, and other events not only are impressed on our unconscious and determine our speech, but also can elicit behavioral *actions*.

Recall, too, the discussion in which the door opened just a crack and a person in the hallway had *peeked in*, after which a person just happened to select a story about having a *mouse that would just peek into the garage*. Since the speaker had no awareness that the event of the door's opening and someone peeking in had activated his linguistic act, it seems that this context shaped or influenced (I will resist the term *caused*) his behavior. I have observed numerous other actions that were unconsciously "caused" by events in the immediate conversational environment. In fact, my subliteral findings are all based on such "subliminal" perception of events affecting both language and behavior.

The man's subliterally "caused" actions can also be viewed as belonging to the same class of phenomena as post-hypnotic suggestions. While in hypnosis a person can be given a suggestion to engage in some behavior—like scratching her left earlobe—but not remember the suggestion when she returns to her normal state. Later, when asked why she is scratching her left earlobe, she will not be aware of the real reason. However, often the person will construct a reason, saying it's because her earlobe itches or some other rationalization.

I recall one day getting up from my writing and saying to my wife that I guess I should take out the garbage. She said, "That's what I just asked you to do five minutes ago." I had no recollection of her asking me to take the garbage out. Her request, however, registered in my mind beneath my awareness level and acted as a post-hypnotic suggestion.

In addition, subliterally "caused" actions can also be viewed as belonging to the same class of phenomena as what is called "Subliminal Activation Research."[5] This research involves presenting a stimulus below people's level of awareness, then observing its effect on their behavior. You many recall reading reports on early experiments conducted in movie theaters where either the words "Buy popcorn" or "Buy Coca Cola" were subliminally flashed on the screen in order to increase popcorn and Coke sales.[6] While this experiment was discredited, there has been considerable research on subliminal stimuli showing more positive—albeit still controversial—results.[7]

We could also explain subliteral action from the well-accepted research on what's called *priming effects*.[8] Similar to the subliminal research, priming generally involves visually presenting—for example, the word "ugly" paired with some pictures on a screen just below the awareness level. Other pictures are presented below the level of awareness without being paired with the word "ugly." Then all the pictures are presented so the person can normally see them, and the person is asked to rate the pictures as either pleasant or unpleasant. What we find is that the pictures that were "subliminally" primed with the word "ugly" were consciously judged as less pleasant compared to the pictures that were not subliminally paired with the word "ugly." So, perhaps I haven't crossed the Rubicon with my subliteral analysis of the hatchet killing.

Since I have gone this far out on a limb, I can't resist a related observation about the significance of proper names on the person having the name. I wonder how coincidental it is that one of the most famous U.S.

Supreme Court justices and legal scholars was named *Learned Hand*. Did his name influence his aspirations? I wonder, too, about the more recent controversy regarding the cloning of human beings. Is it completely coincidence that the (rogue?) scientist making all the headlines who wants to begin cloning humans immediately, and who isn't even a biologist but a physicist, is named Richard *Seed*. Do such phenomena occur purely by chance, or are some—certainly not all and likely a small number of primed minds—more general instances of my subliteral cognition effects?

The final two illustrations of apparently unconscious communication are from two books by "Freudian" psychiatrists. I present them as exemplifications of the problem of interpreting unconscious meaning without a systematic method of verifying that meaning. Indeed, these two books provide object lessons for *how not to* analyze unconscious meaning, in contrast to my deep-listening illustrations.

JonBenét Ramsey: A Note from the Underground

Few people haven't heard of little six-year-old JonBenét Ramsey, who was killed in her Boulder, Colorado, home on December 26, 1996. This unsolved but ongoing case still seems to capture our imagination and that of the media. One book on the case, *A Mother Gone Bad,* purports to name JonBenét's killer by revealing an unconscious confession ostensibly hidden within the text of the ransom note.[9] On this basis, the book identifies JonBenét's killer as her mother, Patsy Ramsey.

Written by Andrew G. Hodges, a "Freudian"-oriented psychiatrist, this book, in my view, is an outrageously bad example of revealing unconscious meaning and a mark of scandalous professional irresponsibility. Ironically, Freud would agree with me (recall Chapter 6). In short, it's *a scandalous object lesson in how not to analyze unconscious or subliteral communication.* I will present only a few examples from the book, but they will be sufficient *to illustrate how not to* analyze unconscious meaning and why a systemic method is required to validly analyze unconscious meaning.

So that you don't think this "Freudian" interpretation of the Jon-Benét ransom note is a psychiatric fluke, I will end this chapter by ana-lyzing a book by yet another psychiatrist who purports to reveal unconscious racial meanings. I might note that neither of these books are from the naive or beginning phase in the development of psycho-analysis; they are recent. I might also note, too, that, being psychiatrists, both authors are M.D.s, and have supposedly been trained in research methodology. Both books, *The Isis Papers* and *A Mother Gone Bad*, read like a psychiatry gone mad. But you be the judge.

Where to begin? Contextually, let me point out that even if it's even-tually found that Patsy Ramsey did kill her daughter, in no way does it validate the author's analysis of the ransom note. Typically in the analy-sis of a crime, discovering the motive is important. So the question is, why would Patsy kill her own daughter? The basic idea is that Patsy killed JonBenét when she discovered her husband, John, having sex with the girl; she flew into a rage and killed JonBenét. Why she didn't kill her husband supposedly involved rivalry with her daughter and identification with her husband. For my purposes, we needn't be con-cerned with this latter aspect. So, how are we to know from the ransom note discovered in the house that the murderer was Patsy? Here goes.

The "real" telltale-confession ransom note, we are told in Hodges's book, is hidden within the text of the actual note. This hidden confes-sion note is unconsciously written to the police letting them know who the killer is. The note opens with the ostensible killer's literally telling the reader to "listen carefully." Hodges says that this is really Patsy's un-conscious mind writing to the police, telling them that if they "listen carefully," the note will reveal a confession by the killer (Patsy).

Similarly, the words "Follow our instructions" are said by Hodges to be instructing the police that if they pay close attention to the note, it will lead them to John and Patsy.[10] The note makes reference to a "small foreign faction" who has kidnapped JonBenét. We are told this phrase unconsciously refers to the "foreign part of themselves that appeared small but eventually erupted into a horrible catastrophic act."[11] Part of the reason the author knows the writer of the note is a woman is re-vealed, we are told, by a mistake in spelling. The misspelled word "bussiness" leads us to think of "buss, bustle, and bust" [as in a woman's breast]. It is then said that "A 'buss' is a 'kiss.' Really? The writer has changed John Ramsey's successful business and career into 'kissiness,' which changes him from an aggressive male into a soft feminine character." Now how does the author know that this interpretation is correct?

The author knows it because, he says, "It is consistent with the earlier slip-up in the same sentence that in essence said, 'We (don't) respect your bussiness.'" Now if you are confused, so am I. Not only is there no objective basis for associating the misspelling of "bussiness" with "buss, bustle, and bust" with "kissiness," but the author saying it's consistent with a previous phrase that essentially meant "We don't respect your business," is actually incorrect. The previous phrase actually said, *"We respect your business, but not the country it serves."*[12] The author added the "don't."

To further support his interpretation, the author shows two pictures, one of Patsy and one of JonBenét, both wearing bustles. Let's not forget that this word "bustle" is the author's own free association, somehow derived from the actual misspelled word "bussiness." It doesn't appear in the note itself. The author goes on. And on. And on. All this is just for openers. Certainly this evidence doesn't rise to the level of jacks or better that are needed to open a valid deep-listening game.

Another apparent "slip" of the pen in the ransom note is the misspelled word "posession," which the author says relates to the word "poses," something that both Patsy and her daughter have engaged in for beauty pageants. We are also informed that this misspelled word implies "posse," and Patsy "knew that a posse was after her." Really! The author then concludes his particular analysis by asserting, "It is interesting that in the two words the killer misspells, she *adds* an 's' in 'bussiness' and *leaves one out* of 'possession.' We are told that this matches Patsy's style of trying to add something like a bustle to make up for a deficiency."[13]

Yet another revealing unconscious communication, says Hodges, is the use of the word "attaché." Note that it has an accent mark on the seventh letter, as does the name JonBenét. If this doesn't convince you that

Patsy wrote the note, the author says this will: Note that attaché even rhymes with JonBenét.[14] Unfortunately, there's still more. In the ransom note, a period that is spaced too far from the end of the sentence means that the writer is out of contact with reality. Give me a break![15] (One begins to wonder just who is out of contact with reality here.)

Further, we are told that the use of exclamation marks—which are asserted to be phallic symbols—is said to signify dramatic actions like being on stage at a beauty pageant. That there are three exclamation marks in the note is said to reference the three people involved, Patsy, John, and JonBenét. We are told they also show Patsy's explosive nature and signify her exploding and killing her daughter.[16] We are also told that another clue to the identity of the killer is the references to the "delivery" of the ransom money; it seems that this implies femininity, as in giving birth! Similarly, we are told that the references in the ransom note to "bank" and "delivery," means, "Patsy unexpectedly came across her husband molesting JonBenét—taking her valuables from her, i.e., intruding into JonBenét's 'bank.'" The author says that this follows from his previous line of reasoning, "and stays with the same symbolic meaning: 'Bank' is a woman, and the woman we're talking about is Jon-Benét."[17] Please *bear* with me; I simply must *belabor* Hodges's examples a little longer.

Hodges suggests that the phrase in the note "If the money is . . . *tampered* with, she dies" reveals that Patsy and John had "*tampered*" with JonBenét's little body.[18]

And how about this one? Hodges says that the writer of the note misspells "kindergartner" with an extra *e* (that is, "kindergartener"). On this basis, he asks, "Was it Patsy's way of saying, 'e-gads'—revealing that she wanted to change the fact that JonBenét was growing up?"[19] E-GADS! Where does this come from?

This next series of interpretations of unconscious meanings is perhaps the real clincher of a psychiatry gone mad (though it's difficult to judge from among the many in the book). Hodges thinks he has struck gold with his wildly free-associative analysis of the ransom note. While there is gold in "them thar hills," most of what he dredges up is pure iron pyrite (fool's gold).

For example, from my perspective one of the possible subliteral clues in the ransom message involves the signed ending of the note with the letters *S.B.T.C.* These initial were supposed to represent the "political" group who was to have kidnapped JonBenét. Before I get to Hodges's more reasonable analysis of these letters, let me show how loosey-goosey things can get without the use of a systematic method.

Hodges says that Patsy or John Ramsey may have made up the initials S.B.T.C. on a whim, or they may have been a random selection. "One thing is certain," he says, "S.B.T.C. came out of their deeper minds." So far, so good—maybe. But now he produces something that would be the envy of most paranoid schizophrenics. Because Patsy had been fighting cancer, Hodges says, "it's only fitting that the ransom note end with a capital 'C' since cancer is known as 'the big C.'"[20] Further, he says that the letters *T.C.* could represent *The Cancer*. He then suggests that the letters S.B.T.C. could represent the hypothetical phrase that he makes up, "*Slain By The Cancer*." Is this even remotely believable? Next, he says that the letters *S.B.* and *T.C.*, "could also represent '*Son of a B*— *The Cancer. Saved because of the cancer*' is another possibility as, in the beginning, the cancer did open Patsy's eyes to the next world and more important matters."[21]

Moreover, Hodges says that "S.B. is common slang for 's.o.b.' which has several meanings itself. People use this expression when they're in a jam. Used as a degrading term it literally means son of a bad woman or not quite so literally, the child of a bad woman." As far as I know, S.B. is not used as short for S.O.B, at least in the United States (I checked with a colleague in the United Kingdom, and as far as he know, this short-ened form is not used there either).

While I think Hodges is stretching his psychoanalysis of Patsy be-yond the breaking point, I believe he is correct when he says of the ini-tials S.B.T.C that "Surely the initials have some significance to Patsy Ramsey." Again, so far, so good. But then, he says, "Being the artist that she is, Patsy likes to put a special hidden message into her communica-tions, particularly at the end of an event because she is acutely sensitive to separations."[22] The use of these initials, however, could apply to John Ramsey (and perhaps others who knew them) as well. In my view,

Hodges then goes off the deep end once again. In order to make the gender of this phrase (*Son* of a bitch) fit, he says that "Patsy could even be revealing . . . she had turned JonBenét into a *masculine* sort of person for the purposes of gaining power—she had symbolically turned her daughter into a son. This fits with the showy finish of the ransom note."[23] It's showy, all right.

Further, Hodges claims that the "T.C. could refer to 'T.L.C.' (tender loving care), almost the exact opposite of 'S.B.'" From S.B. meaning S.O.B, to T.C. meaning T.L.C.? According to Hodges, "Here Patsy could be revealing her other side, the good mother. The S.B./T.C. split could represent Patsy's bad mother/good mother split, with Patsy's evil part coming first." If you think this is "showy," the following is downright obscenely flamboyant: According to Hodges, "'T.C.' is not far from 'T.S.' ('tough s—')." Not far from T.S.?—Say what! As possible evidence that his interpretation is correct, he notes that T.S. is "an incredibly common expression that suggests Patsy is confessing that life was cruel to JonBenét (and to her as well). Maybe that's how Patsy viewed her cancer-'T.S.' and she inflicted that same bad break on JonBenét." I am at a loss for words here.

All this is just the tip of the author's psychiatric interpretations of the unconscious-meaning iceberg. To illustrate further would get so convoluted that you simply wouldn't believe I was doing the author justice. Some of his associations may possibly be correct on some deep unconscious level, but we can't even begin to verify them other than with the wildest of free associations. That's the problem. Again, let me say that in terms of the ransom note, like Hodges, I too am convinced that within the womb of the writer's unconscious mind gestates hidden meaning. Unlike Hodges' birthing method, however, my natural-language method is quite different. (Am I revealing here that I think Patsy is the murderer?)

Hodges continues to interpret the letters S.B.T.C., but dismisses what I think is the most important point regarding the letters. Hodges notes that during World War II, John Ramsey was stationed at *Subic Bay Training Center*, the exact letters of S.B.T.C., but dismisses this observation as having no real significance. In fact, the subliteral significance of these letters is that they are much too coincidental. Now this doesn't necessarily suggest that the writer of the note was John or Patsy Ramsey, since anyone who knew of John's military experience could have used them consciously or unconsciously. Along with other subliteral material (see below) it does, however, strongly suggest that the writer or writers of the note were not strangers to the family.

Hodges does finally make what I think is a potentially significant—and I emphasize *potential*—analysis of the letters *S.B.T.C.* It seems that one of Patsy's favorite passages from the King James Bible was Psalms 118. During her bout with cancer, she had apparently claimed several verses in this psalm as she turned to God for help. In addition, in a book about healing cancer that Patsy had been reading, Psalm 118 appears. Hodges, points out that one of Patsy's favorite verses reads: "God is the Lord, who has *shown us the light; bind the sacrifice with cords,* even unto the horns of the altar" (verse 27). According to Hodges, the first significant aspect of this verse is the phrase "bind . . . with cords," which was how JonBenét was bound, and possibly S.B.T.C. can be loosely translated to mean *Sacrifice Bound* (with) *the Cords,* though this part of the interpretation is a bit of a stretch.

The second significant aspect Hodges suggests is, "Various Christian endeavors use 'T.C.' to mean 'through Christ' or 'Through the Cross.' A capitalized 'T' even looks like a Roman cross (on which Jesus was crucified)." He concludes that "'S.B.T.C.' may also mean 'saved *by the cross,'*" maintaining that another possible meaning is: "*salvation belongs to Christ,*" as Patsy Ramsey was looking for salvation. Gaining downhill momentum, he says, "This fits in even a deeper, almost certainly unconscious way with the idea that Patsy's 'S.B.' side is taken care of through forgiveness." Indeed, we are even asked to believe that S.B.T.C. may have derived from John or Patsy's awareness of the TCBY yogurt initials!

Just before the initials *S.B.T.C.* on the ransom note was the word "Victory." Hodges slips and slides all over the psychoanalytic free associations on this one, too. He suggests that the word "Victory" reveals Patsy's hidden feeling of victory over cancer and references again to Patsy's favorite biblical psalm, 118, which in some translations includes the word *victory* ("and now He has given me the victory").[24] Hodges offers at least a half dozen other associations to the word *Victory*.

His association of the word *victory* to Psalm 118 is interesting subliterally, especially given the ransom amount of $118,000. But Hodges misses another association that likely ties the Subic Bay initials to someone who had intimate knowledge of John's military life: Both during and after the war, the class of ship that was stationed at Subic Bay was called victory ships.

The third intriguing aspect of Psalm 118 relates to the unconscious meaning of numbers (see Chapter 7). Just as I suggested that the use of the letters S.B.T.C., which are the same letters as the initials of Subic Bay Training Center, was too coincidental not to be subliterally meaningful, I think that the number of Psalm 118, which is the same as the ransom note's request for $118,000, is likewise too coincidental not to be subliterally meaningful—especially given that John Ramsey had received $118,000 as a bonus that year. Like the letters *S.B.T.C.*, the ransom amount of $118,000 strongly suggests only that the writer or writers of the note were not strangers to the family. Noticing and connecting the significance of the ransom amount of $118,000 to Psalm 118, Hodges seems to have begun to get this one right. But it's a cosmic leap to name Patsy Ramsey as the killer on this basis (though it would appear that she may somehow have been involved in the writing of the note).

Based on my deep-listening method for analyzing numbers, I would hypothesize that the other numbers in the ransom note are also of significance. Another possibly significant deep-listening clue is likely suggested by the inclusion of the last two zeros in the mentioning of $118,000.00. These are not included in the related numbers mentioned, $100,000 and $18,000. I would also conjecture that the numbers *$100* and *$20*, referring to the denominations that the ransom money was to be in, and 8 and 10 Am, referring to time, are significant as well. Without sufficient information, I would only guess from my own experience with how subliteral numbers are used that what stands out are the separations in each series of numbers (by commas and decimal point) into sets of 3s and 2s, with the one exception of the number 8.

Based on my past analysis of the deep meaning of numbers I would further suggest that the separations in a series of numbers refer to how many people are being referenced and may indicate the gender of those being referenced by the numbers. For example, in the $118,000.00, the two "1's" in the "11(8)" likely indicate two people of the same gender with the 8 indicating a person of the opposite gender. The zeros (reflecting a set of three and a set of two) likely indicate nothing since they are "zeros," or could be some other significant set of people in the mind of the writer of the note. The same analysis may refer to the other numbers mentioned (again, see Chapter 7). The significance of these numbers is that they could provide a concrete set of clues that in the event of their correct deciphering would provide a matrix revealing a coherent and consistent set of unconscious meanings that would serve to internally cross-check these numbers and probably to cross-check the subliteral analyses from words and phrases.

Under the best of circumstances the analysis or the interpretation of unconscious meaning should only be used as possible "clues," not as conclusive evidence—as Hodges does. You will recall from Chapter 6 (on caution, and O.J.'s dream) that even Freud understood the limits of interpreting unconscious meaning. When guided by a systematic methodology, unconscious meaning has the potential for being a valuable aid in solving problems or in yielding "evidence," just like hypnosis is currently used in criminal investigations. In most all states, evidence or other information obtained by hypnosis is not admissible in courts of law. It still has value, however, in leading to evidence that can independently (from hypnosis) be verified and used in court.

Now, consider this: Did you ever notice and wonder why the female form of the name *Frances* is spelled with an *e* and the male form of *Francis* with an *i*? Why not the reverse? The obvious answer is that our ancestor's unconscious minds understood that the *i* being an elongated shape was a penis/phallic symbol, whereas the oval shape of the *e* was a symbol of the female vagina. Just joking, folks!

You see how easy all this symbolic interpretation stuff is? That's the very problem, though. It's too easy. Unfortunately, there are many—presumably Hodges and the next author, Frances Crest Welsing—who would agree with this "interpretation" about the unconscious significance of the differential spelling of the names Frances and Francis.

Washington's White Penis

The last exemplification of *how not to* analyze unconscious or subliteral communication is a book by Frances Crest Welsing, a black "Freudian" psychiatrist, entitled *The Isis Papers*.[25] Before we venture into the symbolic muck and quagmire of the book, I need to make a few general comments. The author correctly recounts the clear history of prejudice and stereotypes by whites against African-Americans in the United States. My quarrel with this book is not its own blatant racism, but its—unfortunately typical—simple-minded analysis (I purposely use this phrase) of unconscious meaning. It almost makes Hodges's book *A Mother Gone Bad* look good. But not quite.

The author maintains that in the middle of predominantly black Washington, D.C., stands a white penis: It's called the Washington Monument.[26] Further, we are told that if one views the Washington Monument from a certain angle and distance, visually it appears to be beside the *domed* Jefferson Memorial, with this juxtaposition revealing a penis with a testicle![27] It only goes downhill from here, folks.

Are you ready for this: We are told that the Christian cross is an unconscious representation of black male genitalia, with its vertical line representing the penis, its horizontal line representing two testicles. The justification for this racist sexual analysis of the Christian cross is that if we see a Christmas tree, we are told, schematically, it's an inverted cross. (I should note, in the spirit of postmodernism, that I am not in the least personally offended by this analysis of the Christian cross.) So the Christmas tree also unconsciously represents black male genitalia (e.g., picture an arrowhead, which can be seen as the same shape as a Christmas tree with its broken-off shaft as the remaining part of the tree trunk). Even the swastika, the symbol of a pure Aryan race, is said to conceal a hidden cross.[28]

How does this psychiatrist know that the Christian cross represents whites' obsession with black male genitalia? First, because she says whites are fearful of being genetically annihilated by the powerful genetic material of black males. Second, the cross signifies "castrated" black male genitalia, and whites have historically been concerned with black male sexuality and have often castrated black males. Though this history is correct, how it gets translated into the Christian cross and the Christmas tree's representing black male genitalia is, at best, an imaginative leap of cosmic proportions.

Even most "ball" games are said to express this unconscious concern by whites of genetic annihilation. "The large brown football is kicked through an upright opening (the goalposts) that can be viewed as the uplifted legs of a white female in the act of sexual intercourse."[29] Moreover, we are told that white balls used in games are usually small (for example golf), whereas brown or black balls are usually larger.[30]

The unconscious motive behind games using either white or brown balls is symbolic of controlling black genetic material. These games reflect whites' reaction to this fear in that the games implicitly (symbolically) represent the explicit game of world domination of people of color by whites. In other words, controlling the black or brown balls is an unconscious playing out of whites' fear of genetic annihilation and their consequent defensive reaction of world domination of people of color. Welsing notes that most players in games that use black or brown balls are black men, but says that doesn't invalidate her argument because blacks weren't always most of the players and because, in any event, the teams are owned by white males.

What about games that have white balls in them, like pool? Well, as we all know, the last ball to be ejected from the table is a black eight ball and the last ball standing is the white cue ball. And what about games like bowling, played mostly by whites using a big black ball to knock down white pins, which are seen as representing white penises? Isn't this a contradiction? Not to Welsing. It isn't because in such a system of "interpreting" unconscious meanings, anything goes. According to Welsing, the white "bowler sees himself as master and possessor of the larger black ball and thereby in control of the harm to the white male genital apparatus (the white pins)."[31] Come, now.

The same reasoning is used to explain Jane Goodall and Diane Fossey, two white scientists who are famous for studying chimpanzees and gorillas, which are seen as unconsciously representing blacks. Goodall and Fossey are said to be unconsciously forming an alliance with this powerful (black) genetic material.[32] How racist can you get?

In Welsing's system, whether white ball or black ball—she wins. Another example of "she wins" is her analysis of the white male's formal black tuxedo: Even though "the 'tails' hang in the back, they remain phallic symbols."[33] With Welsing's interpretations I guess even Bugs Bunny isn't "safe."

It's clear that Welsing is aware of the Freudian cliché that if it's longer than its wide, it's a penis symbol. Evidently she hasn't heard of Freud's other legacy: Sometimes a cigar is just a cigar (incidentally, Welsing doesn't miss the chance to note that white men like to smoke big brown or black cigars). Frances Crest Welsing is not joking. She's deadly serious.

Indeed it seems to Welsing that white folk not only have black penis envy but also have something called Melanin Envy. Melanin is, of course, what people of color have more of than white folk; it protects the skin from the sun. Welsing, however, sees melanin as having other functions. Welsing, an M.D., asserts that blacks are able to interpret symbols better than whites because blacks have more melanin and "melanin is capable of absorbing a broader spectrum of energy frequencies or data. . . . Melaninated people are functioning with a sixth sense, the additional sensory system being that of melanin pigmentation, while Westerners function with only five senses."[34] What can I possibly say to this, except that in effect, Welsing provides us with an almost perfect textbook example of a closed paranoid system of thinking.

Welsing builds an unassailable racial edifice to protect her fanciful interpretation of unconscious meanings from both white folk who are genetically rendered incapable due to our melanin deficiency and from other black folk who disagree with her; if blacks disagree, it must be because they have been brainwashed by whites. In all fairness, there has been no shortage of racist white psychiatrists in history who have woven similar "scientific" fantasies. Since the origin of institutional psychiatry beginning with Benjamin Rush (a signer of the Declaration of Independence) in the eighteenth century and through Nazi racist psychiatry in the twentieth century, racism has not been uncommon. But this doesn't justify new forms of it. Finally, even if all Welsing asserts had an element of truth, the point is we need systematic methods of verification. Now for a few closing words on verifying deep listening.

Method and Meaning

As explained before, the selection of a word during a conversation occurs in two stages. First, because words have multiple meanings, our brain reviews all possible meanings of a word that we are aware of. Then from the context of the discussion, our brain chooses the assumed appropriate meaning for the word in the context of its use. What Hodges and Welsing seem to do, however, is to assume that nearly all the possible meanings of a word are meaningful within a single context In a word, this is ridiculous.

An example is Hodges's freely associating to the misspelling of the word "bussiness" and coming up with "buss, bustle, and bust" and finally somehow coming up with the word "kissiness." Or his associating to the misspelled word "posession," which is said to relate to the word "pose," something that both Patsy Ramsey and her daughter have engaged in for beauty pageants, and to "posse," concluding that Patsy knew that a posse was after her. Say what?!

We can see that the analysis of unconscious meanings without a methodology is like a language without a grammar. It's grammar, a.k.a. syntax, that creates meaning in language, not just the words or semantics. Without syntax, words yield mostly serendipitous nonsense. Worse yet, it leads to dangerous conclusions. At the very least, some of the examples of unconscious meaning and action "slips" in this chapter are fascinating to analyze, to think about, and to ponder for their potential significance on our everyday behavior. But as I have cautioned throughout this book and particularly in Chapters 6 and 9, we must be extremely careful in attributing too much meaning to them.

While unconscious *stimuli* (note I don't say unconsciously "intended" stimuli), cognitive operations, and the subliteral expressions deriving from those stimuli may demonstrate valid psychological phenomena, it doesn't necessarily follow that they were unconsciously intended. Neither does it follow that the "meanings" imply conscious significance for the person uttering them in term of their beliefs or actions. Such meanings may only reflect our automatic cognitive machinery at work.

Again, even Freud knew the difference between what he called *psychical reality* and *material reality*. By analogy, would you hold someone responsible for, and define them as a person based on the content of their nightly dreams? Even with the detailed methodology that I have developed to analyze subliteral meaning, the intent of the method is not so much to enable the valid assignment of responsibility to a speaker for what she or he says as it is to analyze and understand the cognitive machinery undergirding spoken language. Once more, this is a most important point, a point that Hodges's and Welsing's analysis of unconscious meaning totally disregards.

Back to the Future of Deep Listening

So what's in the future for deep listening? Certainly, much more research on subliteral cognition and language needs to be done. While you have seen throughout this book many of the mental mechanisms our minds use to secretly reveal hidden meaning, I have only scratched the surface in terms of illustrating an even wider array of cognitive operations employed by our minds without our knowing it. Discovering more of these operations will help us to further understand how our minds work.

As we have also seen, in terms of assessing the degree of intent that appears to lie beneath a person's deep talk, further careful research is needed to avoid attributing intentional meaning (e.g., racist intent) where it doesn't exist. Finally, as I briefly noted in Chapter 5, research needs to be conducted on whether and how deep talk can be used therapeutically.

Even as it stands now, however, deep listening will continue to be useful in the context of listening to friends, media, and coworkers.

Notes

Preface

1. Bob Dylan, from the album *Highway 61 Revisited* (Warner Bros., 1965).
2. S. Freud, *The Psychopathology of Everyday Life* (New York: Norton, 1960), 272.

Introduction

1. R. E. Haskell, *Between the Lines: Unconscious Meaning in Everyday Life* (Cambridge, Mass.: Perseus Books, 1999). Also see www.perseuspublishing.com/authors.html at Perseus Books' web page.

2. *Details*, June 1999, 34.

3. *Great Dialogues of Plato*, translated by W. H. Rouse (New York: New American Library, 1956).

4. Also see R. E. Haskell, "An Analogical Methodology for the Analysis and Validation of Anomalous Cognitive and Linguistic Operations in Small Group (Fantasy Theme) Reports," *Small Group Research* 22 (1991): 443–474.

5. See H. R. Pollio, M. K. Smith, and M. R. Pollio, "Figurative Language and Cognitive Psychology," *Language and Cognitive Processes* 5 (1990): 141–167; H. Fine, H. R. Pollio, and C. Simpkinson, "Figurative Language, Metaphor and Psychotherapy," *Psychotherapy: Theory, Research and Practice* 10 (1973): 87–91; H. R. Pollio, J. M. Barlow, H. J. Fine, and M. R. Pollio, *Psychology and the Poetics of Growth: Figurative Language in Psychology, Psychotherapy and Education* (Hillsdale, N.J.: Lawrence Erlbaum, 1977).

Chapter 1

1. A. S. Reber, *Implicit Learning and Tacit Knowledge: An Essay on the Cognitive Unconscious* (New York: Oxford University Press, 1993), 25, 69.

2. See, for example, J. Piaget, *Play, Dreams and Imitation of Childhood* (New York: W. W. Norton, 1962).

3. A. H. Maslow, ed., *Motivation and Personality*, 2d ed. (New York: Harper and Row, 1970).

4. See R. E. Haskell, *Reengineering Corporate Training: Intellectual Capital and the Transfer of Learning* (Newport, Conn.: Quorum Books, 1998).

5. For a more elaborated explanation of the subliteral mind and other concepts in this book, see my *Between the Lines: Unconscious Meaning in Everyday Conversation.*

6. See R. E. Haskell, "The Matrix of Group Talk: An Empirical Method of Analysis and Validation," *Small Group Behavior,* 2 (1982): 419–443.

Chapter 2

1. S. Freud, *A General Introduction to Psychoanalysis* (New York: Washington Square Press, 1960), 40.

2. CNN, August 20, 1998.

3. CNN, September 13, 1998.

4. CNN, *Burden of Proof,* August 7, 1998.

5. See B. J. Baars, J. Cohen, G. H. Bower, and J. W. Berry, "Some Caveats on Testing the Freudian Slip Hypothesis: Problems in Systematic Replication." In B. J. Baars, ed., *Experimental Slips and Human Error* (New York: Plenum Press, 1992), 308.

6. There is a serious and eternal controversy revolving around the reality of unconscious meaning that splits psychologists into two basic camps. It involves, on the one hand, psychologists in one camp who want to explain human behavior as it occurs in everyday life and who want to apply the rigorous research findings that exist to explain and support these explanations of everyday life events. On the other hand, psychologists in the other camp are oriented to "pure research" and get very upset when their rigorously controlled research is generalized to support explaining everyday life events. In reality these two camps are extreme ends of a continuum. The two camps seldom talk to or respect each other. I like to think of myself as belonging to both camps. Unfortunately, those at the extreme end in the first camp tend to see my more rigorous methodology for analyzing subliteral language as belonging to the second camp, while those in the second camp tend to see applying my findings and transferring their related research as belonging to the first camp. As members of the reading public you, and the mass media, get caught in the middle of these two camps and the result is often confusion.

Technically, it's understandable why the "purists" object to their carefully constrained and controlled research being applied to everyday events. By design, their research is so tailored to special experimental conditions that these conditions may not be applicable to the conditions prevailing in everyday life. More practically, however, it has always seemed to me that we must try to connect laboratory research with everyday life (There are other differences between these two camps as well, but I can't go into them here). Overlaid on this more general split, there is one more:. Freud's ghost haunts deep listening. Contrary to popular knowledge, Freud is not held in great esteem by rigorous researchers. Thus most cognitive scientists have understandably been reluctant to deviate from their tightly controlled experimental laboratory methods in examining unconscious processes. As I suggested in a similar context elsewhere, it evidently remains a fear that if the meticulous experimental door to the unconscious is opened to other methodologies, "All manner of Freudian specters will be let loose in the cognitive laboratories." If psychologists in the first camp have been too loosey-goosey, those in the second camp have been too obsessive compulsive.

7. *Commonwealth v. Anthony Johnson*, Appeals Court of Massachusetts Hampden Sr. No. 96-P-0759 700 N.E., 2nd 270 Cite as: 45 Mass. App. Ct. 473 700 N.E. 2nd 270. Argued November 25, 1997. Decided September 17, 1998. I would like to thank Professor William Kaplin, School of Law, Catholic University of America, for locating this case for me.

8. G. Beyer, K. Redden, and M. Beyer, *Modern Dictionary for the Legal Profession*, 2d ed. (Buffalo, N.Y.: William & Hein, 1996).

9. See W. Key, *Subliminal Seduction* (New York: New American Library, 1987).

10. See R. F. Bales, *Personality and Interpersonal Behavior* (New York: Holt, Rinehart & Winston, 1970); D. L. Smith, *Hidden Conversations: An Introduction to Communicative Psychoanalysis* (London: Tavistock/Routledge, 1991); D. S. Whitaker and M. Lieberman, *Psychotherapy Through the Group Process* (New York: Atherton, 1964).

Chapter 3

1. Depending on whether you are religious or secular, the master template will change. Many psychologists—perhaps most—would consider the Parent Template as the master template. From this perspective, it's our childhood experience with parents that generalizes to a later belief in an all-powerful God.

2. See R. E. Haskell and G. Hauser, "Rhetorical Structure: Truth and Method in Weaver's Epistemology," *Quarterly Journal of Speech* 64 (1978): 233–245.

3. See, again, R. F. Bales, *Personality and Interpersonal Behavior* (New York: Holt, Rinehart & Winston, 1970); D. L. Smith, *Hidden Conversations: An Introduction to Communicative Psychoanalysis* (London: Tavistock/Routledge, 1991); D. S. Whitaker and M. Lieberman, *Psychotherapy Through the Group Process* (New York: Atherton, 1964); see also P. Slater, *Microcosm: Structural, Psychological and Religious Evolution in Groups* (New York: Wiley & Sons, 1966).

Chapter 4

1. See J. Bruner, *Acts of Meaning* (Cambridge, Mass.: Harvard University Press, 1990), 77.

2. *The Merv Griffin Show*, September 14, 1977.

3. I would like to thank my colleague John Heapes for this illustration. See my *Between the Lines* for more on names used subliterally.

Chapter 5

1. R. Pirsig, *Zen and the Art of Motorcycle Maintenance* (New York: Bantam Books, 1974), 11.

2. R. E. Haskell, "Anatomy of Analogy: A New Look," *Journal of Humanistic Psychology* 8 (1968): 161–169; see also R. E. Haskell, ed., *Cognition and Symbolic Structures: The Psychology of Metaphoric Transformation* (Norwood, N.J.: Ablex Publishing, 1968).

3. M. Hesse, *Models and Analogies in Science* (New York: Sheed and Ward, 1963).

4. See, for example, D. Gentner, "Structure Mapping: A Theoretical Framework for Analogy," *Cognitive Science* 7 (1983): 155–170; M. L. Gick and K. J. Holyoak, "Analogical Problem Solving," *Cognitive Psychology* 12 (1980): 306–355.

5. Socrates said, "I am myself a great lover of these processes of division and generalization; they help me to speak and to think. And if I find any man who is able to see 'a One and Many' in nature, him I follow, and 'walk in his footsteps as if he were a god.'" See Plato, *Phaedrus*, translated by W. E. Helmbold and W. G. Rabinowitz (New York: Bobbs-Merrill, 1956). Later, Aristotle echoed the same view: "The greatest thing by far is to be a master of metaphor. It is the one thing that cannot be learned from others. It is the mark of genius." See L. Cooper, *The Rhetoric of Aristotle* (New York: Appleton-Century-Crofts, 1960), 101.

6. See R. E. Haskell, *Transfer of Learning: Cognition, Instruction, and Reasoning* (San Diego: Academic Press, 2000).

7. R. E. Haskell, "Analogical Transforms: A Cognitive Theory of the Origin and Development of Equivalence Transformation, Part I," *Metaphor and Symbolic Activity* 4 (1989): 247–259.

8. See T. Kuhn, *The Structure of Scientific Revolutions* (Chicago: University of Chicago Press, 1970).

9. R. E. Haskell, "An Analogic Model of Small Group Behavior," *International Journal of Group Psychotherapy* 28 (1978): 27–54.

10. See D. Kahn, *The Codebreakers: The Story of Secret Writing* (New York: Scribner, 1967).

11. R. E. Haskell, "Empirical Structures of Mind: Cognition, Linguistics and Transformation," *The Journal of Mind and Behavior* 5 (1984): 29–48.

12. R. E. Haskell, "The Matrix of Group Talk: An Empirical Method of Analysis and Validation," *Small Group Behavior* 2 (1982): 419–443.

13. R. E. Haskell, "Cognitive Structure and Transformation: An Empirical Model of the Psycholinguistic Function of Numbers in Discourse," *Small Group Behavior* 13 (1983): 165–191.

14. See, for example, the following early works: H. Fine, H. Pollio, and C. Simpkinson, "Figurative Language, Metaphor and Psychotherapy," *Psychotherapy: Theory, Research and Practice* 10 (1973): 87–91; H. R. Pollio, J. M. Barlow, H. J. Fine, and M. R. Pollio, *Psychology and the Poetics of Growth: Figurative Language in Psychology, Psychotherapy and Education* (Hillsdale, N.J.: Lawrence Erlbaum, 1977); D. Gordon, *Therapeutic Metaphors* (Cupertino, Calif.: Meta Publications, 1978); E. Rossi, ed., *The Collected Works of Milton H. Erickson*, four volumes (New York: Irvington, 1980).

15. R. F. Bales, *Personality and Interpersonal Behavior* (New York: Holt, Rinehart and Winston, 1970).

16. G. Gibbard and J. Hartman, "The Significance of Utopian Fantasies in Small Groups," *International Journal of Group Psychotherapy* 23 (1973): 125–147; J. Hartman and G. Gibbard, "A Note on Fantasy Themes in the Evolution of Group Culture." In G. Gibbard, J. Hartman, and R. Mann, eds., *Analysis of Groups.* (San Francisco: Jossey-Bass, 1974); R. Mann, *Interpersonal Styles and Group Development* (New York: Wiley, 1967); P. Slater, *Microcosm: Structure, Psychological and Religious Evolution in Groups* (New York: John Wiley, 1966); T. Mills, *Group*

Transformation (Englewood Cliffs, N.J.: Prentice-Hall, 1964); D. Dunphy, "Phases, Roles, and Myths in Self-Analytic Groups," *Journal of Applied Behavioral Sciences* 4 (1968): 195-225.

17. See H. E. Durkin, *The Group in Depth* (New York: International University Press, 1964); H. Ezriel, "A Psychoanalytic Approach to the Treatment of Patients in Groups," *Journal of Mental Science* XCVI (1950): 774–779; H. Ezriel, "Experimentation Within the Psychoanalytic Session, *British Journal of the Philosophy of Science* 7 (1956): 29–48; C. Morocco, "The Development and Function of Group Metaphor," *Journal for the Theory of Social Behavior* 9 (1979): 1, 15–27; W. Schutz, *Here Comes Everybody: Bodymind and Encounter Culture* (New York: Harrow, 1971).

S. H. Foulkes and E. J. Anthony, *Group Psychotherapy* (Baltimore: Penguin, 1957); P. Mullahy, *Psychoanalysis and Interpersonal Psychiatry: The Contributions of Harry Stack Sullivan* (New York: Science House, 1970); D. S. Whitaker and M. Lieberman, *Psychotherapy Through the Group Process* (New York: Atherton, 1964); I. Yalom, *The Theory and Practice of Group Psychotherapy* (New York: Basic Books, 1970).

18. L. DeMause, "Historical Group Fantasies," *Journal of Psychohistory* 7 (1979): 1–70.

19. See E. G. Bormann, "Fantasy and Rhetorical Vision: The Rhetorical Criticism of Social Reality," *Quarterly Journal of Speech* 58 (1972): 396-407; G. P. Mohrmann, "An Essay on Fantasy Theme Criticism," *The Quarterly Journal of Speech* 68 (1982): 109–132; M. P. Farrell, "Collective Projection and Group Structure: The Relationship Between Deviance and Projection in Groups," *Small Group Behavior* 10 (1979): 81–100.

20. My thanks to Dr. David Livingstone Smith.

21. S. Freud, *The Interpretation of Dreams,* 1st English edition (London: George Allen and Unwin Ltd., 1954).

22. S. Freud, *The Psychopathology of Everyday Life,* translated by J. Strachey (New York: W. W. Norton, 1960).

23. S. Freud, *Jokes and Their Relation to the Unconscious,* translated by J. Strachey (New York: W. W. Norton, 1963). For years, I have had to deal with the pop psychology notions from students in my courses. Pop psychology books are characterized by wild speculation, based only on a mental health professional's personal everyday experience, not scientific research. This is done by people who should know better. At least in psychology, personal experience is not a good basis for knowing how the mind or the world really works. I consider pop psychology as (1) psychological information, (2) widely disseminated to the general public, (3) that is simplified and distorted, (4) has little or no rigorous evidence to support it, (5) but which is believed to be true.

24. An interesting and thorough history of the unconscious mind can be found in H. Ellenberger, *The Discovery of the Unconscious: The History and Evolution of Dynamic Psychiatry* (New York: Basic Books, 1970); L. L. Whyte, *The Unconscious Before Freud* (New York: Mentor Books, 1960); D. L. Smith, *Freud's Philosophy of the Unconscious* (Dordrecht, Netherlands: Kluwer Academic Publishers, 1999).

25. Freud, *The Interpretation of Dreams.*

26. Ellenberger, *The Discovery of the Unconscious,* 209.

27. E. J. Caropreso and C. S. White, "Analogical Reasoning and Giftedness: A Comparison Between Identified Gifted and Nonidentified Children," *Journal of Educational Research* 87(5) (1994): 271–278.

28. J. Lacan, "The Insistence of the Letter in the Unconscious." In Jacques Ehrmann, *Structuralism* (Garden City, N.Y.: Doubleday Anchor Books, 1966).

29. Smith is not only a philosopher of mind, he is a scholar on the history of psychoanalysis. More importantly, he is trained in the philosophy of science. Not being an expert on Freud, I thank and rely on Dr. Smith's extensive knowledge and scholarship on psychoanalysis and its many interpretations and controversies. Any glaring mistakes, however, are mine. I would also like to note that relative to the amount of expounding about Freud, there are few real "experts" on what Freud really said, especially about unconscious communication. See D. L. Smith, *Hidden Conversations: An Introduction to Communicative Psychoanalysis* (London: Tavistock/Routledge, 1991).

30. Smith, *Hidden Conversations*, 52.

31. S. Freud, *The Unconscious* (1915), in the standard edition of the complete psychological works of Sigmund Freud. Volume 14, translated and edited by James Strachey (London: Hogarth Press, 1901), 174.

32. D. L. Smith, *Hidden Conversations: An Introduction to Communicative Psychoanalysis* (London: Tavistock/Routledge, 1991).

33. For a general view, see my *Between the Lines*, ch. 12, and R. Langs, *Unconscious Communication in Everyday Life* (New York: Jason Aronson, 1983); see also R. Langs, *Clinical Practice and the Architecture of the Mind* (London: Karnac Books, 1995); R. Langs, *Empowered Psychotherapy* (London: Karnac Books, 1993); R. Langs, *Science, Systems and Psychoanalysis* (London: Karnac Books Brunner/Mazel, 1992).

34. From Smith, *Hidden Conversations*, 146.

35. Under the best of conditions, in the popular culture and media talking about unconscious material generally means that the person is a "shrink," that is, a psychotherapist. This is what psychology means in the popular media-mind. It isn't so. Most psychologists are not psychotherapists. Moreover, being a "shrink" is only one small part of the profession of psychology.

36. See R. E. Haskell, "Unconscious Communication: Communicative Psychoanalysis and Subliteral Cognition," *Journal of the American Academy of Psychoanalysis* 27, (1999): 471–502.

37. See my early article: R. E. Haskell, "The Analogic and Psychoanalytic Theory," *The Psychoanalytic Review* 55 (1969): 662–680.

38. H. Werner and B. Kaplan, *Symbol Formation: An Organismic Developmental Approach to Language and the Expression of Thought* (New York: Wiley, 1963).

39. To my knowledge there have been only two experiments that directly relate to deep listening. See M. P. Farrell, "Collective Projection and Group Structure: The Relationship Between Deviance and Projection in Groups," *Small Group Behavior* 10 (1979): 81–100; M. Horwitz and D. Cartwright, "A Projective Method for the Diagnosis of Group Properties," *Human Relations* 6 (1952): 397–410.

Chapter 6

1. See R. F. Bales, *Personality and Interpersonal Behavior* (New York: Holt, Rinehart & Winston, 1970), 139.

2. R. E. Haskell, ed., *Cognition and Dream Research* (New York: Institute of Mind and Behavior, 1986); also published as a special double issue of the *Journal of Mind and Behavior*.

3. Freud, *Interpretation of Dreams*, 67.

4. Ibid., 620.

5. From S. Freud, *A General Introduction to Psychoanalysis*, translated by J. Riviere (New York: Washington Square Press, 1961).

6. Ibid., 73.

Chapter 7

1. T. Dantzig, *Number: The Language of Science* (Garden City, N.Y.: Doubleday Anchor Books, 1930), 5.

2. R. E. Haskell, "Cognitive Structure and Transformation: An Empirical Model of the Psycholinguistic Function of Numbers in Discourse," *Small Group Behavior* 13 (1983): 165–191.

3. See Tobias Dantzig's fascinating classic, *Number: The Language of Science* (Garden City, N.Y.: Doubleday Anchor Books, 1930).

4. See, for example, E. Cassirer, *Mythological Thought* (London: Yale University Press, 1955).

5. For examples of the pathological use of numbers in schizophrenia see Kasanin's classic work, J. S. Kasanin, ed., *The Language and Thought of Schizophrenia* (New York: W. W. Norton, 1964).

6. N. Fodor, "The Psychology of Numbers," *Journal of Clinical Psychopathology* 8 (1947): 525–556; C. G. Jung, *Dreams,* translated by R.F.C. Hull (Princeton, N.J.: Princeton University Press, 1974); W. Stekel, *The Interpretation of Dreams* (New York: Liveright, 1943).

7. E. Gutheil, *The Handbook for Dream Analysis* (New York: Liveright, 1951).

8. S. Freud, *The Interpretation of Dreams,* first English edition (London: George Allen & Unwin Ltd., 1954).

9. See, for example, R. N. Shepard, D. W. Kilpatric, and J. P. Cunningham, "The Internal Representation of Numbers," *Cognitive Psychology* 7 (1975): 82–138.

10. The literal topic of "We narrowed them all down to 3 different options" subliterally refers to the emergence of the 3 dominant members. Psycholinguistically, it is important to note that the member telling the story is a part of the triad. As the literal story line notes, "*we*" (subliterally meaning the 3 dominant member) narrowed them (meaning the total group membership) down to three "options" (meaning the emergence of the 3 dominant members). For members who were not a part of this triad to have introduced this topic with the particular wording "We narrowed them down" would not have been congruent with the here-and-now situations because they didn't control the topics being discussed in the group and, therefore, didn't narrow the leadership down to three people. This is what I call psychosociometric validity (see *Between the Lines* appendix).

11. The phrase *lucky spots* has linguistic legitimacy because it's a phrase commonly used in one variation or another to refer to desirable status positions. That the "Three Lucky Spots" is a bar is also significant. Logically, the topic simultaneously relates to both a part (that is, member) of and the whole group (that is, a bar). In other words, the number 3 is not just an isolated number; it's associated with a group, a bar, just as the three leaders are part of a whole *group*. Again, this story, too, has psychosociometric validity in that it was introduced by a member who belonged to the three lucky status spots. Again, the number 3

corresponds to the actual triadic leadership structure of the conversation. The reference to *lucky spots* in the name of the bar is an additional *semantic association* that subliterally corresponds to the status of the 3 dominant members who were the leaders. The concern of members is that they are being evaluated on their leadership and interpersonal and communication skills. Thus in this situation, the 3 dominant members who occupy the *3 lucky spots*, are perceived as being the recipients of excellent evaluations.

12. It's interesting here to ask why the member making this statement would specifically select "3" drinks as indicating too many? This would certainly not be a typical number of drinks that would be considered too many, especially by young people. This particular number selected for indicating too many drinks is not normative and is so extreme that it functions as a clue that something subliteral is happening.

13. The statement "the 3rd day" is still another reference to the triad, which includes (as in most of the topics above) a larger unit, a "bus," which represents the rest of the group.

14. Once again, the number 3 in this topic corresponds to the actual group leadership composition, with the number 3 being part of a larger group (total). Like the 3 people in the bar, the "3 seniors" were a disrupting influence and removed. Emotionally, the rest of the here-and-now group would like to remove the threatening triad. Once again, psychosociometrically, the member telling this story was not a member of the triad—which is subliterally being criticized via this story.

15. Like the other topics reflecting the triad in this group, the "3 old greyhound buses" story corresponds not only to the triad but also to its being part of a larger whole; that is, the 3 buses were part of an airport system.

16. In terms of other association-type connections, the phrase "and they wouldn't serve any of them" is deep talk for the fact that the rest of the group would not accept the leadership of the three leaders, that is, they would not *serve* as followers.

17. On another level, the "being *under* 21" subliterally references the remaining members of the group, who were all younger than the three leaders, that is, they were literally all *under 21* years old. As partial verification of this analysis almost immediately connected to this phrase was the statement "Over half of them were *under* age." As in the literal story, the younger female members constituted the majority and were under the age of 21.

18. The particular phrasing of this topic is equally revealing. In the phrasing *This 1 Girl Who Was with These 2 Guys*, note the use of pronouns. The use of the pronouns "this" and "these" were used, as if the people being talked about were present, instead of the more appropriate "that" one girl and "those" two guys. This *tense shift* psychologically and linguistically links the story with the here-and-now conversational situation. Any number of phrasings could have been used. For example, it could have been said, that "*there* was a girl who was with two guys," or so forth.

19. There were three other references in this session's protocol with the number 3 in them. To simplify things, I didn't use them. In any event, they would not have changed the meaning of the number that I have used. The three other numerical references were what I call double numbers like 33 and 30; if I used them the total number of group topics and total number of group members would have been 16, not 13. This wouldn't have changed my basic analysis of the numbers as it would have been a reference to the total group membership including the three absent members. I might note that this fact might also support

my tentative analysis of the 13 topics equaling the 13 members (present) because including the three extra numerical references ends with same result.

20. Quoted in R. Palmer, *Hermeneutics* (Evanston, Ill.: Northwestern University Press, 1969), 140.

Chapter 8

1. L. Carroll, *Alice in Wonderland*, ch. 7.

2. For similar themes, see R. E. Haskell, "An Analogic Model of Small Group Behavior," *International Journal of Group Psychotherapy* 28 (1978): 27–54.

3. I wish to thank my colleague John Heapes for this deep-talk narrative.

4. A psychoanalytic colleague of mine has suggested that removing my sport jacket was in fact a "seductive" move on my part. More factually, I would say that it may have been *perceived* as seductive.

Chapter 9

1. A. Gresson, "Postmodern American and the Multicultural Crisis: Reading *Forest Gump* as the "Call Back to Whiteness," *Taboo: The Journal of Culture and Education* 1. (1996): 26.

2. See J. Waller, *Face to Face: The Changing State of Racism Across America* (New York: Plenum/Insight Books, 1998).

3. Gallup Organization, April 19–22, 1990, survey reported in *American Enterprise*, September/October 1990.

4. An indication of denial or of ignorance during the O.J. Simpson criminal case was whites' saying that the mostly black jury engaged in jury nullification (that is, not abiding by the evidence and the law). Even if jury nullification occurred, little mention was made by white juries engaging in jury nullification for years when an African-American was on trial.

5. A couple of the illustrations in this chapter are from R. E. Haskell, "Social Cognition and the Non-Conscious Expression of Racial Ideology," *Imagination, Cognition and Personality* 6 (1987): 75–97. For more illustrations see my book *Between the Lines*.

6. All the illustrations in this chapter reflect African-American and white relations. This is not by design. The populations that I have lived and worked in have not been diverse enough to provide me with occasions for recognizing subliteral narratives about other minority groups. In addition I assume that having black friends for over twenty years has sensitized me to deep listening in black and white. The illustrations also are limited to ones created by whites. African-Americans, too, create deep talk about race. I chose not to present any of these because of space considerations. In any event, I might note that, at least in my experience, deep talk about race by blacks—strangely enough—is not as negative as that by whites (see my book *Between the Lines*).

7. See A. Gresson, *The Recovery of Race in America* (Minneapolis: University of Minnesota Press, 1995); A. Gresson, *The Dialectics of Betrayal: Sacrifice, Violation and the Oppressed* (Norwood, N.J.: Ablex Publishing, 1982).

8. A. Montague, *Man's Most Dangerous Myth: The Fallacy of Race,* 4th ed. (Cleveland: World, 1964).

9. See C. West, *Race Matters* (New York: Vintage Books, 1994).

10. NBC, 9:30 PM EST, September 4, 1999.

11. The stereotype of watermelons is not dead. A few years ago there was a popular country song about a lonely old gray-haired black gentleman sweeping the floor in a nearly empty bar as he thought about the failure of most human endeavors. The story teller in this song is "pourin' blended whiskey down." After thinking over his life, the song ends with the old black man concluding that there are only three things "worth a solitary dime." The three things are reflected in the title of the song: "Old Dogs, Children, and *Watermelon* Wine." Peruse some old books about African-Americans and you will find that blacks and watermelons have historically been closely associated. Interestingly, and ironically, watermelons were indigenous to the Kalahari Desert. They were brought to North America by European colonists and African slaves.

12. *New York Times,* New England edition, January 29, 1999, A8.

13. *New York Times*, February 2, 1999.

14. This event doesn't seem to want to go away. Over a year and a half later (August 16, 2000), the issue was presented on the (Catherine) *Crier Today* program (see www.courttv.com/onair/shows/criertoday). The show was based on a series of articles from the *Akron Beacon Journal* by two Pulitzer Prize-winning journalists, Carl Chancellor and Bob Dyer (see www.ohio.com/bj/), who have written a number of articles on the "niggardly" incident. In one of the stories (Feburary 7, 1999) the chairman of the NAACP, Julian Bond, disavowed the incident, saying that this whole episode speaks loudly to where we are on issues of race. Even "imagined slights are catapulted to the front burner."

15. When I have told of this incident and my analysis of it to friends and students, the response has often been, "Rob, why didn't you write an editorial about this?" My answer was, "I did." It was, of course, rejected. It was rejected with no reply by two national circulation newspapers. In my view, this rejection further points to the disavowal of racial problems in American society.

16. Italics added. Ethically (see Chapter 6), because of a lack of contextual data to validate this example, and because it could socially stigmatize the author, I am omitting the 1992 citation to the book from which this example was gleaned. I will provide it only for certain research purposes.

17. "Famous Howard Cosell Quotes," *Washington Post,* April 24, 1995; italics added.

18. *NBC Nightly News,* July 27, 1999.

19. If more convincing is needed to show that the stereotype of the black male as an animalistic "buck" is still current, one only has to search the Internet using the words "big black buck." What one finds is a host of pornographic type cites with all of the classic sexual stereotypes of the black male.

20. "Net Profits," *Time,* January 13, 1992, p. 64. I would like to thank my former student Mary Donahue for finding this equivalent photo and headline for me.

21. For a modern version of research on the role of psychological associations, see A. G. Greenwald, D. E. McGhee, and J.L.K Schwartz, "Measuring Individual Differences in Im-

plicit Cognition: The Implicit Association Test," *Journal of Personality and Social Psychology* 74 (1998): 1464–1480. See also http://buster.cs.yale.edu/implicit/.

22. Since the publication of my *Between the Lines,* it has come to my surprised attention that because I notice so many racial incidences and explain their unconscious associations, some readers believe this shows that I must be prejudiced. How else, the reasoning goes, could I access, recognize, and be attuned to so many stereotypes and racist perceptions and reasoning? This perception disturbs me greatly, not only because it's untrue, but because it logically faulty. The answer to why I recognize the many incidences that I do is this: First, being a social and cognitive psychologist, it's my job to know about these racial and gender issues. Second, I grew up during times when racism was much more socially acceptable than it is now. Consequently, my mind, too, has been culturally filled with the racial myths, images, and stereotypes. Third, having for over twenty years a best friend and colleague who is black has sensitized me to racial issues. Finally, my friend taught me a great deal about racism.

23. See R. E. Haskell, "Social Cognition, Language, and the Non-Conscious Expression of Racial Ideology," *Imagination, Cognition and Personality* 6 (1986-1987): 75; italics added.

24. B. L. Duncan, "Differential Social Perception and Attribution of Intergroup Violence: Testing the Lower Limits of Stereotyping of Blacks," *Journal of Personality and Social Psychology* 34 (1976): 590–598.

25. See, for example, E. J. Vanman, B. Y. Paul, T. A. Ito, and N. Miller, "The Modern Face of Prejudice and Structural Features That Moderate the Effect of Cooperation on Affect," *Journal of Personality and Social Psychology* 73 (1997): 941–959.

26. See, for example, J. A. Bargh, M. Chen, and L. Burrows, "Automaticity of Social Behavior: Direct Effects of Trait Construct and Stereotype Activation on Action," *Journal of Personality and Social Psychology* 71 (1996): 230–244; B. Wittenbrink, C. M. Judd, and B. Park, "Evidence for Racial Prejudice at the Implicit Level and Its Relationship with Questionnaire Measures," *Journal of Personality and Social Psychology* 72 (1997): 262–274.

27. A. G. Greenwald, D. E. McGhee, and J.L.K. Schwartz, "Measuring Individual Differences in Implicit Cognition: The Implicit Association Test," *Journal of Personality and Social Psychology* 74 (1998): 1464–1480. See also http://buster.cs.yale.edu/implicit/.

28. With this experimental research on "priming" having been presented, consider this: After the initial hullabaloo over the "niggardly" incident that I discussed above, the fact that the white aide was gay was hardly mentioned in the press, and probably rightly so as it doesn't seem relevant to the story. And the gay issue is nearly as emotionally incendiary as the racial issue. In the same series of articles in the *Akron Beacon Journal* (January 29, 1999), the fact that the white aide was gay wasn't mentioned. However, I don't think it was coincidental that the accusers of the gay mayoral aide were quoted as saying that they were wrong and "we went off, *half-cocked.*" As for the journalist using the headline "APOLOGIES *FLOW WRONG DIRECTION* IN D.C.," with its implicit references to something "flowing" into something in the wrong direction and to the AC/DC vernacular meaning; and as for the word "mustered" as in mustering up an apology, with its direct lexical access to common dictionary associations calling "troops together," to cause to "*come* together," to leave or be "*discharged,*" I won't comment, except to ask again: Why these particular words were

selected in this context out of the at least a hundred different ones that could have been used? And finally why did I return to this end note hours later to add the adjective "mayoral" (*may* plus *oral*) to describe the mayor's assistant? The automatic nature of deep talk is indeed, relentless. No, I'm not homophobic; but like those who are, I have been subject to the cultural stereotypes and lexicon (see endnote 22).

Chapter 10

1. See D. A. Norman, *The Psychology of Everyday Things* (New York: HarperCollins, 1988); D. A. Norman, "Categorization of Action Slips," *Psychological Review* 88 (1981): 1–15. See also D. Norman, "Post-Freudian Slips," *Psychology Today,* April 1980.

2. *Journal Sentinel,* July 28, 1998.

3. I wish to thank Keith Edwards, the reporter of the story, for a copy of the police report.

4. Julius Caesar and his army in 49 B.C. crossed the Rubicon river in north-central Italy, a crossing that began a civil war.

5. On the nature of this process—and its controversial aspects, see N. F. Dixon, *Subliminal Perception: The Nature of a Controversy* (London: McGraw-Hill, 1971); N. F. Dixon, *Preconscious Processing* (New York: Wiley & Sons, 1981).

6. H. Brean, "Hidden Sell Technique Is Almost Here: New Subliminal Gimmicks Now Offer Blood, Skulls, and Popcorn to Movie Fans," *Life,* March 31, 1958, p. 102.

7. L. H. Silverman and J. Weinberger, "Mommy and I Are One," *American Psychologist* 40 (1985): 1296–1308; R. E. Haskell, "Logical Structure and the Cognitive Psychology of Dreaming," in R. E. Haskell, ed., *Cognition and Dream Research* (New York: Institute of Mind and Behavior, 1986), 215–248); S. Sohlberg, A. Billinghurst, and S. Nyléén, "Moderation of Mood Change After Subliminal Symbiotic Stimulation: Four Experiments Contributing to the Further Demystification of Silverman's 'Mommy And I Are One' Findings," *Journal of Research in Personality* 32 (1998):33–54.

8. See, for example, J. A. Bargh, M. Chen, and L. Burrows, "Automaticity of Social Behavior: Direct Effects of Trait Construct and Stereotype Activation on Action," *Journal of Personality and Social Psychology* 71 (1996): 230–244.

9. A. G. Hodges, *A Mother Gone Bad* (Birmingham, Ala.: Village House Publishers, 1998).

10. Ibid., 120.

11. Ibid., 7.

12. Ibid., 8–9.

13. Ibid., 14; italics added.

14. Ibid., 22.

15. Ibid., 28.

16. Ibid., 65.

17. Ibid., 29.

18. Ibid., 81; italics added.

19. Ibid., 143.

20. Ibid., 77.

21. Ibid.; italics added.

22. Ibid., 77.

23. Ibid.; italics added.

24. Ibid., 67.

25. F. C. Welsing, *The Isis Papers* (Chicago: Third World Press, 1991).

26. Ibid., xii.

27. Ibid., 111.

28. Ibid., 67.

29. Ibid., 137.

30. Ibid., 134.

31. Ibid., 136.

32. Ibid., 66.

33. Ibid., 148.

34. Ibid., 175–176.

Index

AAAS. *See* American Association for the Advancement of Science

Abdul-Jabar, Kareem, xxiii–xxiv, 171–172, 173–174, 175

Abel (Biblical character), 47, 60, 69

Acrostics, 95

Action slips, xxiv, 181–184

Advertisements, 38–42

African Americans, 120, 158, 161. *See also* Racism

Alcoholics Anonymous, xx

Allen, Woody, 112–113

American Association for the Advancement of Science (AAAS), 119

Analogical thinking, 91–92

Archetypes, xxii, 47–50, 120. *See also* God archetypes

Aristotle, 92

Army cryptography, 94

Associations, 22

Associative selection, 129

Authority figures, xxii, 48–49, 93–94. *See also* God archetypes

Baars, Bernard, 36–37

Bales, Robert Freed, 99–100, 111

Bellevue Hospital, 169–170

Bernstein, Carl, 28–29

Between the Lines (Haskell), xiii, xiv, xviii, 115–116, 169–170

Bible, 47–48, 60–61, 115, 194–195

Bion, Alfred, 154

Blitzer, Wolf, xxii, 27–31

Boredom, 76–77

Bragging, 77–78

Brand names, 85–86

Bronze Age (3500 B. C.), 94–95

Bruner, Jerome, 71

Buck fever, 169

Buffalo Springfield, 181

Burden of Proof, xxii, 29–31

Cain (Biblical character), 47, 60, 69

California, 121–122

Caropreso, Edward, 103

Carroll, Lewis, 139

Carson, Johnny, 147–148

Censoring, 22

Champollion, Jean Francois, 97

Children, xvi, 9–11

Christian Bible, 47–48, 60–61, 115, 194–195

Christianity, 48, 195–196

CIA, 44, 49

Clinton, Bill, xxii, 27–31

CNN news, xxii, 27–31

Coded speech, xv, 7, 93–99, 174

Cognitive operations, 91–92, 127, 129

Comedians, 115

Communicative psychotherapy, 108–109

Compliments, 79–83

Conflicts, 22

Context, 115–116

Conversations

conditions of, 21–22
free-flowing, xvi
meaning of, 114–116
phatic communion, 2
subliteral, xvii–xix, 19–20, 116–121
volume of, 8–11
workplace, xix, 6–7
Cosell, Howard, 171
Cosmological meaning of numbers,
    127–128
Cossack, Roger, xxii, 29–31
Creative writing, 112–113, 115, 172
Crusoe, Robinson, 100
Cryptography, 94

Dantzig, Tobias, 125
Darwin, Charles, 92, 103, 139–140
Deconstructing Harry, 112–113
Deep action. *See* Action slips
Deep listening
    ethics of, 111–114
    future of, 108–110
    principles of, 20–23
    usefulness of, xix–xxi
    validating, 116–121
Deep listening examples
    CNN unpresidented matrix map,
        31
    composite "buck" matrix map, 173
    composite numbers stories matrix
        map, 133
    and Freud, 91–108. *See also* Freud,
        Sigmund
    Grateful Dead live in concert matrix
        map, 6
    In Defense of Whores matrix map,
        119
    lost child of the tribe session
        template, 60
    many called but few chosen session
        template, 67–68
    mysterious mind of god session
        template, 53

professor's compliment matrix map,
    81
women under the influence matrix
    map, 143
written word of god session
    template, 55–56
Deep Throat, 29
Defoe, Daniel, 100
de Gaulle, Charles, 99
Derivatives, 108
Disney, Walt, 96
DNA, xiv
Double entendres, xiv, 11
Dreams, 121–124
Dr. Frankenstein, 141–142
Dr. J. *See* Erving, Julius
Dr. Strangelove, 84
Duncan, Birt, 176
Dupuytren's contracture, 32–33

Egyptian hieroglyphics, 97
Einstein, Albert, 112
Ellenberger, Henri, 102
Ellis, Albert, 54–55
Emotions, 22
Epistemology, 98
Erving, Julius ("Dr. J."), xxiv, 171–172,
    175
Esau (Biblical character), 47, 60, 69
Ethics, xxiii, 48, 111–114
Ethnicity. *See* Racism
Euphemisms, 158–159
Experimental Slips and Human Error
    (Baars), 36–37

Facial muscle activity, 177–178
Failed accomplishments, 107
FBI, 44, 49
Fehlleistungen, 107
Fiddler on the Roof, 33–36
"Figures" of speech, xxiii, 125. *See also*
    Numbers
Foreman, George, xxiii, 162–165

Fossey, Diane, 198–199
Free flowing conversation, xvi
Free will, 17–19
Freud, Sigmund, 25, 101–108, 181, 201
    dreams, 121–124, 129
    slips of the tongue, xiv, xx, 25–26,
        104, 106
    terminology, 19
    unconscious communication, xxiii

Gallup Poll, 158
Garrett, Alvin, 171
Gay men. *See* Sexual orientation
Gender, xxiii, 182. *See also* Women
*A General Introduction to
    Psychoanalysis* (Freud), 123
Genesis (Bible), 115
Genetics, 182
God archetypes, xxii, 47–50
    lost child of the tribe, 57–60
    many called but few chosen,
        60–69
    mystery, 50–54
    written word, 54–57
Goodall, Jane, 198–199
Graham, Billy, 51, 52
Graham, Virginia, 76
Grateful Dead, xxii, 1–6, 19, 83
Greek tragedies, 72
Greenwald, Anthony, 178–179
Gresson, Aaron David, 157, 161,
    168
Griffin, Merv, 76
Groups, 13–17
    dynamics, 99–101
    psychotherapy, xix–xx
    research in, xviii
    support, xx
    videotaping of, 44–45
    See also T-groups
A Guide to Rational Living (Ellis),
    54–55
Gutheil, Emil, 129

Hand, Learned, 188
Haskell, Claudette, 40
Haskell, Melyssa, 40, 74–75
Heidegger, Martin, 137
Hieroglyphics, 97
Hiroshima, 112
Hispanics, 158, 170
Hitler, Adolf, 112
Hodges, Andrew G., 188–189, 200
Homosexuality. *See* Sexual orientation
Hypnosis, 186–187, 196

IAT. *See* Implicit Association Test
Ideograms, 97
Implicit Association Test (IAT),
    178–179
Incompetent leaders, 86–89
Ink-blot tests, 177
The Interpretation of Dreams (Freud),
    101, 122, 129
The Isis Papers (Wesling), 189,
    197–200
Ito, Lance, 121
Ivory towers, 87

Jacob (Biblical character), 47, 60, 69
Jews, 33–35
Johnson, Andrew, 30
Johnson, Magic, 174
*Jokes and Their Relation to the
    Unconscious* (Freud), 101
Journal Sentinel, 184–185
Judeo-Christian ethics, 48. *See also*
    Christianity
Jung, Carl, 47
Kaplan, Bernard, 110
Kubrick, Stanley, 84
Ku Klux Klan, 158
Kula Ring, 92–93

Lacan, Jacques, 104
Langs, Robert, 108–109
Larry King Live, 30

Leadership in T-groups, 21, 49–50, 86–89, 93–94
Leakey, Louis, 92
Leakey, Mary, 92
Leibnitz, Gottfried, 73
Lewinski, Monica, xxii, 27–31
Lexical accessing and selection, 5, 23, 167
Lexicons, 5
Linear B, 97
Literary templates, 72
Losses (personal), 56–57

Mailer, Norman, xxiii, 162–165
Male dominance, 140–142
Malinowski, Bronislaw, 92
Manhattan Project, 111–112
Mann, Thomas, 102
Man's Most Dangerous Myth (Montague), 161
Mapping, 23
Maslow, Abraham, 12
Material reality, 201
Matrix maps. See Deep listening examples
Meaning of conversations, 114–116
Melanin envy, 199
Menomonie (Wisc.), 185
Mental schemas, 23
Metaphors, xiv, xvi, 91–92
   and communication, 3
   and psychotherapy, xix–xx
   and subliteral mind, 19
Milwaukee Journal Sentinel, 184–185
Mind reading, 23, 112
Model building, 91–92
Modern Dictionary for the Legal Profession, 38
Monads, 73
Montague, Ashley, 161
A Mother Gone Bad (Hodges), 188–189
Muhammad Ali, xxiii, 162–163
Muscle activity, 177–178

Myers, Piers, 108
Mystical meaning of numbers, 127–128
Mythical meaning of numbers, 128

NAACP, 166
Nagasaki, 112
Names. See Proper names
Napoleon, 97
Nation of Islam, 158
National Security Agency (NSA), 94
Nazi racism, 200
Need to know, 11–13
New Age numerology, 125
New York Times, 165
Nixon, Richard, 28–29
Norman, Donald, 181
NSA. See National Security Agency
Numbers, xxiii, 96–97, 125–138, 195–196

Olduvai Gorge, 92
Oppenheimer, J. Robert, 112
"Oreos," 161
Oxford English Dictionary, 79

Parapraxes, 104, 106. See also Slips of the tongue
Parton, Dolly, 147–148
Pathological meaning of numbers, 128–129
People magazine, 171–172
Personal losses, 56–57
Personal names. See Proper names
Phatic communion, 2
Phonograms, 97
Physical events, 42–46
Pinker, Steven, 165–167
Pirsig, Robert, 91
Plato, xv, 92
Plimpton, George, xxiii, 162–165
Preconscious minds, 104–106

Prejudice, 160–162, 175–179. *See also* Racism; Sexual orientation; Women
Priming effects, 178, 187
Privacy templates, 69
Professor and the Madman, 79
Proper names, 7, 83–86, 178–179
Psalms (Bible), 194–195
Psychical reality, 201
Psychoanalytic meaning of numbers, 128–129
Psycholinguistics, 3
The Psychopathology of Everyday Life (Freud), 101, 181
Psychotherapy, xix–xx, 9–11, 108–109, 114
Ptolemy, Claudius, 98
Puns, xiv, 40–42, 148–149
Pythagoras, 101, 127–128

Racism, xxiii–xxiv, 157–179, 197–200. *See also* African Americans
Ramsey, John, 192, 193–194
Ramsey, JonBenét, xxiv, 188–195
Ramsey, Patsy, 188–195, 200
Random talk, xvi
Ransom notes, 189–195
Reber, Arthur, 1
Relationships, 71–89
Reynolds Company, 148–149
Rivalry templates, 69
Robin Hood, 10–11
Rorschach tests, 177
Rosetta Stone, 97
Rudolf, Deborah, 172
Rudolf, Eric, 172
Rush, Benjamin, 199–200
Rutherford, Ernest, 91–92

Samuel (Book of the Bible), 47
Schemas, 23
Schopenhauer, Arthur, 102–103
Secret codes, 93–99

Seduction, 144–147
Seed, Richard, 188
Semmelweis, Ignaz, 100
Sexual dominance, 140–142
Sexual orientation, 151–156
Sexual seduction, 144–147
Sexual tension, xxiii
Shakespeare, William, 72, 102
Silences, 22
Simpson, O. J., xxiii, 121–122, 158
Single parenting, 142–144
Sins of the fathers, 35–37
Slips of the mind, 27–38, 45–46
Slips of the pen, 123–124, 190
Slips of the tongue, xiv, xx, 11, 25–26, 45–46, 104, 106
Small-group dynamics, 99–101
Smith Brothers, 85
Smith, David Livingstone, 9–11, 34, 105, 107, 108
Social censoring, 22
Social dominance, 140–142
Socrates, 92
Sodomy, 152
Speech, xv, 93–99
Spock, Benjamin, 87
Spooner, William Archibald, 25–26
Starr, Kenneth, 28
Star Trek, 10–11
Star Wars, 15
Stereotypes. *See* Racism; Women
Subliminal activation research, 187
Subliminal perception, 178
Subliteral conversations, xvii–xix, 19–20, 116–121
Subliteral numbers. *See* Numbers
Subordinates, 72
Support groups, xx
Symbol Formation (Werner and Kaplan), 110
Symbolism in television advertising, 148–151

T.A.T. *See* Thematic Apperception Test
Television
   advertisements, 38–42
   Burden of Proof, xxii, 29–31
   CNN news, xxii, 27–31
   commercials, 147–151
   Johnny Carson, 147–148
   Larry King Live, 30
   Merv Griffin, 76
   Pete Williams, 172
   Star Trek, 10–11
   Today show, 57, 59
   War on AIDS, 174
   and women, 147–151
Thematic Apperception Test (T.A.T.),
   177
Therapy, xix–xx, 108–109, 114
T-groups. *See* Training groups
Time magazine, 172–174
Today show, 57, 59
Topic selections, 22, 52–53
Training groups (T-groups), xvi, 3,
   23–24
   and God templates, 49–69
   leadership style, 21, 49–50, 86–89,
     93–94
   videotaping, 44
Transitional topics, 53
Triadic themes, 130–137
Trobriand Islands, 92

Unconscious communication, 104–107
Upjohn Company, 85
U.S. Army, 94

Validating deep listening, 116–121
van Susteren, Greta, 30–31
Ventris, Michael George, 97
Vestigial remains of racial
   conditioning, 176
Videotaping groups, 44
Vikings, 32–36
Volume of speech, 8–11

Wallace, Alfred Russell, 107
War on Aids, 174
Washington Monument, 197
Welsing, Frances Crest, 196–197
Werner, Heinz, 110
The White Negro (Mailer), 165
White, Stephen, 103
Williams, Anthony, xxiii, 165–166
Williams, Pete, 172
A Woman Under the Influence, 141–142
Women, 120, 139–156
Woodward, Bob, 28–29
Workplace conversations, xix, 6–7
World War II, 112
Writing, 112–113, 115, 172